"It is immensely gratifying to be able to co  the fortieth anniversary of its remarkable a to us critically important stories that have l and in engaging young activists who will be able work. A crucial contribution to the hope society." —Noam Chomsky

"Project Censored is a national treasure in American life serving to remind us of how crucial it is to be vigilant about making the truth heard in the public sphere and what it means to criticize those who censor in order to defile both the truth and democracy itself. Project Censored has once again produced a work that is as crucial to educating the American public as it is to making a valuable call to save American democracy. This is a brilliant, startling, and informative book that every young person, adult, student, and concerned citizen should read. *Censored 2018* inspires, energizes, and gives new meaning to the notion that critical citizens are at the core of a strong democracy and that informed resistance is not an option but a necessity." —Henry A. Giroux, McMaster University Professor for Scholarship in the Public Interest and the Paulo Freire Distinguished Scholar in Critical Pedagogy, McMaster University, Canada

"As trivia, celebrity gossip, blow-by-blow descriptions of the latest foibles of the political elites, entertainment, and corporate-approved stories replace journalism, real news happens increasingly on the fringes, where it is more easily marginalized and ignored. Project Censored rescues the most important stories you should have read but probably never saw from oblivion." —Chris Hedges, bestselling author of *War is a Force That Gives Us Meaning* and *Wages of Rebellion*

"Project Censored is a lifeline to the world's most urgent and significant stories. The Project's list of the top stories that get very little mainstream media traction should in fact drive the reporting agendas of every major news outlet." —Naomi Wolf, author of the bestselling books *The Beauty Myth*; *The End of America*; and *Give Me Liberty*

"Project Censored brings to light some of the most important stories of the year that you never saw or heard about. This is your chance to find out what got buried." —Diane Ravitch, author of *The Death and Life of the Great American School System*

"The systematic exposure of censored stories by Project Censored has been an important contribution." —Howard Zinn, author of *A People's History of the United States*

"[Project Censored] is a clarion call for truth telling." —Daniel Ellsberg, *The Pentagon Papers*

"Project Censored . . . has evolved into a deep, wide, and utterly engrossing exercise to unmask censorship, self-censorship, and propaganda in the mass media." —Ralph Nader, consumer advocate, lawyer, author

"Project Censored provides the kind of fearless and honest journalism we so desperately need in these dangerous times." —Peter Kuznick, professor of history, American University, and coauthor, with Oliver Stone, of *The Untold History of the United States*

"[Project Censored] shows how the American public has been bamboozled, snookered, and dumbed down by the corporate media. It is chock-full of 'ah-ha' moments where we understand just how we've been fleeced by banksters, stripped of our civil liberties, and blindly led down a path of never-ending war." —Medea Benjamin, author of *Drone Warfare*, and cofounder of Global Exchange and CODEPINK

"Most journalists in the United States believe the press here is free. That grand illusion only helps obscure the fact that, by and large, the US corporate press does not report what's really going on, while tuning out, or laughing off, all those who try to do just that. Americans—now more than ever—need those outlets that do labor to report some truth. Project Censored is not just among the bravest, smartest, and most rigorous of those outlets, but the only one that's wholly focused on those stories that the corporate press ignores, downplays, and/or distorts." —Mark Crispin Miller, author, professor of media ecology, New York University

"At a time when the need for independent journalism and for media outlets unaffiliated with and untainted by the government and corporate sponsors is greater than ever . . . we are fortunate to have an ally like Project Censored." —Dahr Jamail, independent journalist

"[Project Censored's] efforts to continue globalizing their reporting network could not be more timely or necessary." —Kristina Borjesson, award-winning freelance journalist

"Project Censored continues to do the work they've been persistently pursuing since 1976: Exposing the secrets that those in power would prefer to keep hidden and the corruption that should be scandalous, but isn't, because the corporate media won't cover it." —David Rovics, musician and activist

"One of the most significant media research projects in the country." —I.F. Stone, American muckraker

"Project Censored is one of the organizations that we should listen to, to be assured that our newspapers and our broadcasting outlets are practicing thorough and ethical journalism." —Walter Cronkite, anchor, *CBS Evening News*, 1962–1981

CENSORED 2018

PRESS FREEDOMS IN A "POST-TRUTH" WORLD

The Top Censored Stories and Media Analysis of 2016–17

Andy Lee Roth and Mickey Huff
with Project Censored

Foreword by
Deepa Kumar
Cartoons by
Khalil Bendib

Seven Stories Press
New York • Oakland • London

Seven Stories Press
140 Watts Street
New York, NY 10013
www.sevenstories.com

ISBN 978-1-60980-781-8 (paperback)

ISBN 978-1-60980-782-5 (electronic)

ISSN 1074-5998

9 8 7 6 5 4 3 2 1

Book design by Jon Gilbert

Printed in the USA

Contents

CHAPTER 2: Post-Truth Dystopia: Fake News, Alternative Facts, and the
Ongoing War on Reality—Junk Food News and News Abuse for 2016–17
by Nolan Higdon and Mickey Huff, with student writers and researchers
Aimee Casey, Gabriella Custodio, Elsa Denis, Thomas Field, Alisha
Huajardo, Justin Lascano, Aubrey Sanchez, Edwin Sevilla, Hannah
Soule, Kelly Van Boekhout, Kristen van Zyll de Jong, Michael Vega,

CHAPTER 3: Media Democracy in Action
introduction by Andy Lee Roth, with contributions by Rachael Jolley
(Index on Censorship), Chase Palmieri (Tribeworthy), Mahsood Ebrahim
and Julianne Rodriguez (Citrus College), Kevin Gosztola and Rania
Khalek (Unauthorized Disclosure), and Gennie Gebhart (Electronic

CHAPTER 4: The New American Authoritarianism: How the Corporate Media
Normalized Racism in 2016

CHAPTER 5: Trump Universe

CHAPTER 6: Defamation as Censorship in the Social-Media Era:
Who Counts as a Media Defendant?

Sifting and Winnowing in the "Post-Truth" Era

Deepa Kumar

Oxford Dictionaries selected "post-truth"—defined as "relating to or denoting circumstances in which objective facts are less influential in shaping public opinion than appeals to emotion and personal belief"—as its 2016 word of the year. Oxford explained its choice by stating that, while the word has been in use for about a decade, two events, Brexit and the Trump election victory, marked a spike in the public use of the term.

Donald Trump has indeed displayed a shocking disregard for science, for facts, and for any evidence-based research. He dismissed decades of scientific research on global warming, calling it a "hoax," and even disputed the size of the audience at his inauguration. His list of lies and falsehoods is so long that various news media organizations have taken to counting and documenting them. *The New York Times* wrote that it "has logged at least one false or misleading claim per day on 91 of his first 99 days."[1]

While this work is essential in an era in which "emotion" and "personal belief," as Oxford states, have overtaken objective facts, to scrutinize only the Far Right—the forces of Brexit or the Trump administration—misses a deeper dynamic in which right-wing and establishment liberalism have both played a part in the generation of a "post-truth" society.

In a piece titled "The Art of Spin," Patrick Barrett and I argued that the 2016 election was remarkable for the "unprecedented debasement of the national political discourse" that characterized it.[2] This was caused only in part by Trump's incoherent ramblings and lack of substantive knowledge, along with his predilection for explicitly sexist and racist appeals, outright lies, and scathing personal insults and threats directed against his opponents and their supporters. No less significant was the Clinton campaign's extensive use of propaganda and misdirection.

Both the Trump and the Clinton campaigns skillfully deployed long-held beliefs among their bases, rejecting fact and resorting to emotion to shore up two unpopular candidates. Trump appropriated beliefs popular among evangelicals and the Far Right, such as climate science denial and creationism, while Clinton and her supporters drew on feminism and identity politics to silence critics and bolster her base.

Thus, left-wing critics of Clinton were called "brogressives," "brocialists," and "manarchists" as a way to shame and silence them, while those who chose not to vote for Clinton were attacked for exercising "privilege." As we wrote, this charge is based on the idea that "only privileged people (by virtue of their class position, race, gender, legal status, or sexual orientation) have the luxury of criticizing or opposing Clinton, ostensibly because they are immune to the harmful effects that taking such a position will have on the most vulnerable members of society."

Emotional blackmail of a left-wing variety was deployed to paper over the reality that millions of vulnerable people have been attacked by the Clintons. It is a fact that welfare "reform" negatively impacted millions of poor women, that Bill Clinton's 1994 crime bill exacerbated mass incarceration and imprisoned hundreds of thousands more brown and black people, and that the draconian Iraq sanctions led to the death of half a million Iraqi children. While these were policies of Bill Clinton, Hillary Clinton directly supported them. It is this experience in the White House, and the "two-for-one" presidency, that the Clinton campaign repeatedly touted as the reason why she was the most experienced candidate to ever run for the presidency. Yet these facts and most others seemed to matter little in an emotionally charged political environment.

In short, emotional appeals based on long-held beliefs among both conservatives and liberals were used effectively by the Trump and Clinton campaigns to usher in what Oxford refers to as the "post-truth" era.

The same can be said of the media. While Fox News, the *New York*

Post, and the right-wing media have long peddled their pet theories as fact, with complete and total disregard for the truth and evidence-based research, the liberal establishment media have also played a part in obscuring and distorting reality. Numerous media scholars have explained how a for-profit media system generates news that reinforces the status quo, distorts reality, and fails to meet the needs of a democratic society.

It is here that the work of groups like Fairness and Accuracy In Reporting (FAIR) and Project Censored is vital in pointing to the ways in which the establishment media fail to cover important stories or offer coverage that is supportive of the power elite. The "post-truth" phenomenon had haunted the US public sphere long before Oxford made its declaration in 2016.

However, no group of journalists, analysts, or scholars is beyond reproach. Indeed, it would be folly to think that some of us are never swayed by emotion and that our beliefs and politics do not inform our thinking and writing. We too inhabit a "truth-deficient" landscape and are susceptible to viewing the world through our own lenses, accepted theories, and value systems.

It is not a question of striving for neutrality, a position which itself is not possible in a society riven by conflicting interests and social and political struggles and which only serves to obscure one's normative agenda and worldview. But while it is not possible to be "neutral on a moving train" (as Howard Zinn once famously put it), it is possible to strive for accuracy in our pursuit of knowledge and truth—that is, to be open to new evidence and new facts, including (if not especially) those that conflict with our current assumptions and preferred ways of understanding the world. Thus, rather than dismissing new evidence out of hand because it does not fit our existing theories, the challenge we face is to adjust the latter to account for the former as we seek to expand our knowledge of the world.

This principle is at the core of academic freedom and it applies as much to journalism as it does to scholarly research. In this post-truth moment it's worth recalling the landmark case involving Richard T. Ely, an economics professor at the University of Wisconsin–Madison who came under attack in the 1890s, a period of great social and political conflict, for his pro-labor views. In 1894 the UW Board of Regents ruled in Ely's favor, producing a defense of academic freedom that has been widely cited ever since:

> As Regents of a university with over a hundred instructors supported by nearly two millions of people who hold a vast diversity of views regarding the great questions which at present agitate the human mind, we could not for a moment think of recommending the dismissal or even the criticism of a teacher even if some of his opinions should, in some quarters, be regarded as visionary. Such a course would be equivalent to saying that no professor should teach anything which is not accepted by everybody as true. This would cut our curriculum down to very small proportions. We cannot for a moment believe that knowledge has reached its final goal, or that the present condition of society is perfect. We must therefore welcome from our teachers such discussions as shall suggest the means and prepare the way by which knowledge may be extended, present evils be removed and others prevented. We feel that we would be unworthy of the position we hold if we did not believe in progress in all departments of knowledge. In all lines of academic investigation it is of the utmost importance that the investigator should be absolutely free to follow the indications of truth wherever they may lead. Whatever may be the limitations which trammel inquiry elsewhere we believe the great state University of Wisconsin should ever encourage that continual and fearless sifting and winnowing by which alone the truth can be found.[3]

One hundred and twenty-three years later, we once again face a similar set of obstacles in our pursuit of knowledge and truth at a time of intensifying social and political conflict. It is therefore incumbent on all of us to redouble our commitment to that pursuit as we seek answers to "the great questions which at present agitate the human mind" and struggle for social justice.

We live in an extraordinarily complex and ever-changing world that is not given to simple, much less simplistic, explanations. The pursuit of truth is therefore an ongoing project, in which the flourishing of competing explanations is in fact essential to its success. Journalists, scholars, and critical thinkers must resist the temptation to "call out," to shame or otherwise silence dissenters through emotional appeals. Instead, if we are to explain the world adequately—and set about to change it for the better—then we must engage in a process of genuine debate, distinguished by the "continual and fearless sifting and winnowing" encouraged in the UW Regents' statement from 1894.

DEEPA KUMAR is an associate professor of journalism and media studies at Rutgers University. She received the 2016 Dallas Smythe Award for her influential scholarship and activism. She is author of *Outside the Box: Corporate Media, Globalization, and the UPS Strike* and *Islamophobia and the Politics of Empire*. She has written dozens of articles that have appeared in scholarly journals, independent media, and the mainstream media.

Notes

1. Linda Qiu, "Fact-Checking President Trump through His First 100 Days," *New York Times*, April 27, 2017, https://www.nytimes.com/2017/04/29/us/politics/fact-checking-president-trump-through-his-first-100-days.html.
2. Deepa Kumar and Patrick Barrett, "The Art of Spin," *Jacobin*, November 6, 2016, https://www.jacobinmag.com/2016/11/spin-clinton-campaign-feminist-privilege-politics/.
3. "Report of the Board of Regents Investigating Committee," University of Wisconsin Board of Regents, September 18, 1894, republished in Theodore Herfurth, "Sifting and Winnowing," *Wisconsin Electronic Reader*, http://digicoll.library.wisc.edu/WIReader/WER1035-Chpt1.html.

Introduction

Mickey Huff and Andy Lee Roth

*The truth comes as conqueror only because we have lost
the art of receiving it as guest.*

—Rabindranath Tagore (1861–1941)[1]

THE TRUTH AS CONQUEROR IN A "POST-TRUTH" WORLD

The Indian poet and Nobel laureate Rabindranath Tagore personified
truth as either a guest or a conqueror, depending on our attitude toward
it. As welcome guest, truth could enlighten and enhance our lives; as
conqueror, it compels us to face reality, whether we like it or not.

In her foreword to this book, Deepa Kumar noted that Oxford Dictionaries selected "post-truth" as its 2016 Word of the Year.[2] A decade
earlier, late-night satirist Stephen Colbert had coined a similar term,
"truthiness," which Oxford later defined as "the quality of seeming or
being felt to be true, even if not necessarily true." Oxford Dictionaries
noted that *post-truth* extended the notion of *truthiness* to "a general
characteristic of our age."[3]

In the twenty-first century, denial of truth has become so ubiquitous that our political leaders invoke "alternative facts" and mock
the "reality-based community."[4] In a "post-truth" era, the society's
most popular news is characterized by statements taken out of context, headlines driven by clickbait, and unabashed lies. Not surpris-
ingly, this "characteristic of our age" has spawned curious offspring,
including "alternative facts" and so-called "fake news."

At a time when government and the corporate media regard
the truth as an uninvited guest—when reporters who question the

veracity of authorities are denied access to sources, are chastised or censored, or are even physically removed—Tagore's vision of truth as conqueror once again emerges in full force. Project Censored stands alongside a dedicated community of investigators and scholars in defiant opposition of those who promote and profit from "post-truth" narratives. In gathering a diversity of voices in pursuit of a common cause, *Censored 2018* affirms the crucial role of a free and fearless press in the dogged belief that a well-informed populace is the best defense against the tyranny of the corrupt.

"FAKE NEWS" AS A WEAPON

The corporate media and political class popularized the concept of "fake news" during the 2016 presidential election. Historically "fake news" had indicated a form of satire, not intended to be interpreted as actual reporting. In contemporary context, the concept has been recast to describe information that "is clearly and demonstrably fabricated . . . packaged and distributed to appear as legitimate news."[5] Over the course of the 2016 election, the use of "fake news" developed further. Initially it referred specifically to (false) news stories intended to produce profits for the stories' creators when those stories went viral on social media, to the detriment of a misled public. In fact, many in the corporate press and the Democratic Party blamed "fake news" for the election's outcome,[6] which resulted in a dark-horse Republican candidate and long-time reality TV celebrity winning the Electoral College while losing the popular vote by a margin of nearly three million votes. This attention sparked increased public interest in the phenomenon of "fake news"—attention that was certainly warranted, given the findings from a November 2016 Stanford University study showing that alarming numbers of middle school, high school, and college students could not distinguish advertisements from news stories and fake news stories from real ones. The study concluded:

> Overall, young people's ability to reason about the information on the Internet can be summed up in one word: bleak. Our "digital natives" may be able to flit between Facebook

and Twitter while simultaneously uploading a selfie to Instagram and texting a friend. But when it comes to evaluating
information that flows through social media channels, they
are easily duped.[7]

A Pew Research Center poll from late 2016 found that 64 percent
of the American public believed fake news "caused a great deal of
confusion."[8]

On the campaign trail and as president, Donald Trump used the
term "fake news" in a second, different way—as "a weaponized epithet" to attack journalists or news media outlets with which he disagreed.[9] In this usage, power is wielded by applying the label "fake
news" to any news story, person, or organization that one seeks to
discredit or dismiss. For example, during a January 2017 press conference, President-Elect Trump used the label as a justification for
refusing to take a question from CNN reporter Jim Acosta. "I'm
not going to give you a question," Trump told Acosta. "You are fake
news!"[10]

Another way to attempt to counter information with which one dis-
agrees is by citing "alternative facts," as happened after Trump's inauguration. In his first appearance before the White House press corps,
Sean Spicer, Trump's press secretary, claimed, "This was the largest
audience to ever witness an inauguration—period." Subsequently,
on *Meet the Press*, Trump's counselor, Kellyanne Conway, sought to
defend Spicer and his claim, by asserting that Spicer "gave alternative
facts."[11] As Chuck Todd, the host of *Meet the Press*, responded, "Alternative facts are not facts. They're falsehoods."[12]

Although the corporate media and political elites brought "fake
news" and "alternative facts" to public attention during the 2016
presidential election, the underlying concerns that each raises are not
new. "Fake news" and "alternative facts" are part and parcel of what is
more commonly understood as *propaganda*, which we at Project Censored have analyzed as a form of censorship. Further, these terms and
concepts are not unique to US history. As German studies scholar
Petra S. McGillen described in a recent historical review of fake news,
"By the 1850s, the phenomenon was so widespread in Germany
that it had become its own genre—the 'unechte Korrespondenz,' or

'fake foreign correspondent's letter,' as people in the German news trade called it."[13] McGillen explained that, as news reporting became increasingly standardized, with newspapers covering similar stories using formulaic language and conventional formats, local reporters could pose as foreign correspondents by imitating the style and form used by actual foreign correspondents. This nineteenth-century ruse in some ways anticipated the downsizing of newsrooms due to corporate consolidation in the past two decades, as we once again see a proliferation of fake news and propagandistic reports in what is now called an "echo chamber." These same techniques of misrepresentation, coupled with digital technology, make falsehoods even easier to propagate.

There have been numerous examples of promulgating falsehoods as truths throughout US history. Recall the early European settlers who claimed to have "bought" land from Native Americans; the oft-repeated assertion that slavery would be "civilizing" for those who were subjected to it;[14] the shameful fact that runaway slaves, overwhelmingly African American, were diagnosed with a "medical condition," drapetomania, conjured in the 1850s by physician Samuel A. Cartwright;[15] the allegation that communists had infiltrated the US (and that President Eisenhower was a "conscious, dedicated agent" of the communist conspiracy);[16] and the manifold false pretexts for war, including the Gulf of Tonkin incident and Iraq's nonexistent weapons of mass destruction.[17] The list is long, and could go on. Note that today's fake news is tomorrow's fake history.

THE FREE PRESS AS "ENEMY OF THE PEOPLE"

Like fake news, hostility toward the press is also nothing new. In the US, the Nixon administration made a policy of demonizing the media, especially as it grappled with declining public support for the war in Vietnam and the 1970 Kent State massacre. Then–vice president Spiro Agnew, with infamous alliteration penned by speechwriter William Safire, referred to the press as "nattering nabobs of negativism" who "formed their own 4-H club—the 'hopeless, hysterical hypochondriacs of history.'"[18] This preceded Nixon's 1971 attack on the *New York Times*, when his administration attempted to suppress the release of the Pentagon Papers and silence whistleblower Daniel Ellsberg—a case Nixon took to the Supreme Court and lost.

While hostility toward the press has historically run in cycles, it has been increasing lately as whistleblower protections and respect for journalists have measurably decreased. The Obama administration prosecuted more whistleblowers than all previous US administrations combined, and Trump has run at full throttle in attacking the press, making those attacks a staple of both his campaign and his presidency.

Throughout the 2016 election campaign, Trump treated the press as "a prop, or a punching bag," leading Emily Bazelon to predict in a November 2016 *New York Times Magazine* article that "[t]he new president will be a man who constantly accuses the media of getting things wrong but routinely misrepresents and twists facts himself."[19] Trump urged his supporters at rallies to attack the press as throngs chanted, "Lock them up!" As Indira A.R. Lakshmanan of the Poynter Institute observed, "His attitude worsened when he won. Trump turned 'fake news' from a factual description of online hoaxes into a weaponized epithet against any critic."[20]

In one of his first post-inauguration appearances, President Trump gave a speech from the CIA headquarters stating that he was engaged in "a running war with the media" and that journalists were "among the most dishonest human beings on earth." At a Republican policy retreat in late January he said there was "nothing fair about the media. Nothing." At the same time, Trump's chief strategist Steve Bannon, former CEO of the right-wing news site Breitbart, said the media, which he referred to as "the opposition party," had been "humiliated" by the election's outcome. Bannon quipped, "The media should be embarrassed . . . and keep its mouth shut and just listen for awhile."[21] Trump surrogates used the attack on the press as a key talking point throughout his first hundred days in office.

In February 2017, during a series of public Tweets, Trump wrote, "The FAKE NEWS media (failing @nytimes, @NBCNews, @ABC, @CBS, @CNN) is not my enemy, it is the enemy of the American People!" The term "enemy of the people" carries significant connotations, having been used historically by despots against journalists and dissidents, sometimes to justify ethnic cleansing. Trump has used it, proudly and repeatedly, against the free press.[22]

Trump's systemic hostility toward the news media has set an example others have been willing to follow. Montana's 2017 special election for the House of Representatives saw GOP candidate Greg Gianforte confront *Guardian* reporter Ben Jacobs after refusing to answer questions at a campaign event. Gianforte verbally abused Jacobs before body-slamming him to the ground. Said Jacobs, "Mr. Gianforte's response was to slam me to the floor and start punching me. He injured my elbow, broke my glasses and thrust me into a national spotlight I did not seek or desire."[23] Despite his assault on a journalist, Gianforte went on to win the special election, with many of his supporters cheering on his actions as if they were part of a professional wrestling melodrama rather than a congressional election. Gianforte admitted his own guilt to misdemeanor assault charges, apologized, and was sentenced to forty hours of community service and twenty hours of anger management classes.[24]

It is heartening to see resistance to this violent attitude toward journalists. Numerous free press organizations protested Gianforte's actions, including PEN America, the Committee to Protect Journalists (CPJ), and the Society of Professional Journalists, among others. Gianforte had to pay some restitution, including a donation to the CPJ. Gabe Rottman of PEN America said, "A member of the House hasn't physically assaulted someone this severely since the Civil War, and we are unaware of any historical precedent for a lawmaker beating up a reporter . . . Amid a climate of escalating hostility toward the press it is essential for the House to send a clear message to its members and to the nation that hostile treatment of the press will not be tolerated or ignored."[25] But, as this book goes to print, Gianforte has been sworn in as the sole federal representative to the House from the state of Montana.

These attacks on the press come at a time when we need a strong fourth estate the most, to help educate and inform the American public about key issues of our day. The US public is becoming dangerously uninformed. Recall that in December 2015, Public Policy Polling conducted an opinion poll asking, "Would you support or oppose bombing Agrabah?" Some 30 percent of 532 Republican primary voters polled said yes; 13 percent opposed; and 57 percent said they were not sure.[26] Agrabah is the fictional kingdom from Disney's animated classic, *Aladdin*. Democrats should not be too smug about these results: 19 percent of the Democrats polled said they would support bombing Agrabah, while 36 percent opposed doing so.[27]

Public ignorance has risen to the point that Stanford University science historian Robert Proctor decided to establish a new field of study, agnotology. Proctor coined the term after studying tactics used by the tobacco industry to downplay the dangers of smoking. "I was exploring how powerful industries could promote ignorance to sell their wares. Ignorance is power . . . and agnotology is about the deliberate creation of ignorance."[28] Similarly, David Dunning of Cornell University warned that the Internet has made it much easier to spread propaganda, which would include "fake news" and "alternative facts." Dunning stated, "While some smart people will profit from all the information now just a click away, many will be misled into a false sense of expertise. My worry is not that we are losing the ability to make up our own minds, but that it's becoming too easy to do so."[29] Dunning noted that, by suggesting "easy solutions to followers that are either unworkable or unconstitutional," Trump contributed to the rampant spread of ignorance on both sides of the political spectrum during the presidential primaries.

A "post-truth" society celebrates the triumph of partisan opinion over reasoned argument, "alternative" facts over empirical ones, and even fake news over well-documented investigative reporting.[30] At a time when public trust in news media is not only in decline but also deeply divided along partisan lines, a recent Pew Research Center poll found that Democrats were more than twice as likely as Republicans to support a watchdog role for the press in holding those in public office accountable. The gap of 47 percentage points between the two groups is the largest recorded since 1985, when Pew began tracking the phenomenon.[31] Similarly, a study from Duke University's Sanford School of Public Policy found conservatives were far more likely to distrust fact-checking organizations than their liberal counterparts, and to attack fact-checkers as "incompetent journalists."[32]

If we are to remain a free and democratic society, we need critical thinking tools to verify the integrity of the news and information we receive. It is not enough to examine the spread of public ignorance or the depths of the partisan divide between segments of the public;

something must be *done* about them. There is a glimmer of hope. According to a 2017 Reuters survey, people are starting to become more critical of news and information sources. After reading a news item on social media, 74 percent double-check with sources they trust, and 88 percent check multiple sources for important stories.[33] So despite some of the grim details of our "post-truth" world, there are signs that people are becoming more critical. It is in times like these that we need a free and independent press more than ever, one that Project Censored has celebrated and supported for over forty years.

INSIDE *CENSORED 2018*

As noted in the introduction to Chapter 1, Project Censored can be understood as "an ongoing empirical investigation of the corporate news media's blind spots and lacunae, its third rails and 'no go' zones." Chapter 1 presents the twenty-five most important but under-reported news stories of 2016–2017. The list highlights expert news coverage by independent reporters and organizations that work in service of a well-informed public. Each of these stories has been "censored" by the corporate news media in the broad sense of the term established by Project Censored's founder, Carl Jensen, who defined censorship as "the suppression of information, whether purposeful or not, by any method—including bias, omission, underreporting or self-censorship—that prevents the public from fully knowing what is happening in its society."[34] From the Pentagon paying a public relations firm to produce fake al-Qaeda videos (story #3) and the Big Data and dark money behind the 2016 presidential election (story #5), to widespread lead contamination across the US (story #1) and the nation's growing maternal mortality rates (story #8), independent news reporters have provided vital information about fundamental public issues that the corporate news media have inadequately covered or altogether ignored.

In Chapter 2, we examine Junk Food News and News Abuse. The former refers to the journalistic folly that corporate news organizations all too often publish and broadcast in the place of genuinely important and newsworthy stories. Among this year's Junk Food News, the White House Correspondents' Association Dinner,

Olympic crimes and behavior, and the Best Picture Oscar's snafu at the Academy Awards were all corporate media favorites, while the same media failed to report on numerous stories related to the seriousness of climate change. Under the rubric of News Abuse, we examine the skewed framing, glaring biases, and party-line propaganda that serve to undermine the public's understanding of stories that are in fact important and newsworthy. In 2016–2017, we tracked News Abuse coverage of the 2016 presidential election, failures of the mass media and educational system, and the roles that so-called "fake news" and "alternative facts" have played in creating a "post-truth" world.

Media Democracy in Action provides crucial counterbalance to the Junk Food News and News Abuse documented in Chapter 2. Chapter 3 highlights organizations, resources, and research that exemplify the vital links between media activism and democracy—from venerable organizations, such as the Index on Censorship, to promising new ones, including Tribeworthy and the *Unauthorized Disclosure* podcast. This chapter introduces readers to tools they can use to engage more directly and effectively in media democracy themselves—from the aforementioned Tribeworthy's Crowd Contested Media to the Electronic Frontier Foundation's Privacy Badger and HTTPS Everywhere web browser extensions. This chapter also presents a simple but effective method for analyzing news stories in terms of whom journalists treat as newsworthy, and how these choices shape news content.

In Chapter 4, Nolan Higdon and Nicholas Baham III critically examine news coverage of the 2016 presidential election. They describe how, "in an effort to garner ratings and advertiser funds at the expense of the democratic process, the US media normalized racism by providing precious media time and space to racists." Higdon and Baham identify four factors that contributed to this process of normalization and resulted in Donald Trump's election: The corporate news media (1) failed to think critically about race; (2) gave Trump leeway in their pursuit of advertiser revenues; (3) traded journalistic integrity for access to the new administration; and (4) mistakenly expected racist arguments to collapse under their own weight. The corporate media's failures, Higdon and Baham warn, serve as "fertile ground" for the normalization of a new American authoritarianism.

For several years now, Project Censored has sought to feature a graphic chapter. Those efforts have yielded stirring results with the inclusion of Adam Bessie and Peter Glanting's "Trump Universe" in Chapter 5. Drawing on a visual vocabulary informed by Jack Kirby's Galactus and Dr. Doom, among others, and with text that invokes Ursula Le Guin and namechecks Rod Serling's *Twilight Zone* and George Orwell's *1984*, Bessie and Glanting measure the gravity of "Trump Universe" and encourage us to engage not as characters from already familiar dramas, but as the authors of our own stories.

In Chapter 6, Elizabeth Blakey examines how the courts use a different First Amendment standard, "one that creates a higher likelihood of liability in defamation lawsuits," for social-media speakers than they apply to traditional journalists. Blakey provides a succinct, clear primer on whom the courts define as a *media defendant* in defamation cases, how these definitions vary in jurisdictions across the country, and what's at stake. Uneven regulation of social media, often based on "antiquated" understandings of news production and publishing, has led to ambiguity in who is granted status as a media defendant. The result, she writes, is an "uneven hierarchy" between speakers, "some with more privileges and liberties than others," that is unconstitutional and creates censorship problems that bode poorly for "the future of public speaking via social media."

In 1988, Edward S. Herman and Noam Chomsky published *Manufacturing Consent*, which introduced their Propaganda Model of news and presented substantial evidence of its utility. The Propaganda Model identified five news filters that narrowed "the premises of [news] discourse and interpretation, and the definition of what is newsworthy in the first place."[35] For its thirtieth anniversary, Herman provides an assessment of the Propaganda Model's twenty-first-century relevance. Against the backdrop of declining advertising revenues for legacy news media and the arrival of Google, Facebook, and other new giants in digital advertising, Herman examines corporate news coverage of the Bush administration's case for the invasion of Iraq in 2003 and provides a comparative analysis of establishment reporting on the 2009 elections in Iran and Honduras. As Herman shows, thirty years on, the explanatory power of the Propaganda Model has not diminished.

Ralph Nader concludes this year's volume with "Breaking Through Power: Mass Media Blacks Out the Super Bowl of Citizen Action." Nader describes how, in May and September of 2016, he and the Center for Study of Responsive Law convened in Washington, DC, "the greatest number of civic advocates, thinkers, innovators, and whistleblowers ever brought together for civic mobilization in American history." The result, Nader reports, was a "black out" of the event and its more than 180 distinguished, newsworthy speakers by the nation's and the region's most prominent news organizations. Nevertheless, the Breaking Through Power events amounted to "a major show of civic presence in the nation's capital," and they demonstrated that "the interconnected whole of grassroots action in the United States is greater than the sum of its parts."

"A STIMULUS FOR CRITICAL REFLECTION"

A democratic civilization will save itself only if it makes the language of the image into a stimulus for critical reflection— not an invitation for hypnosis.

—Umberto Eco[36]

The cover of *Censored 2018* features original art by Hilary Allison.[37] As a living room floods (perhaps as a result of human-triggered climate change?) the television broadcasts imagery of a blaze. An array of fire extinguishers suggests that the household's members had followed the media's agenda by preparing for fire. But the fire extinguishers are useless for countering the reality of the rising tide. (Somewhere out of view, perhaps on the side table or tucked in the cushion of a couch, we might find an alternative newsweekly, with a feature story warning of flooding.)

Allison's imagery of a television screen that distracts its viewer from direct reality will remind some readers of Ray Bradbury's *Fahrenheit 451*, in which members of the public are distracted from impending war by wall-sized screens that bombard them with nonsense.[38]

The screen in Allison's cover image does not broadcast nonsense, but it has evidently misled its audience about what element poses the greatest risk in this scene—not fire, but water. As such, *Censored 2018*'s cover also suggests a fundamental insight from Umberto Eco, the Italian novelist, literary critic, and philosopher. In a 1979 essay, "Can Television Teach?," Eco questioned whether TV led to hypnosis or critical reflection. Nearly thirty years later, screens not only convey information and imagery to us in our living rooms, but also wherever we go, thanks to smartphones, tablet computers, and other mobile communication devices—and Eco's question about the relationship between "the language of the image" and the future of democracy remains crucial.

We present *Censored 2018* as a stimulus not only for critical reflection but also for engaged action. It is not enough to be informed that a flood is coming (or that the threat of fire might be *misinformation*). That knowledge prepares us to act effectively, but we must still engage. At the risk of seeming immodest, we see Project Censored as part of the "interconnected whole of grassroots action" described by Ralph Nader in this book's concluding chapter. We invite you to join us in vigorously supporting both a truly free and independent press and critical media literacy, as two crucial bulwarks against a rising "post-truth" tide of alternative facts, fake news, and propaganda. In standing up for fearless reporting, we ally ourselves with the Truth as conqueror, fighting back against the spin to win its place as our most welcome guest.

Notes

1. *The English Writings of Rabindranath Tagore, Volume Seven: Lectures, Addresses* (New Delhi, Atlantic Publishers & Distributors, 2007), 674.
2. Oxford defined "post-truth" as describing "circumstances in which objective facts are less influential in shaping public opinion than appeals to emotion and personal belief." "Word of the Year 2016 is…," English Oxford Living Dictionaries, November 8, 2016, https://en.oxforddictionaries.com/word-of-the-year/word-of-the-year-2016.
3. Ibid.
4. In 2004, Ron Suskind described a 2002 conversation with an unnamed senior advisor to President George W. Bush. In that conversation, Suskind reported, the aide (widely believed to have been Bush's deputy chief of staff, Karl Rove) "said that guys like me were 'in what we call the reality-based community,' which he defined as people who 'believe that solutions emerge from your judicious study of discernible reality.' I nodded and murmured something about enlightenment principles and empiricism. He cut me off. 'That's not the way the world really works anymore,' he continued. 'We're an empire now, and when we act, we create our own reality.'" Ron Suskind, "Faith, Certainty and the Presidency of George W. Bush," *New York Times Magazine*, October 17, 2004, http://www.nytimes.com/2004/10/17/magazine/faith-certainty-and-the-presidency-of-george-w-bush.html. See also Mark Danner, "Words in a Time

of War," *Los Angeles Times*, June 1, 2007, http://www.latimes.com/la-oe-danner1juno1-story. html. Danner observed that, from the point of view expressed by the Bush aide, "Those in the 'reality-based community' are figures a mite pathetic, for we have failed to realize the singular new principle of the new age: Power has made reality its bitch."

5. Allison Butler, "Post-Election, Post-Truth: Using Comprehensive Media Literacy to Assess and Evaluate News and Current Events," Mass Media Literacy, January 31, 2017, posted online at the Global Critical Media Literacy Project, gcml.org/wp-content/uploads/2017/02/fakenews. pdf; for a comprehensive list of related terms, see "Understanding the Fake News Universe: A Guide to Fake News Terminology," Media Matters, December 15, 2016, https://www.media-matters.org/research/2016/12/15/understanding-fake-news-universe/214819#d1.

6. See, for instance, Mathew Ingram, "Hillary Clinton Blames the Russians, Facebook, and Fake News for Her Loss," *Fortune*, May 31, 2017, http://fortune.com/2017/05/31/clinton-fake-news/. For more on how the Democratic Party and corporate media blamed the election's outcome on "fake news" while creating some of their own, see Chapter 2 of this volume.

7. "Evaluating Information: The Cornerstone of Civic Online Reasoning," Stanford History Education Group, November 22, 2016, https://sheg.stanford.edu/upload/V3LessonPlans/Executive%20 Summary%2011.21.16.pdf.

8. Michael Barthel, Amy Mitchell, and Jesse Holcomb, "Many Americans Believe Fake News is Sowing Confusion," Pew Research Center, December 15, 2016, http://www.journalism. org/2016/12/15/many-americans-believe-fake-news-is-sowing-confusion/.

9. Indira A.R. Lakshmanan, "President Trump's War on the Press is Dangerous. He's Discrediting a Profession He Fears," Poynter Institute, May 25, 2017, http://www.poynter.org/2017/president-trumps-war-on-the-press-is-dangerous-hes-discrediting-a-profession-he-fears/461352/.

10. Rebecca Savransky, "Trump Berates CNN Reporter: 'You are Fake News,'" The Hill, January 11, 2017, http://thehill.com/homenews/administration/313777-trump-berates-cnn-reporter-for-fake-news.

11. See "Kellyanne Conway Denies Trump Press Secretary Lied: 'He Offered Alternative Facts'— Video," *Meet the Press*, NBC, January 22, 2017, posted on the *Guardian*, January 22, 2017, https://www.theguardian.com/us-news/video/2017/jan/22/kellyanne-conway-trump-press-secretary-alternative-facts-video.

12. Ibid. For further analysis of Conway's exchange with *Meet the Press* host Chuck Todd, see the introduction to Chapter 1 of this volume.

13. Petra S. McGillen, "Techniques of 19th-Century Fake News Reporter Teach Us Why We Fall for It Today," The Conversation, April 5, 2017, https://theconversation.com/techniques-of-19th-century-fake-news-reporter-teach-us-why-we-fall-for-it-today-75583.

14. For one example of this argument, see the text of Senator James Henry Hammond's March 1858 speech before the US Senate, in which he asserted, "Our slaves are black, of another and inferior race. The status in which we have placed them is an elevation. They are elevated from the condition in which God first created them, by being made our slaves." See "The 'Mudsill' Theory," Africans in America, Public Broadcasting Service (PBS), no date, http://www.pbs. org/wgbh/aia/part4/4h3439t.html.

15. Drapetomania—which might alternatively have been "diagnosed" as the longing for *freedom*— caused slaves to flee captivity, and Cartwright proposed, as professional medical treatment, either "whipping the devil" out of slaves or cutting off their big toes to prevent their escape. See Kevin White, *An Introduction to the Sociology of Health and Illness* (London: SAGE, 2007), 46–48.

16. Michael Seiler, "Robert Welch, Founder of Birch Society, Dies at 85," *Los Angeles Times*, January 8, 1985, http://articles.latimes.com/1985-01-08/news/mn-7296_1_john-birch-society.

17. Norman Solomon, *War Made Easy: How Presidents and Pundits Keep Spinning Us to Death* (New York: Wiley, 2006).

18. David Remnick, "Nattering Nabobs," *New Yorker*, July 10, 2006, http://www.newyorker.com/ magazine/2006/07/10/nattering-nabobs; these lines were from a speech given by then–vice president Spiro Agnew at the California Republican state convention, September 11, 1970.

19. Emily Bazelon, "Stop the Presses," *New York Times Magazine*, November 27, 2016, 53.

20. Lakshmanan, "President Trump's War on the Press."
21. "The Trump Administration's War on the Press," Media Matters, February 1, 2017, https://www.mediamatters.org/trumps-war-on-the-press.
22. See, e.g., Amanda Erickson, "Trump Called the News Media an 'Enemy of the American People.' Here's a History of the Term," Washington Post, February 18, 2017, https://www.washingtonpost.com/news/worldviews/wp/2017/02/18/trump-called-the-news-media-an-enemy-of-the-american-people-heres-a-history-of-the-term/.
23. Christopher Mele, "Montana Republican Greg Gianforte is Sentenced in Assault on Reporter," New York Times, June 13, 2017, https://www.nytimes.com/2017/06/13/us/politics/greg-gianforte-sentenced.html; "SPJ Joins Groups Asking that Gianforte be Disciplined for Violence against Reporter," Society of Professional Journalists, June 5, 2017, http://www.spj.org/news.asp?ref=1512.
24. Mele, "Montana Republican Greg Gianforte is Sentenced."
25. Ibid.
26. Jana Kasperkevic, "Poll: 30% of GOP Voters Support Bombing Agrabah, the City from Aladdin," Guardian, December 18, 2015, https://www.theguardian.com/us-news/2015/dec/18/republican-voters-bomb-agrabah-disney-aladdin-donald-trump.
27. Ibid. In the same poll, 54 percent of Republican primary voters supported banning Muslims from entering the US, and 46 percent supported the creation of a national database of Muslims in the US. The study also found that 25 percent of those polled wanted to make Islam illegal in the US, and the same number approved of the US policy of interning Japanese-Americans during World War II.
28. Georgina Kenyon, "The Man Who Studies the Spread of Ignorance," BBC, January 6, 2016, http://www.bbc.com/future/story/20160105-the-man-who-studies-the-spread-of-ignorance. Project Censored has examined agnotology previously; see Censored 2015: Inspiring We the People, eds. Andy Lee Roth and Mickey Huff with Project Censored (New York: Seven Stories Press, 2014), 134–35, 171.
29. Kenyon, "The Man Who Studies the Spread of Ignorance."
30. Or, as Pico Iyer summarized in equation form, the dismaying tacit belief that "hearsay + opinion + guesswork = truth." See Pico Iyer, "What Do We Know?," New York Times, December 31, 2016, https://www.nytimes.com/2016/12/31/opinion/sunday/what-do-we-know.html.
31. Michael Barthel and Amy Mitchell, "Americans' Attitudes about the News Media Deeply Divided Along Partisan Lines," Pew Research Center, May 10, 2017, http://www.journalism.org/2017/05/10/americans-attitudes-about-the-news-media-deeply-divided-along-partisan-lines/.
32. Erik Wemple, "Study: Conservatives Despise the Fact-Checking Industry," Washington Post, June 9, 2017, https://www.washingtonpost.com/blogs/erik-wemple/wp/2017/06/09/study-conservatives-despise-the-fact-checking-industry/; to see the full study, Rebecca Iannucci and Bill Adair, "Heroes or Hacks: The Partisan Divide over Fact-Checking," Duke Reporters' Lab, Sanford School of Public Policy, June 2017, https://drive.google.com/file/d/0BxoyrEbZxrAMNm9HV2tvcXFma1U/view.
33. Ricardo Bilton, "Reuters' New Survey Suggests that Readers are Getting (a Bit) Smarter about Verifying Breaking News," Nieman Lab, June 8, 2017, http://www.niemanlab.org/2017/06/reuters-new-survey-suggests-that-readers-are-getting-a-bit-smarter-about-verifying-breaking-news/.
34. Carl Jensen, ed., Censored: The News That Didn't Make the News—And Why (Chapel Hill: Shelburne Press, 1993), 7.
35. Edward S. Herman and Noam Chomsky, Manufacturing Consent: The Political Economy of the Mass Media (New York: Pantheon, 1988), 2.
36. Umberto Eco, "Can Television Teach?" Screen Education, No. 31 (1979), 15–24, 15. We thank Bill Yousman for alerting us to this quotation.
37. See http://www.hilaryallison.com/ and @Haha_Hilary. Allison also created the cover art for Censored 2016: Media Freedom on the Line, eds. Mickey Huff and Andy Lee Roth with Project Censored (New York: Seven Stories Press, 2015).
38. We discussed Bradbury's classic novel in the introduction to Censored 2013: Dispatches from the Media Revolution, eds. Mickey Huff and Andy Lee Roth with Project Censored (New York: Seven Stories Press, 2012), 21–27.

CHAPTER 1

THE TOP *CENSORED* STORIES AND MEDIA ANALYSIS OF 2016–17

Compiled and edited by Andy Lee Roth

INTRODUCTION

This year's listing of Project Censored's most important but under-reported independent news stories is best understood against two historic backdrops—one dating back to late 2016, and the other spanning more than four decades, back to 1976—as united by an observation made a century ago by the sociologist Max Weber.

"Inconvenient Facts"

A hundred years ago, on November 7, 1917, in a lecture hall on the campus of Munich University, one of Germany's most eminent social scientists and political economists, Max Weber, gave a lecture on science as a "calling" and its relevance to politics. Social scientists continue to debate the arguments on science and politics that Weber articulated in this lecture, but one of its most famous points remains directly relevant here.

Weber told his Munich University audience that the primary duty of a competent teacher was to teach students to acknowledge "inconvenient facts"—by which, he explained, he meant facts that are inconvenient for the students' "own political views," before adding that there are inconvenient facts "for every political position, including my own." If teachers compel their students to accustom themselves to the existence of such facts, this achievement is "more than merely intellectual," Weber told his audience. Indeed, at the risk of sounding "too emotive," he said we might think of this result as an "ethical achievement."[1] Weber's lecture framed science, in the broadest sense of the term, as a calling to knowledge.

Journalism rests on similar commitments to those articulated by Weber in his "Science as a Vocation" lecture. Like Weber, many journalists distinguish between facts and value judgments, and they strive to be objective in their work. This comparison leads in many interesting directions, but here we'll pursue just one: When we think of journalists as watchdogs and muckrakers, and of journalism as the fourth estate, we probably harbor something akin to Weber's directive for teachers—that a good journalist should dig for and bring to public attention inconvenient facts.

"Alternative Facts"

Perhaps this is what Chuck Todd, the host of NBC's *Meet the Press*, was doing when he challenged Kellyanne Conway—counselor to President Donald Trump—during the January 22, 2017 broadcast of *Meet the Press*. During this broadcast, Conway explained that White House Press Secretary Sean Spicer, in his first appearance before the press, "gave alternative facts" when he inaccurately described the crowd for Trump's inauguration as "the largest ever."[2] When Conway sought to defend the White House press secretary by claiming that Todd was being "over-dramatic" in response to Spicer's "alternative facts," Todd interrupted her and directly countered her claims.[3]

Conway's stipulation of "alternative facts" in defense of Spicer's empirically false claim epitomized an attitude that had led Oxford Dictionaries to name "post-truth" as its Word of the Year in 2016.[4] The exchange over "alternative facts" between Conway and Todd, which lasted less than a minute but generated days of subsequent news coverage and commentary, could be viewed as evidence that *Meet the Press*, and perhaps by extension the nation's establishment news organizations, could still perform their crucial democratic role as the fourth estate, as watchdogs that alert the public to abuses of government authority.

Forty-Two Years of Documenting
Underreported News Stories

Shift now to the second backdrop that provides meaningful context for this year's list of the most important but underreported news stories. This is the forty-second such list that Project Censored has compiled and reported since Carl Jensen founded the Project at Sonoma State University in 1976.[5] Over more than four decades, and now extending geographically to encompass a digitally-networked coalition of college and university campuses across North America and around the world, students, faculty, community experts, and an esteemed panel of international judges have identified, vetted, and publicized news stories of critical importance that have been reported by independent journalists and news organizations, despite inadequate or nonexistent coverage by US corporate news media.

Put another way, the Project can be understood as an ongoing empirical investigation of the corporate news media's blind spots and lacunae, its third rails and "no go" zones. To the already existing database of 1,025 such news topics and stories, *Censored 2018* adds twenty-five further data points.

Crucially, however, this year's top *Censored* stories, along with the thousand-plus stories that preceded them, not only document the shortcomings of the US corporate news media; they also spotlight the crucial work of a truly independent and increasingly networked fourth estate. The news reporting recognized in each year's list of the top *Censored* stories is "good work" in the most deep and meaningful sense of that modest term—it is work of "expert quality that benefits the broader society."[6]

If the corporate news media were prepared to respond as immediately and forcefully as Todd did to Conway, to the abuses of power and "inconvenient facts" captured in the twenty-five independent news reports that follow, then there would be no need for this year's list of the top *Censored* news stories, much less forty-some years of such lists. But, with due respect to Chuck Todd, it was far simpler to counter Conway's defense of Spicer's "alternative facts" than it is to confront the reality that, for instance, the Pentagon paid a UK public relations firm to produce fake al-Qaeda videos (this year's #3 story), the fossil fuel industry has effectively "colonized" energy and climate science research at the nation's most prestigious universities (#21 on this year's list), and maternal mortality is a growing threat in the US (story #8). The "inconvenient facts" underlying each of these stories challenge not only fundamental institutions in our society, but also cherished notions about who we are and the values we hold sacrosanct.

For whatever reasons, in 2016–2017 the most prominent establishment news organizations in the US proved unwilling to cover these news stories and twenty-two more like them, which are detailed below. Fortunately, independent journalists and news organizations have done the proper investigative work, and have published their findings even when the corporate media have not. Though many of these stories are far from good news, the efforts undertaken by these news reporters truly constitute good work, and these efforts to confront the truth should be an inspiration to us all. Whether fighting "fake news" and its pernicious consequences or investigating how corporate news more generally functions as propaganda, we are responding to Weber's calling to knowledge and engaging in a version of what he described as the task of addressing "inconvenient facts."[7]

An Overview of This Year's Top *Censored* Stories

Each of the independent news stories presented in this chapter stands on its own, and matters in its own right, as evidence of a public issue that we must face, and sometimes also as indication of what is possible when we do address public issues collectively. But, as suggested by this introduction's emphasis on a broader perspective spanning more than four decades of *Censored* news stories, it's also important to consider connections among the stories that constitute this year's Top 25 list.

In the sciences, grouping similar things together is often referred to as "lumping"—while the opposite, parsing different things as separate, is known as "splitting."[8] When we lump things together, we allow perceived similarities to outweigh differences. Finding common themes across news stories helps to contextualize each item as a part of the larger narratives shaping our times.

For example, four stories in this year's list focus on climate change (#15, "Shell Understood Climate Change as Early as 1991—and Ignored It," #16, "'Resilient' Indian Communities Struggle to Cope with Impacts of Climate Change," #17, "Young Plaintiffs Invoke Constitutional Grounds for Climate Protection," and #21, "Fossil Fuel Industry 'Colonizing' US Universities"). Together, these stories present a constellation of "inconvenient facts" for President Trump's well-documented equivocations on climate science and his "America First" approach to the Paris climate agreement and the G7 climate change declaration.

Racial inequalities inform at least a half dozen of the stories, including #4, "Voter Suppression in the 2016 Presidential Election," #8, "Maternal Mortality a Growing Threat in the US," #14, "Judges across US Using Racially Biased Software to Assess Defendants' Risk of Committing Future Crimes," and #18, on the number of transgender murders. Racial inequality also plays a major part in story #1, on widespread lead contamination, and #25, about how juvenile court fees punish children for their families' poverty. These stories present "inconvenient facts" for politicians and pundits who assert that the US is a "post-racial" society.

A handful of stories focus on issues involving the courts—not only as crucial venues in which injustices can be addressed (for example, #22, "Lawsuit against Illinois Department of Corrections Exposes Militarization of Law Enforcement inside Prisons," and #17, "Young Plaintiffs Invoke Constitutional Grounds for Climate Protection"), but also, in some cases, as sites where inequalities are reproduced (as in #14, "Judges across US Using Racially Biased Software to Assess Defendants' Risk of Committing Future Crimes," and #18, "Rise in Number of Transgender People Murdered").

Health issues unite several of the stories on this list (see #1, #6, and #8). The Pentagon features in at least two stories (#2 and #3), as does government surveillance (#11, #12, and #23). Documentary films produced by the Shell Oil Company feature in a pair of stories (#15 and #21).

There are more connections to be identified. As we have noted in previous *Censored* volumes, the task of identifying common topical themes, within each year's story list and across multiple years, transforms the reader from a passive recipient of information into an active, engaged interpreter.[9] We invite you to engage with this year's story list in this way.

Beyond the intrepid reporters and independent organizations that have brought this year's collection of stories to the public, this chapter would not exist without the active, engaged, and collective effort of more than 310 student researchers and 27 faculty evaluators from 12 college and university campuses across the US and Canada. Working under the organizational umbrella of Project Censored's Validated Independent News program, they identified, vetted, and summarized more than two hundred independent news stories, from which the Top 25 of 2016–2017 have been selected. Our researchers, too, have wrestled with "inconvenient facts." This direct, hands-on training in critical thinking and media literacy is a crucial aspect of Project Censored's mission to prepare a next generation—including many who are on their way to becoming leaders in their communities—to cultivate a wary attitude toward corporate media, to support high quality independent journalism, and to recognize and champion the crucial role of a free press for democracy.

For each story synopsis that follows, we identify not only the names and publication sources of the original news story, but also the names and campus affiliations of the students and faculty members who investigated whether the story received any coverage in the corporate media and who wrote the initial synopsis of the news story. We identify the student researchers and faculty evaluators, not only to give credit where credit is due—the independent press is so diverse and extensive today that no single small group of people can keep track of it—but also to inspire other students and teachers, who might want to do this work themselves, to join us. Those interested can learn more about how to do so in this volume or on the Project Censored website.[10]

The brief synopses that follow are not meant to replace the original news reports on which they are based. Instead, they summarize the stories' key points, hopefully in ways that lead interested readers back to the original reports themselves. The following "Note on Research and Evaluation of *Censored* News Stories" provides more detail on the vetting process and how we rank the stories.

ACKNOWLEDGMENTS: Geoff Davidian provided resolute assistance and keen editorial judgment in helping to prepare this year's slate of several hundred Validated Independent News stories for the Top 25 vote by our panel of judges. Tom Field responded with expert research assistance and astute news judgment each time we presented him with some of the thornier issues the stories brought up. Brittany Ayala, Ama Cortes, Elsa Denis, Jess Parry, and Miranda Webster assisted with the final review of this year's *Censored* stories.

A NOTE ON RESEARCH AND EVALUATION
OF *CENSORED* NEWS STORIES

How do we at Project Censored identify and evaluate independent news stories, and how do we know that the Top 25 stories that we bring forward each year are not only relevant and significant, but also trustworthy? The answer is that each candidate news story undergoes rigorous review, which takes place in multiple stages during each annual cycle. Although adapted to take advantage of both the Project's expanding affiliates program and current technologies, the vetting process is quite similar to the one Project Censored founder Carl Jensen established over forty years ago.

Candidate stories are initially identified by Project Censored professors and students, or are nominated by members of the general public, who bring them to the Project's attention through our website.[11] Together, faculty and students vet each candidate story in terms of its importance, timeliness, quality of sources, and corporate news coverage. If it fails on any one of these criteria, the story is not included.

Once Project Censored receives the candidate story, we undertake a second round of judgment, using the same criteria and updating the review to include any subsequent, competing corporate coverage. Stories that pass this round of review get posted on our website as Validated Independent News stories (VINs).[12]

In early spring, we present all VINs in the current cycle to the faculty and students at all of our affiliate campuses, and to our national and international panel of judges, who cast votes to winnow the candidate stories from several hundred to twenty-five.

Once the Top 25 list has been determined, Project Censored student interns begin another intensive review of each story using LexisNexis and ProQuest databases. Additional faculty and students contribute to this final stage of review.

The Top 25 finalists are then sent to our panel of judges, who vote to rank them in numerical order. At the same time, these experts—including media studies professors, professional journalists, and a former commissioner of the Federal Communications Commission, among others—offer their insights on the stories' strengths and weaknesses.[13]

Thus, by the time a story appears in the pages of *Censored*, it has undergone at least five distinct rounds of review and evaluation.

Although the stories that Project Censored brings forward may be socially and politically controversial—and sometimes even psychologically challenging—we are confident that each is the result of serious journalistic effort, and therefore deserves greater public attention.

THE TOP *CENSORED* STORIES AND MEDIA ANALYSIS OF 2016–17

1

Widespread Lead Contamination Threatens Children's Health, and Could Triple Household Water Bills

Joshua Schneyer and M.B. Pell, "Unsafe at Any Level: Millions of American Children Missing Early Lead Tests, Reuters Finds," Reuters, June 9, 2016, http://www.reuters.com/investigates/special-report/lead-poisoning-testing-gaps/.

M.B. Pell and Joshua Schneyer, "Off the Charts: The Thousands of U.S. Locales Where Lead Poisoning is Worse Than in Flint," Reuters, December 19, 2016, http://www.reuters.com/investigates/special-report/usa-lead-testing/.

Farron Cousins, "America is Suffering from a Very Real Water Crisis That Few are Acknowledging," DeSmogBlog, January 24, 2017, https://www.DeSmogBlog.com/2017/01/24/america-suffering-very-real-water-crisis-few-are-acknowledging.

Student Researchers: Jessie Eastman and Allison Kopicki (North Central College)

Faculty Evaluator: Steve Macek (North Central College)

In December 2016, M.B. Pell and Joshua Schneyer of Reuters reported that nearly three thousand neighborhoods across the US had levels of lead poisoning more than double the rates found in Flint, Michigan at the peak of its contamination crisis. Blood tests showed that more than 1,100 of those communities had rates of lead contamination "at least four times higher" than had been found in Flint.

In January 2016, President Obama had declared a federal emergency in Flint, based on lead contamination of the city's water supply. In that case, corrosive river water leached lead from old pipes; as a result, 5 percent of the children screened in Flint had high blood lead levels. By comparison, the Centers for Disease Control and Prevention (CDC) estimate that 2.5 percent of all US children under the age of six—approximately 500,000 children—have elevated blood lead levels.[14]

In early 2016, Flint's lead-contaminated water featured prominently and frequently in the news; however, news about the health plight of Flint's residents quickly peaked, and it never emphasized the full scope of the issue. Unlike Flint, the "lead hotspots" identified in Pell and Schneyer's report have received "little attention or funding."

Pell and Schneyer wrote that the communities affected by lead poisoning "stretch from Warren, Pennsylvania . . . where 36 percent of

children tested had high lead levels, to . . . Goat Island, Texas, where a quarter of tests showed poisoning. In some pockets of Baltimore, Cleveland and Philadelphia, where lead poisoning has spanned generations, the rate of elevated tests over the last decade was 40 to 50 percent." Across the US, they reported, "legacy lead"—which includes not only leached lead from faulty plumbing but also crumbling paint and industrial waste—continues to thwart national efforts to eradicate childhood lead poisoning.

As part of a special series of investigations on lead poisoning across the US, titled "Unsafe at Any Level," Pell and Schneyer requested testing data at the neighborhood level from all fifty states. Their focus on census tracts and zip code areas allowed them to identify neighborhoods "whose lead poisoning problems may be obscured in broader surveys," such as those focused on statewide or countywide rates.[15]

Twenty-one states responded with data, allowing Pell and Schneyer to identify 2,606 census tracts and 278 zip code areas with rates of lead poisoning at least double Flint's rate.[16] Interactive maps embedded in their December 2016 report detail their findings for census tracts and zip code areas in the cities of St. Joseph, Missouri; Milwaukee; South Bend, Indiana; Cleveland; Baltimore; Fresno; Los Angeles; and Buffalo. As one expert, Dr. Helen Egger, chair of Child and Adolescent Psychiatry at NYU Langone Medical Center's Child Study Center, told Pell and Schneyer, "The disparities you've found between different areas have stark implications . . . The national mean doesn't mean anything for a kid who lives in a place where the risks are much higher."

Nevertheless, just eleven US states, plus Washington, DC, mandate blood lead tests for all children; some other states mandate tests for children in areas with known exposure risks. But even in states that require testing, Schneyer and Pell reported, "more than half the children were missing a test." The "sweeping" testing gap they documented in their June 2016 report leaves children "vulnerable to prolonged lead exposure, among the most insidious, and preventable, early health risks. Lead poisoning can lead to a lifetime of severe mental and physical ailments."

The World Health Organization has linked lead exposure to children's physical ailments—including anemia, kidney dysfunction, and high blood pressure—and developmental issues—such as impaired peripheral nerve function and decreases in growth, hearing, and IQ.[17] "By school age," Schneyer and Pell wrote, "children with a history of lead exposure can exhibit poor attention and impulse control, with lower intelligence and academic performance—a stigma that can follow them through life." Their article quoted Dr. Morri Markowitz, director of the lead poisoning program for the Children's Hospital at Montefiore in New York City: "The lower your IQ, the more trouble learning, the more likely you are to drop out of school, to be delinquent, to be incarcerated."

In January 2017, Schneyer and Pell reported that, based on their previous investigation, "From California to Pennsylvania, local leaders, health officials and researchers are advancing measures to protect children from the toxic threat. They include more blood-lead screening, property inspections, hazard abatement and community outreach programs."[18]

As Farron Cousins reported for DeSmogBlog in January 2017,

"Lead pipes are time bombs" and water contamination is to be expected. The US relies on an estimated 1.2 million miles of lead pipes for municipal delivery of drinking water, and much of this aging infrastructure is reaching or has exceeded its lifespan. Citing Pell and Schneyer's December 2016 Reuters report, Cousins characterized Flint as "just a tiny piece in a much larger story" about a US water crisis characterized by both contamination *and* lack of affordability.

Declaring this the "Era of Infrastructure Replacement," in 2012 the American Water Works Association estimated that a complete overhaul of the nation's aging water systems would require an investment of $1 trillion over the next twenty-five years, which could triple the cost of household water bills.[19] As Cousins reported, a Michigan State University study, conducted by Elizabeth A. Mack and Sarah Wrase and published in January 2017, found that, "while water rates are currently unaffordable for an estimated 11.9% of households, the conservative estimates of rising rates used in this study highlight that this number could grow to 35.6% in the next five years."[20] (11.9 percent equates to 13.8 million US households; 35.6 percent would amount to 40.9 million households.[21]) As Cousins concluded, "While the water contamination crisis will occasionally steal a headline or two, virtually no attention has been paid to the fact that we're pricing a third of United States citizens out of the water market."

In May 2017, *Democracy Now!* reported that thousands of homeowners in Flint, Michigan, were facing tax liens and ultimately foreclosures if they failed to pay outstanding water bills, despite the fact that officials acknowledge that Flint's water is still unsafe to drink without a filter.[22]

2
Over Six Trillion Dollars in Unaccountable Army Spending

Dave Lindorff, "The Pentagon Money Pit: $6.5 Trillion in Unaccountable Army Spending, and No DOD Audit for the Past Two Decades," This Can't Be Happening!, August 17, 2016, http://thiscantbehappening.net/node/3262.

Thomas Hedges, "The Pentagon Has Never been Audited. That's Astonishing," *Guardian*, March 20, 2017, https://www.theguardian.com/commentisfree/2017/mar/20/pentagon-never-audited-astonishing-military-spending.

Student Researcher: Elsa Denis (Diablo Valley College)

Faculty Evaluator: Mickey Huff (Diablo Valley College)

According to a July 2016 report by the Department of Defense's Office of Inspector General (DoDIG), over the past two decades the US Army has accumulated $6.5 trillion in expenditures that cannot be accounted for, because two government offices—the Office of the Assistant Secretary of the Army and the DoD's Defense Finance and Accounting Service—"did not prioritize correcting the system deficiencies that caused errors . . . and did not provide sufficient guidance for supporting system-generated adjustments."[23] In the bureaucratic language of the report, the expenditures themselves are referred to as "unsupported adjustments" and the lack of complete and accurate records of them are described as "material weakness." In other words, as Dave Lindorff reported, the DoD "has not been tracking or recording or auditing all of the taxpayer money allocated by Congress—what it was spent on, how well it was spent, or where the money actually ended up."

In 1996, Congress enacted legislation that required all government agencies—including not only the Department of Defense but also the federal government's departments of education, veterans affairs, and housing and urban development, for instance—to undergo annual audits. As Thomas Hedges reported for the *Guardian* in March 2017, "the Pentagon has exempted itself without consequence for 20 years now, telling the Government Accountability Office (GAO) that collecting and organizing the required information for a full audit is too costly and time-consuming."[24]

As Lindorff wrote, in fiscal year 2015 total federal discretionary spending—which includes everything from education, to housing and community development, to Medicare and other health programs—amounted to just over $1.1 trillion, and the $6.5 trillion in unaccountable Army expenditures represents approximately fifteen years' worth of military spending.

The DoD Inspector General issued its report at a time when, in Lindorff's words, "politicians of both major political parties are demanding accountability for every penny spent on welfare," and they have also been engaged in pervasive efforts "to make teachers accountable for student 'performance.'" Yet, he observed, "the military doesn't have to account for any of its trillions of dollars of spending . . . even though Congress *fully a generation ago* passed a law requiring such accountability."

Mandy Smithberger, director of the Strauss Military Reform Project at the Project on Government Oversight, told Lindorff, "Accounting at the Department of Defense is a disaster, but nobody is screaming about it because you have a lot of people in Congress who believe in more military spending, so they don't really challenge military spending." Similarly, Rafael DeGennaro, director of the Audit the Pentagon coalition, told the *Guardian*, "Over the last 20 years, the Pentagon has broken every promise to Congress about when an audit would be completed . . . Meanwhile, Congress has more than doubled the Pentagon's budget." Notably, since 2013 Congressional representative Barbara Lee (D-CA) has introduced bipartisan legislation that would penalize the DoD financially for failing to complete its required audit. One of the act's cosponsors, Michael Burgess, a Republican representative for Texas, told the *Guardian* that the Pentagon "should have been audit-ready decades ago."

As *Censored 2018* goes to print, the next deadline for a DoD audit is scheduled for September 2017.

Corporate media have not covered the $6.5 trillion in unaccountable Army expenditures, as documented in the July 2016 DoDIG study, and reported by Dave Lindorff. In December 2016, the *Washington Post* published an article about a "buried" January 2015 DoD report, which had found "$125 billion in administrative waste" in Pentagon business operations. As the *Post* reported, "After the project documented far more wasteful spending than expected, senior defense officials moved swiftly to kill it by discrediting and suppressing the results."[25] The Huffington Post and TomDispatch cross-posted William Hartung's May 2016 piece, "The Pentagon's War on Accountability," which made many of the same points raised by Lindorff, but did not address the $6.5 trillion in unaccountable Army expenditures.[26] CounterPunch and OpEdNews reposted Lindorff's original report.

3

Pentagon Paid UK PR Firm for Fake Al-Qaeda Videos

Crofton Black and Abigail Fielding-Smith, "Fake News and False Flags: How the Pentagon Paid a British PR Firm $500 Million for Top Secret Iraq Propaganda," Bureau of Investigative Journalism, October 2, 2016, http://labs.thebureauinvestigates.com/fake-news-and-false-flags/.

Student Researcher: Matthew Misiano (Indian River State College)

Faculty Evaluator: Elliot D. Cohen (Indian River State College)

The Pentagon paid a British PR firm more than $660 million to run a top-secret propaganda program in Iraq from at least 2006 to December 2011, Crofton Black and Abigail Fielding-Smith reported for the Bureau of Investigative Journalism in October 2016. The UK-based PR firm Bell Pottinger produced short TV segments made to appear like Arabic news stories and insurgent videos, according to a former employee.

According to Bell Pottinger's former chairman, Lord Tim Bell, his firm had worked on a "covert" military operation "covered by various secrecy agreements." He said that he reported to the Pentagon, the CIA, and the National Security Council on his firm's work in Iraq. According to a former employee, Martin Wells, who worked as video editor in Iraq, the firm's output was approved by former General David Petraeus—then–commander of the coalition forces in Iraq—and on occasion by the White House.

The Bureau reported that Bell Pottinger's work consisted of three types of products, including TV commercials portraying al-Qaeda in a negative light, news items intended to look like they had been "created by Arabic TV," and—the third and most sensitive type—fake al-Qaeda propaganda films. Wells, the firm's former video editor, said that he was given precise instructions for production of fake al-Qaeda films, and that US Marines would take CDs of these films on patrol to drop in houses that they raided. Codes embedded in the CDs linked to a Google Analytics account, which allowed US military personnel to track a list of IP addresses where the CDs had been played, providing crucial intelligence for US operations. "Key people who worked in that unit deny any involvement with tracking software as described by Wells," the Bureau of Investigative Journalism report noted.

Black and Fielding-Smith reported that the US used contractors because "the military didn't have the in-house expertise and was operating in a legal 'grey area.'" Documents show that Bell Pottinger employed as many as three hundred British and Iraqi staff at one point; and its media operations in Iraq cost more than $100 million per year on average. After a 2012 buyout, Bell Pottinger changed ownership. Its current structure, Black and Fielding-Smith clarified, has "no connections with the unit that operated in Iraq, which closed in 2011."

Black and Fielding-Smith reported that the Bureau of Investigative Journalism "traced the firm's Iraq work through US army contracting censuses, federal procurement transaction records and reports by the Department of Defense (DoD) Inspector General, as well as Bell Pottinger's corporate filings and specialist publications on military propaganda." They also interviewed former officials and contractors involved in information operations in Iraq.

In a year when pundits and politicians of all stripes as well as members of the public and the establishment press crowed over "fake news," the US corporate media completely ignored the story of how one of the most powerful US government institutions, the Department of Defense, secretly used taxpayer money to create fake news of its own.

4

Voter Suppression in the 2016 Presidential Election

Ari Berman, "Welcome to the First Presidential Election Since Voting Rights Act Gutted," *Rolling Stone*, June 23, 2016, http://www.rollingstone.com/politics/news/welcome-to-the-first-presidential-election-since-voting-rights-act-gutted-20160623.

Sarah A. Harvard, "How Did the 'Shelby County v. Holder' Supreme Court Decision Change Voting Rights Laws?," Mic, July 29, 2016, https://mic.com/articles/150092/how-did-the-shelby-county-v-holder-supreme-court-decision-change-voting-rights-laws.

Ari Berman, "This Election is being Rigged," *Nation*, October 17, 2016, https://www.thenation.com/article/this-election-is-being-rigged/.

A.J. Vicens, "John Roberts Gutted the Voting Rights Act. Jeff Sessions is Poised to Finish It Off," *Mother Jones*, November 28, 2016, http://www.motherjones.com/politics/2016/11/voting-rights-act-whats-to-come-jeff-sessions-trump.

Ari Berman, "GOP Voter Suppression and the Trump Win," part of the feature "The Overlooked, Under-Reported and Ignored Stories of 2016," Moyers & Company, December 28, 2016, http://billmoyers.com/story/overlooked-reported-ignored-stories-2016/.

Ari Berman, "Wisconsin's Voter-ID Law Suppressed 200,000 Votes in 2016 (Trump Won by 22,748)," *Nation*, May 9, 2017, https://www.thenation.com/article/wisconsins-voter-id-law-suppressed-200000-votes-trump-won-by-23000/.

Student Researcher: Kätchen McElwain (University of Vermont)

Faculty Evaluator: Rob Williams (University of Vermont)

The Voting Rights Act of 1965 addressed discrimination in voting by requiring all state and local governments with a history of racial discrimination to get preclearance from the federal government before making any changes to their voting laws or procedures. In 2013, the Supreme Court ruled 5–4 in *Shelby County v. Holder* that a key provision of the Voting Rights Act, the section that determined which state and local governments must comply with the Act's preapproval requirement, was unconstitutional and could no longer be used.[27] As Ari Berman and other independent journalists reported, this made 2016 the first presidential election in fifty years without the full protections guaranteed by the Voting Rights Act. The director of media and campaigns for the Leadership Conference on Civil and Human Rights, Scott Simpson, told *Mother Jones*, "The Shelby decision is when this election began for people of color."

Specifically, as a result of the *Shelby* decision, changes to voting laws in nine states and parts of six others with long histories of racial discrimination in voting were no longer subject to federal government approval. Since *Shelby*, fourteen states, including many southern states and key swing states, implemented new voting restrictions, in many cases just in time for the election.[28] Texas implemented a photo-ID law that resulted in one of the lowest voter turnouts in the country. In North Carolina a voter-ID requirement permitted just a few acceptable forms of identification: According to data from the state's board of elections, over 300,000 registered voters lacked even one accepted form of ID. Arizona made changes to its voting laws that the Department of Justice had previously rejected due to minority voter discrimination. Florida converted to English-only elections in many counties, and also changed poll locations at the last minute.

In May 2017, Berman reported on an analysis of the effects of voter suppression, by Priorities USA. The analysis, he wrote, showed that strict voter-ID laws in Wisconsin and other states resulted in a "significant reduction" in voter turnout in 2016, with "a disproportionate impact on African-American and Democratic-leaning voters." According to the Priorities USA data, Wisconsin's strict voter-ID requirements reduced turnout by 200,000 votes.[29] As Berman noted, Donald Trump won the state by just over 22,000 votes.

Beyond Wisconsin, Priorities USA found additional evidence that newly enacted voter-ID restrictions suppressed the African American vote. For instance, comparing counties where African Americans constitute less than 10 percent of the population, the study found voter turnout rose 1.9 percent from 2012 to 2016 in counties with no changes to voter-ID laws, but decreased by 0.7 percent in counties where voter-ID requirements had become stricter. Similarly, for counties where African Americans make up more than 40 percent of the population, the study found a decrease of 2.2 percent in voter turnout from 2012 to 2016 for counties where ID laws did not change, and a decrease of 5 percent in counties with new voter-ID requirements. As Berman concluded, "This study provides more evidence for the claim that voter-ID laws are designed not to stop voter impersonation fraud, which is virtually nonexistent, but to make it harder for certain communities to vote."

Although independent publications like *Rolling Stone*, the *Nation*, and *Mother Jones* have covered the impacts of *Shelby v. Holder* on the 2016 election, the establishment press has not adequately covered the full extent of this change. As Berman noted in an article published by Moyers & Company in December 2016, the topic of "gutting" the Voting Rights Act did not arise once during the twenty-six presidential debates prior to the election, and "[c]able news devoted hours and hours to Trump's absurd claim that the election was rigged against him while spending precious little time on the real threat that voters faced."

In May 2017, the Brennan Center for Justice at New York University's School of Law identified thirty-one states that have introduced ninety-nine bills in 2017 to "restrict access to registration and voting." Thirty-five of these bills in seventeen states, the Brennan Center reported, have seen "significant legislative action," meaning those bills have been approved "at the committee level or beyond."[30] Furthermore, the Brennan Center report noted, "The majority of states acting to restrict voting are legislating on topics where courts previously acted to protect voters."

5

Big Data and Dark Money behind the 2016 Election

Hannes Grassegger and Mikael Krogerus, "The Data That Turned the World Upside Down," Motherboard (VICE), January 28, 2017, https://motherboard.vice.com/en_us/article/how-our-likes-helped-trump-win.

Carole Cadwalladr, "Robert Mercer: The Big Data Billionaire Waging War on Mainstream Media," Guardian, February 26, 2017, https://www.theguardian.com/politics/2017/feb/26/robert-mercer-breitbart-war-on-media-steve-bannon-donald-trump-nigel-farage.

Jane Mayer, interviewed by Nermeen Shaikh and Amy Goodman, "Jane Mayer on Robert Mercer and the Dark Money Behind Trump and Bannon," Democracy Now!, March 23, 2017, https://www.democracynow.org/2017/3/23/jane_mayer_on_robert_mercer_the.

Travis Gettys, "Before Helping Trump Win with Data Mining, Cambridge Analytica Tipped Elections with Old-Fashioned Tricks," Raw Story, March 24, 2017, http://www.rawstory.com/2017/03/before-helping-trump-win-with-data-mining-cambridge-analytica-tipped-elections-with-old-fashioned-tricks/.

Jane Mayer, "The Reclusive Hedge-Fund Tycoon Behind the Trump Presidency," New Yorker, March 27, 2017, http://www.newyorker.com/magazine/2017/03/27/the-reclusive-hedge-fund-tycoon-behind-the-trump-presidency.

Student Researchers: Maura Rocio Tellez (San Francisco State University) and Olivia Jones (University of Vermont)

Faculty Evaluators: Kenn Burrows (San Francisco State University) and Rob Williams (University of Vermont)

Right-wing computer scientist and hedge-fund billionaire Robert Mercer was the top donor to Donald Trump's presidential campaign, contributing $13.5 million and helping lay the groundwork for what is now called the Trump Revolution. Mercer also funded Cambridge Analytica, a data analytics company that specializes in "election management strategies" and using microtargeting. As Carole Cadwalladr reported for the Guardian in February 2017, Cambridge Analytica's website boasts that it has psychological profiles based on thousands of pieces of data for some 220 million American voters. As Jane Mayer and other independent journalists reported, Mercer, Cambridge Analytica, and others used these capacities to exploit a populist insurgency among voters and tip the election toward Trump.

Right-wing websites are now dominating Google's search results on certain subjects.[31] Jonathan Albright, a professor of communications at Elon University in North Carolina, mapped the "news ecosystem" and found millions of links to right-wing sites "strangling" the mainstream media. As the *Guardian* and the *New Yorker* reported, Albright has described Cambridge Analytica as a "propaganda machine," using trackers from sites like Breitbart to document people's web histories and target them with messages and advertisements via their Facebook accounts.[32]

Mercer's money also enabled Steve Bannon to fund Breitbart, a right-wing news site established with the express intent of serving as a Huffington Post for the Right. Since 2010, Mercer has donated $95 million to right-wing political campaigns and nonprofits. As Cadwalladr reported in the *Guardian*, Mercer funds the Heartland Institute, a climate change denial think tank, and the Media Research Center, which refers to itself as "America's Media Watchdog" and aims to correct "liberal bias."[33]

In an article for the *New Yorker*, Jane Mayer described Mercer as a "brilliant computer scientist" who has "never given an interview explaining his political views," and yet is "emblematic" of a major shift of power in American politics, from the two main political parties toward "a tiny group of rich mega-donors."[34] Mayer quoted Trevor Potter, president of the Campaign Legal Center, a nonpartisan watchdog group, and former chairman of the Federal Election Commission, on the effects of the 2010 Supreme Court decision, *Citizens United v. Federal Election Commission*: "Suddenly, a random billionaire can change politics and public policy—to sweep everything else off the table—even if they don't speak publicly, and even if there's almost no public awareness of his or her views."

As Mayer reported, Mercer has argued that the 1964 Civil Rights Act was a major mistake, and sources who know Mercer told Mayer that he has stated that the Clintons have had opponents of theirs murdered, and that, during the Gulf War, the US should have simply taken Iraq's oil. As Mayer wrote, "despite his oddities, he has had surprising success in aligning the Republican Party, and consequently America, with his personal beliefs, and is now uniquely positioned to exert influence over the Trump Administration."

Cambridge Analytica is an affiliate of a larger British company known as Strategic Communication Laboratories. As Hannes Grassegger and Mikael Krogerus reported, Alexander Nix, the chief executive officer of Cambridge Analytica, was quoted in a company press release the day after Trump's victory, saying, "We are thrilled that our revolutionary approach to data-driven communication has played such an integral part in President-elect Trump's extraordinary win." Cambridge Analytica began working for the Trump campaign in June 2016, after initially providing analysis for Ted Cruz. (Cambridge Analytica is also believed to have worked for the organization Leave.EU in its Brexit campaign.) According to Nix, Grassegger and Krogerus reported, Cambridge Analytica combined behavioral science based on the measurement of psychological traits, Big Data analysis—premised on the fact that everything we do leaves digital traces—and ad targeting that is aligned "to the personality of an individual."

As Nix told the audience at the Concordia Summit in New York in September 2016, once Cambridge Analytica became involved with the Trump campaign, "Pretty much every message that Trump put out was data-driven." For example, Grassegger and Krogerus reported, on the day of the third presidential debate between Trump and Hillary Clinton, the Trump team "tested 175,000 different ad variations for his arguments, in order to find the right versions above all via Facebook." The results were examples of "dark posts"—sponsored newsfeed-style advertisements that will only be seen by users with specific profiles. These specifically tailored and targeted messages ignored demographics, data Nix dismissed as "a really ridiculous idea." What Nix meant, Grassegger and Krogerus explained, is that "while other campaigners so far have relied on demographics, Cambridge Analytica was using psychometrics." Prior psychometric research has shown that a sample of just sixty-eight Facebook "likes" is sufficient to predict a user's skin color (with 95 percent accuracy), sexual orientation (88 percent accuracy), and affiliation to the Democratic or Republican party (85 percent accuracy).

As Grassegger and Krogerus reported, this new approach informed not only direct messaging to potential Trump voters, but also Trump's canvassers. From July 2016, they used an app, known as Ground Game, to identify the political views and personality types of the inhabitants of a house. As Grassegger and Krogerus wrote, "Trump's people only rang at the doors of houses that the app rated as receptive to his messages. The canvassers came prepared with guidelines for conversations tailored to the personality type of the resident. In turn, the canvassers fed the reactions into the app, and the new data flowed back to the dashboards of the Trump campaign." (Advocates in the Brexit campaign used the same app.) While Clinton and the Democrats relied on traditional demographic data to inform their campaign, Cambridge Analytica and the Trump campaign divided the US population into thirty-two personality types and focused on seventeen specific states. According to Grassegger and Krogerus, data analysis using psychometrics led to the campaign's focus on Michigan and Wisconsin in the final weeks. "The candidate," they wrote, "became the instrument for implementing a big data model." Cambridge Analytica, they reported in January 2017, earned an estimated $15 million overall during the 2016 campaign, and Nix, the company's CEO, is "currently touring European conferences showcasing their success in the United States."

6

Antibiotic Resistant "Superbugs" Threaten Health and Foundations of Modern Medicine

Melinda Wenner Moyer, "Dangerous New Antibiotic-Resistant Bacteria Reach U.S.," *Scientific American*, May 27, 2016, https://www.scientificamerican.com/article/dangerous-new-antibiotic-resistant-bacteria-reach-u-s/.

Madlen Davies, "How Big Pharma's Industrial Waste is Fuelling the Rise in Superbugs Worldwide," Bureau of Investigative Journalism, September 15, 2016, https://www.thebureauinvestigates.com/stories/2016-09-15/how-big-pharmas-industrial-waste-is-fuelling-the-rise-in-superbugs-worldwide.

Katie Morley and Madlen Davies, "Superbugs Killing More People Than Breast Cancer, Trust Warns," *Telegraph*, December 10, 2016, http://www.telegraph.co.uk/news/2016/12/10/superbugs-killing-people-breast-cancer-trust-warns/.

Student Researchers: Yadira Martinez (Sonoma State University) and Bridgette McShea (University of Vermont)

Faculty Evaluators: Roxanne Ezzet (Sonoma State University) and Rob Williams (University of Vermont)

Pharmaceutical companies that produce antibiotics are creating dangerous superbugs when their factories leak industrial waste, Madlen Davies of the Bureau of Investigative Journalism reported in September 2016. Superbugs are bacteria that become resistant to antibiotics. Pharmaceutical factories in China and India—the places where the majority of the world's antibiotics are manufactured—are releasing "untreated waste fluid" into local soils and waters, leading to increases in antimicrobial resistance that diminish the effectiveness of antibiotics and threaten the foundations of modern medicine. A number of the companies have established links to US markets.

After bacteria in the environment become resistant, they can exchange genetic material with other germs, spreading antibiotic resistance around the world, according to an assessment issued by the European Public Health Alliance (EPHA), which served as the basis for Davies's news report.[35] Davies described a case in which a drug-resistant bacterium that originated in India in 2014 has since been found in seventy other countries. Superbugs resulting from pharmaceutical pollution have already killed an estimated 25,000 people across Europe—thus globally posing "as big a threat as terrorism," according to a UK National Health Service official, Chief Medical Officer Dame Sally Davies. In a May 2014 report, Martin Khor quoted Dr. Keiji Fukuda, who coordinated the World Health Organization's work on antimicrobial resistance between 2010 and 2016. According to Fukuda, "A post-antibiotic era, in which common infections and minor injuries can kill, far from being an apocalyptic fantasy, is instead a very real possibility for the 21st century."[36]

At the heart of the issue is how to motivate pharmaceutical companies to improve their production practices. With strong demand for antibiotics, the companies continue to profit despite the negative consequences of their actions. The EPHA assessment recommended five responses that major purchasers of medicines could implement to help stop antibiotic pollution. Among these recommendations are blacklisting pharmaceutical companies that contribute to the spread of superbugs through irresponsible practices, and promoting legislation to incorporate environmental criteria into the industry's good manufacturing practices.

In 2015, World Health Organization head Margaret Chan cautioned that antibiotic-resistant superbugs may signal "the end of modern medicine as we know it."[37] Noting that superbugs "haunt" hospitals and intensive care units around the world, Chan reported that, if current trends continue, "sophisticated interventions," including organ transplants, joint replacements, cancer chemotherapy, and care of pre-term infants, "will become more difficult or even too dangerous to undertake" as common infections "will once again kill." As Katie Morley and Madlen Davies reported in the *Telegraph* in December 2016, data analysis by the UK Sepsis Trust indicated that superbugs now cause more deaths than breast cancer in the UK. The UK Sepsis trust estimates that around 12,000 people in the UK die because of drug resistance each year, a figure that is considerably higher than the government estimate of 5,000 deaths per year due to drug resistance. In 2014, the government recorded 11,433 deaths due to breast cancer.

As Morley and Davies reported, "the full extent of the problem is obscured because the Government statistics are calculated using 'ballpark' figures from foreign studies, not those conducted in the UK." Furthermore, superbugs are "rarely listed on death certificates," and government health officials often lack political, legal, and financial means to establish a rigorous system to monitor the spread of resistance.

In May 2016, *Scientific American* reported that a "dangerous new form of antibiotic resistance has spread to the United States." Bacteria infecting a Pennsylvania woman with a urinary tract infection proved resistant to colistin, which is known as an "antibiotic of last resort." Citing a report published in the journal *Antimicrobial Agents and Chemotherapy*, Melinda Wenner Moyer wrote that "the findings have sounded alarm bells" among scientists who fear that "common infections will soon be untreatable."[38]

In November 2015, Wenner Moyer reported, Chinese and British researchers discovered that a new gene for colistin resistance—known as mcr-1—was circulating among animals and people in China. The case of the Pennsylvania woman is the first to document mcr-1 in the US. Wenner Moyer also noted that in May 2016 the US Department of Agriculture and the Department of Health and Human Services announced that they had discovered colistin-resistant bacteria in an American pig, suggesting that colistin-resistant bacteria have reached

American livestock. If the newly discovered mcr-1 gene is picked up by other bacteria that are already resistant to multiple drugs, then "the world could suddenly be faced with pan-drug-resistant bacteria." As Lance Price, director of the Antibiotic Resistance Action Center at George Washington University's Milken Institute School of Public Health, told *Scientific American*, the results would be "a royal flush—the infection has an unbeatable hand."

Although the threat of antibiotic-resistant microbes is well documented in scientific publications, there is little to no coverage on superbugs in the corporate press. What corporate news coverage there is tends to exaggerate the risks and consequences of natural outbreaks—as seen during the Ebola scare in the US in 2014—rather than reporting on the preventable spread of superbugs by irresponsible pharmaceutical companies.

7
The Toll of US Navy Training on Wildlife in the North Pacific

Dahr Jamail, "Navy Allowed to Kill or Injure Nearly 12 Million Whales, Dolphins, Other Marine Mammals in Pacific," Truthout, May 16, 2016, http://www.truth-out.org/news/item/36037-the-us-navy-s-mass-destruction-of-marine-life.

Student Researcher: Nora Kasapligil (Sonoma State University)

Faculty Evaluator: Elaine Wellin (Sonoma State University)

US Navy training activities are deadly for marine mammals in the North Pacific. In a five-year period, the US Navy has killed, injured, or harassed whales, dolphins, porpoises, sea lions, and other marine wildlife in the North Pacific Ocean nearly twelve million times—legally, according to a report for Truthout by Dahr Jamail. The West Coast Action Alliance (WCAA), a coalition that aims to protect the nation's national and state parks, airspace, and waters, combined data from the Navy's Northwest Training and Testing environmental impact statement and the National Oceanic and Atmospheric Administration's Letter of Authorization for the number of "takes" of marine mammals caused by Navy exercises. A "take" is a type of harm to an animal, with impacts ranging from harassment, resulting in behavioral changes, to death.

The WCAA found that, over a five-year period, the US Navy has been responsible for more than 11.8 million takes of marine mammal species in four North Pacific areas of operation, a figure that Karen Sullivan, a WCAA spokesperson and former endangered species biologist with the US Fish and Wildlife Service, described as "staggering."[39]

The Navy currently does not allow expert civilians or US Fish and Wildlife officials on board their vessels to monitor impacts during training exercises. Instead, Jamail wrote, "the 'technology' the Navy uses to ensure whether marine mammals are present in the vicinity of their exercises is the same 'technology' that has been used since the 17th century—two lookouts at the bow of the ship." Emily Stolarcyk, program manager of the Eyak Preservation Council in Cordova, Alaska, told Truthout, "With the limited observation practiced, the Navy's activities have proved lethal to large marine species. What about the unknown impacts?" As a WCAA report noted, the 11.8 million reported takes do not include impacts on "endangered and threatened seabirds, fish, sea turtles or terrestrial species" due to Navy activities.

As Jamail reported, the Navy's October 2015 environmental impact statement showed substantial increases in a large number of detrimental training activities, including a 778 percent increase in the number of torpedoes launched in inland waters, a 400 percent increase in air-to-surface missile exercises (including some within the Olympic Coast National Marine Sanctuary), and 284 sonar testing events in inland waters. Sonar disrupts marine mammals' abilities to use echolocation to find food, putting them at risk of malnutrition or starvation.

With little oversight on Navy training activities, the public is left in the dark regarding their environmental impacts, including especially how Navy operations impact fish in the North Pacific and marine life at the bottom of the food chain. There has been almost no coverage of these impacts in the corporate press. In July 2016, the *Washington Post* reported on a federal appeals court ruling in San Francisco, which found that the Navy's use of loud, low-frequency sonar had violated marine mammal protection laws.[40]

8

Maternal Mortality a Growing Threat in the US

Elizabeth Dawes Gay, "Congressional Briefing Puts U.S. Maternity on Exam Table," Women's eNews, April 15, 2016, http://womensenews.org/2016/04/congressional-briefing-puts-u-s-maternity-on-exam-table/.

Kiera Butler, "The Scary Truth About Childbirth," *Mother Jones*, January/February, 2017, http://www.motherjones.com/politics/2017/01/childbirth-injuries-prolapse-cesarean-section-natural-childbirth.

Student Researchers: Jane C. Hau (Citrus College) and Hope Matheson (North Central College)

Faculty Evaluators: Andy Lee Roth (Citrus College) and Steve Macek (North Central College)

Each year, more than 65,000 pregnant women in the United States suffer life-threatening complications, including physical and psychological conditions aggravated by pregnancy, and more than 600 die from pregnancy-related causes. Elizabeth Dawes Gay reported that inadequate health care in rural areas and racial disparities are drivers of this maternal health crisis. Nationally, African American women are three to four times more likely than white women to die from pregnancy-related causes, with rates even higher in parts of the US that Gay characterized as "pockets of neglect," such as Georgia, where the 2011 maternal mortality rate of 28.7 per 100,000 live births was nearly double the national average.

Women's Policy Inc., a nonprofit, nonpartisan public policy organization, hosted a briefing in April 2016 for US maternal mortality experts to address problems and present solutions to a panel of congressional staffers, federal employees, and women's health advocates. "The U.S. is the only nation in the developed world with a rising maternal mortality rate," Rep. Lois Capps stated at the meeting. Dr. Keisha Callins identified issues that contribute to the rising maternal mortality rate, including "provider shortages, lack of physical access to care, . . . low educational attainment, poverty, poor access to healthy foods, neighborhood violence and stress." The prevalence of caesarian section (C-section) delivery is another factor. The World Health Organization recommends that no more than 10–15 percent of births should be C-section deliveries; in the US, one in three babies is delivered by C-section.

Gay described a maternal safety bundle initiative—"best practices, guidelines and protocols to improve maternal health care quality and safety"—that has been developed by the Alliance for Innovation on

Maternal Health, or AIM. These "bundles" include "equipping hospital labor units with a fully stocked cart for immediate hemorrhage treatment, establishing a hospital-level emergency management protocol, conducting regular staff drills and reviewing all cases to learn from past mistakes."[41]

Across the US, the number of women who are vulnerable to high-risk deliveries is rising. In addition, doctors rarely warn patients of the potential for serious injuries and complications that can occur following birth, according to a report by Kiera Butler for *Mother Jones*. Women have a right to make informed decisions about their bodies and serious medical situations; however, when it comes to birth and its aftereffects, Butler found that doctors simply are not providing vital information. Though laws in many states require doctors to inform women of the potential complications and dangers that can occur during delivery, no such laws require doctors to inform about potential long-term problems following delivery, or to share the fact that some complications are more prevalent in women who give birth vaginally than in women who deliver by C-section.

This is a big problem for millions of women, as, according to a 2008 study by researchers at the California HMO Kaiser Permanente, 80 percent of women who suffer from pelvic floor disorders are mothers, and women who delivered vaginally are twice as likely to experience these injuries as women who have had a C-section or who have not given birth. According to Butler's *Mother Jones* report, numerous other studies suggest that "50 to 80 percent of women who give birth experience tearing of the pelvic skin and muscles," and, for more than one in ten women who give birth, these injuries are severe enough to damage the anal sphincter muscle, which can lead to loss of bowel and bladder control. Sexual dysfunction, stress urinary incontinence, and pelvic organ prolapse—a chronic and painful condition of the uterus or bladder that often requires multiple surgeries to repair—are some other common conditions more prevalent following vaginal birth than following C-sections, yet doctors rarely discuss these issues with pregnant patients.

Beyond pain and embarrassment, the financial costs of these sometimes preventable conditions are also great. According to Butler, citing the website Healthcare Bluebook, "the typical price for a vaginal hysterectomy, one of the most common fixes for uterine prolapse, is about $14,400, including hospital costs, while a bladder repair surgery for incontinence runs about $28,000." For those who opt not to have surgery, adult incontinence products can be an equally large strain on the wallet. And companies are cashing in; in fact, *Mother Jones* reports that the industry is "projected to grow from $1.8 billion in 2015 to $2.7 billion by 2020, and it is expected to catch up to the baby diaper market within a decade."

The corporate news media have paid limited attention to maternal mortality and morbidity in the US. In 2012, Motherlode, a parenting blog connected with the *New York Times*, published an article, "An Unspoken Risk of Vaginal Birth," that noted the extent to which mainstream publications underestimate the number of women affected by serious injuries sustained during vaginal childbirth.[42] In May 2016, a report in the *Washington Post* addressed the high maternal mortality rates among American women and mentioned a national prevention campaign to avert such deaths.[43] A September 2016 article by Sabrina Tavernise for the *New York Times* provided good, though brief, coverage of the rising rate of maternal mortality in the US.[44]

9
DNC Claims Right to Select Presidential Candidate

Michael Sainato, "Wikileaks Proves Primary was Rigged: DNC Undermined Democracy," *Observer*, July 22, 2016, http://observer.com/2016/07/wikileaks-proves-primary-was-rigged-dnc-undermined-democracy/.

Ruby Cramer, "DNC and Clinton Campaign Operations Started Merging Before Sanders Dropped Out," BuzzFeed, July 27, 2016, https://www.buzzfeed.com/rubycramer/dnc-and-clinton-campaign-operations-started-merging-before-s.

Joshua Holland, "What the Leaked E-mails Do and Don't Tell Us About the DNC and Bernie Sanders," *Nation*, July 29, 2016, https://www.thenation.com/article/what-the-leaked-e-mails-do-and-dont-tell-us-about-the-dnc-and-bernie-sanders/.

Michael Sainato, "DNC Lawyers Argue DNC Has Right to Pick Candidates in Back Rooms," *Observer*, May 1, 2017, http://observer.com/2017/05/dnc-lawsuit-presidential-primaries-bernie-sanders-supporters/.

Student Researchers: Audrey Tuck (University of Vermont) and Tom Field (Diablo Valley College)

Faculty Evaluators: Rob Williams (University of Vermont) and Mickey Huff (Diablo Valley College)

In June 2016, Beck & Lee, a legal firm based in Miami, filed a class-action lawsuit on behalf of supporters of Bernie Sanders against the Democratic National Committee and its former chair, Debbie Wasserman Schultz, alleging that the DNC broke legally-binding neutrality agreements in the Democratic primaries by strategizing to make Hillary Clinton the nominee before a single vote was cast.[45] Transcripts from the hearing on the lawsuit, which took place in a federal court in Fort Lauderdale, Florida, in April 2017, document the DNC's lack of commitment to key articles of its own charter. As Michael Sainato reported for the *Observer*, in that hearing, attorneys for the DNC claimed that Article V, Section 4 of the DNC Charter—which instructs the DNC chair and staff to ensure neutrality in the Democratic presidential primaries—is actually "a discretionary rule" that the DNC "didn't need to adopt to begin with."[46]

Later in the hearing, a DNC attorney asserted that it would have been within the DNC's rights to "go into back rooms like they used to and smoke cigars and pick the candidate that way." Bruce Spiva, the DNC attorney, said, "That's not the way it was done. But they could have. And that would have also been their right." Furthermore, as Sainato reported for the *Observer*, the DNC attorneys argued that specific language used in the DNC charter—including the terms "impartial" and "evenhanded"—could not be interpreted in a court of law. Describing the plaintiff's case as "inchoate," Spiva asserted that any judicial effort to "define what constitutes evenhandedness and impartiality" would "drag the Court . . . into a political question and a question of how the party runs its own affairs."

In response, the attorney representing Sanders's supporters, Jared Beck, told the judge, "Your Honor, I'm shocked to hear that we can't define what it means to be evenhanded and impartial. If that were the case, we couldn't have courts. I mean, that's what courts do every day, is decide disputes in an evenhanded and impartial manner." Earlier Beck argued that the running of elections in a fair and impartial manner was not only a "bedrock assumption" of democracy but also a binding commitment for the DNC: "That's what the Democratic National Committee's own charter says," he told the court. "It says it in black and white. And they can't deny that." Furthermore, Beck contended, Congresswoman Wasserman Schultz and other DNC staff had stated "over and over again in the media" that "they were, in fact, acting in compliance with the charter."

As Sainato has documented in a series of previous reports for the *Observer*, the hearings in the class-action lawsuit against the DNC and its chair follow on the heels of the release of 20,000 DNC emails from January 2015 to May 2016, which WikiLeaks first made public in July 2016. Most of the released emails came from seven prominent DNC staff members. As Sainato reported in July 2016, the leaked emails show that, "[i]nstead of treating Sanders as a viable candidate for the Democratic ticket, the DNC worked against him and his campaign to ensure Clinton received the nomination." Specifically, Sainato wrote, the release provided further evidence that the DNC "broke its own charter" by favoring Clinton as the nominee "long before any votes were cast."

Additional reporters, including the *Nation*'s Joshua Holland, corroborated that the emails showed, in Holland's words, that "by May, DNC staffers wanted Sanders out of the race." But Holland also noted that the emails that caused the most "outrage" among Sanders's supporters were all written after late April. That suggested, Holland wrote, that "committee members' disdain for the Sanders camp didn't reflect their baseline attitude toward a long-shot, anti-establishment challenger from the left. Rather, it appears to have developed over the course of the long race." As Ruby Cramer reported for BuzzFeed in July 2016, the released DNC emails also showed that the DNC and Clinton's campaign had begun merging operations—consolidating research, communications, and media monitoring—before Sanders dropped out of the race. As Cramer explained, "Once a candidate has become the presumptive nominee, it's typical for their campaign and the party to join forces," but the released DNC messages showed that "this process began while Bernie Sanders remained a viable candidate, sooner than previously reported or publicly disclosed."

Much of the reporting and commentary on the DNC's collusion with the Clinton campaign against Sanders in the Democratic primary—including coverage by progressive independent news organizations—has focused on whether or not election fraud took place.[47] As a result of this focus, many members of the public harbor a general sense that Sanders was robbed. By contrast, other news outlets (and segments of the public) have sought to dismiss any consideration of election fraud in the Democratic primary as "conspiracy theory."[48] Regardless of the judge's eventual ruling, the class-action suit against the DNC has spurred corporate news outlets to begin considering criticisms of the DNC's handling of the primaries as a serious, newsworthy topic[49]—even though a reporter for the *Washington Post* described the lawsuit, in passing, as "largely frivolous."[50] Other news commentators noted that the *Post*'s dismissive assessment of the lawsuit appeared to be "the first time" that the paper "has written anything at all about the sensational lawsuit."[51]

Finally, as further indication of the politicized nature of news coverage on this topic, it is noteworthy that even Michael Sainato's reporting—which has consistently used official documents, including the leaked DNC emails and courtroom transcripts, as primary sources—has been repeatedly labeled "opinion"—rather than straight news reporting—by his publisher, the *Observer*.

As *Censored 2018* goes to print, the lawsuit appears to be moving forward to discovery. In that stage of the case, prominent DNC figures, including its former chair, Wasserman Schultz, would likely be called to testify in court on their actions and decisions during the Democratic primary.

10

2016: A Record Year for Global Internet Shutdowns

Devin Coldewey, "Study Estimates Cost of Last Year's Internet Shutdowns at $2.4 Billion," TechCrunch, October 24, 2016, https://techcrunch.com/2016/10/24/study-suggests-internet-shutdowns-may-cost-countries-billions/.

Kevin Collier, "Governments Loved to Shut Down the Internet in 2016—Here's Where," Vocativ, December 23, 2016, http://www.vocativ.com/386042/internet-access-shut-off-censorship/.

Lyndal Rowlands, "More Than 50 Internet Shutdowns in 2016," Inter Press Service, December 30, 2016, http://www.ipsnews.net/2016/12/more-than-50-internet-shutdowns-in-2016/.

Azad Essa, "What Can the UN Do If Your Country Cuts the Internet?" Al Jazeera, May 8, 2017, http://www.aljazeera.com/indepth/features/2017/05/country-cuts-internet-170504064432840.html.

Student Researcher: Hugo Sousa (Citrus College)

Faculty Evaluator: Andy Lee Roth (Citrus College)

Governments around the world shut down Internet access more than fifty times in 2016, Lyndal Rowlands reported for the Inter Press Service (IPS) in December of that year. Around the world, governments shutting down Internet access limited freedom of speech, swayed elections, and damaged economies. "In the worst cases," Rowlands wrote, "Internet shutdowns have been associated with human rights violations," as happened in Ethiopia and Uganda. The IPS report quoted Deji Olukotun, a senior manager at digital rights organization Access Now: "What we have found is that Internet shutdowns go hand in hand with atrocities."

As Kevin Collier reported for Vocativ, Access Now documented fifty-three instances in 2016 in which national governments shut down the Internet for all or part of a country, "throttled" access speeds to make the Internet essentially unusable, or blocked specific communication methods. These fifty-three instances represent a sharp uptick in government shutdowns of the Internet, following on from the fifteen shutdowns identified by Access Now in 2015. As Collier noted, Access Now uses a "conservative metric," counting "repeated, similar outages"—like those which occurred during Gabon's widely criticized Internet "curfew"—as a single instance. (The Vocativ report included a dynamic map chart, designed by Kaitlyn Kelly, that vividly depicts Internet shutdowns around the world, month by month for all of 2016, as documented by Access Now.)

Many countries intentionally blacked out Internet access during elections and to quell protest. Not only do these shutdowns restrict freedom of speech, they also hurt economies around the world. TechCrunch, IPS, and other independent news organizations reported that a Brookings Institution study found that Internet shutdowns cost countries $2.4 billion between July 2015 and June 2016.[52] The biggest losses were in India (an estimated $968 million), Saudi Arabia ($465 million), and Morocco ($320 million). The author of the Brookings study, Darrell West, cautioned that the figures are only estimates, but that the actual economic costs are likely to be even higher. "The $2.4 billion figure is a conservative estimate that likely *understates* the actual economic damage," West wrote, because it does not include "lost tax revenues associated with blocked digital access, impact on worker productivity, barriers to business expansion connected with these shutdowns, or the loss of investor, consumer, and business confidence resulting from such disruptions." Overall, the Brookings study noted, "As long as political authorities continue to disrupt internet activity, it will be difficult for impacted nations to reap the full benefits of the digital economy."

As Olukotun, the Access Now manager, told IPS, one way to stop government shutdowns is for Internet providers to resist government demands. "Telecommunications companies can push back on government orders, or at least document them to show what's been happening, to at least have a paper trail," Olukotun observed. He also called on international organizations—including the International Telecommunications Union, which is the UN agency for information and communication technologies—to issue statements in response to specific incidents.

On July 1, 2016, in a nonbinding resolution signed by more than seventy countries, the UN Human Rights Council lauded the Internet's "great potential to accelerate human progress," and it condemned "measures to intentionally prevent or disrupt access to or dissemination of information online."[53] According to the resolution, "the exercise of human rights, in particular the right to freedom of expression, on the Internet is an issue of increasing interest and importance."

Yet, as Azad Essa reported for Al Jazeera in May 2017, "understanding what this means for internet users can be difficult." For the sixth straight year Freedom House, a US-based freedom of expression watchdog, found that Internet freedom around the world had declined, Essa reported. Freedom House found that two-thirds of the world's Internet users "live in countries where criticism of the government, military, or ruling family [is] subject to censorship."[54] According to their "Freedom on the Net 2016" report, thirty-four of the sixty-five countries studied have been "on a negative trajectory" since June 2015, with the steepest declines in Uganda, Bangladesh, Cambodia, Ecuador, and Libya. Freedom House documented new restrictions on messaging apps, social media users facing unprecedented penalties, governments censoring more diverse content, and security measures threatening free speech and advocacy—even as online activism "reaches new heights." Underscoring the importance of online freedoms, Freedom House noted that in more than two-thirds of the countries studied, "internet-based activism has led to some sort of tangible outcome, from the defeat of a restrictive legislative proposal to the exposure of corruption through citizen journalism."

The UN's special rapporteur on freedom of opinion and expression, David Kaye, told Al Jazeera that advocates of online rights "need to be constantly pushing for laws that protect this space and demand that governments meet their obligations in digital spaces just as in non-digital spaces."

Corporate news coverage of Internet shutdowns tends to focus on specific countries, especially ones in Africa. For instance, in September 2016, CNN reported on the extraordinary Internet shutdown in Gabon.[55] Although this coverage made passing reference to Access Now's findings on Internet disruptions around the world, it focused on the specific details of the shutdown in Gabon, which included Internet "curfews" and the government's total blocking of social media platforms such as Facebook, Twitter, and WhatsApp. A February 2017 *New York Times* report focused on Internet shutdowns in Cameroon, Gambia, and the Republic of Congo.[56] This report also cited the Brookings Institution report on the economic costs of shutdowns. However, corporate coverage tends not to address the larger, global scope of Internet shutdowns—and, unlike independent news coverage, these reports tend not to address how Internet providers might resist government demands.

11

Law Enforcement Surveillance of Phone Records

Aaron Mackey and Dave Maass, "Law Enforcement's Secret 'Super Search Engine' Amasses Trillions of Phone Records for Decades," Electronic Frontier Foundation, November 29, 2016, https://www.eff.org/deeplinks/2016/11/law-enforcements-secret-super-search-engine-amasses-trillions-phone-records.

George Joseph, "Are Police Searching Inauguration Protesters' Phones?," CityLab, January 24, 2017, https://www.citylab.com/equity/2017/01/are-police-searching-inauguration-protesters-phones/514244/.

George Joseph, "Inauguration Protesters Targeted for Facebook Searches," CityLab, February 3, 2017, http://www.citylab.com/crime/2017/02/inauguration-protesters-targeted-for-facebook-searches/515517/.

George Joseph, "Cellphone Spy Tools Have Flooded Local Police Departments," CityLab, February 8, 2017, https://www.citylab.com/equity/2017/02/cellphone-spy-tools-have-flooded-local-police-departments/512543/.

Sarah Lazare, "Law Enforcement Using Facebook and Apple to Data-Mine Accounts of Trump Protest Arrestees," AlterNet, February 22, 2017, http://www.alternet.org/activism/law-enforcement-using-facebook-and-apple-data-mine-accounts-trump-protest-arrestees-o.

Student Researchers: Samantha Bosnich (Sonoma State University) and Tom Field (Diablo Valley College)

Faculty Evaluators: Peter Phillips (Sonoma State University) and Mickey Huff (Diablo Valley College)

In cooperation with AT&T, US federal, state, and local law enforcement agencies have been secretly collecting telephone records since

1987 under a program known as Hemisphere, Aaron Mackey and Dave Maass reported for the Electronic Frontier Foundation (EFF). The Hemisphere database contains "trillions" of domestic and international phone call records, and AT&T "adds roughly four billion phone records" each day, including calls from non-AT&T customers "that pass through the company's switches."

The call records for individuals include phone numbers dialed, calls received, and each call's time, date, and length. Furthermore, Mackey and Maass noted, the collected data allows the Drug Enforcement Agency (DEA) and other law enforcement agencies to undertake "complicated traffic analysis" that can "dynamically map people's social networks and physical locations." Information gleaned from EFF's Freedom of Information Act lawsuits suggests that officials collect and analyze this sensitive data "without a warrant or any judicial oversight," possibly in breach of Fourth Amendment rights. Because Hemisphere permits law enforcement to map personal connections and social networks, Mackey and Maass reported, Hemisphere "also poses acute risks to the First Amendment rights of callers caught in the program's dragnet."

In secret documents obtained by EFF, police tout Hemisphere as a "Super Search Engine" and "Google on Steroids." These descriptions, Mackey and Maass wrote, "confirm EFF's worst fears that Hemisphere is a mass surveillance program that threatens core civil liberties."

The Hemisphere program was unknown until 2013, when a presentation about it was "inadvertently released to a privacy activist," EFF reported. The government and law enforcement agencies have made it their mission to keep this program hidden from the public eye. Police using data collected through Hemisphere were instructed to insure that the program never appeared in the public record. As Mackey and Maass reported, after police obtained private information about someone by using Hemisphere, they would engage in a controversial practice that police call "parallel construction" to obtain the targeted data through traditional subpoenas.[57]

EFF filed Freedom of Information Act requests and sued federal and California law enforcement to access critical information about the Hemisphere surveillance program. The government's secrecy, as well as discrepancies between how it responded to FOIA requests from EFF and the Electronic Privacy Information Center, highlight "the large power imbalance between the government and FOIA requesters seeking records," Mackey and Maass reported. They also noted that the Hemisphere program "could not operate without AT&T's full cooperation."

In December 2016, Maass reported that a group of AT&T shareholders intended to use the company's spring shareholder conference to discuss "contradictions" between the Hemisphere program and AT&T's stated commitment to privacy and civil liberties, and to demand greater transparency about the secret surveillance program.[58]

On the day that Donald Trump was sworn in as president, protests took place a short distance away. Metropolitan Police Department (MPD) officers in Washington, DC, arrested more than two hundred individuals, charging them under felony riot laws and seizing some of their cellphones. AlterNet's Sarah Lazare and CityLab correspondent George Joseph reported that law enforcement was compelling Facebook, Google, and Apple to turn over data for at least some of the people arrested.

An email from Facebook's "Law Enforcement Response Team" to a user explained that the user had ten days to produce court documents that would legally prevent Facebook from honoring a request from the District of Columbia US Attorney's Office for information about their account. Mark Goldstone, a lawyer representing several of the defendants, was quoted as saying that they had received notices from both Apple and Facebook informing them of requests for information by law enforcement. One individual arrested and charged with rioting showed AlterNet a communication from Apple stating that they had received a request from legal authorities requesting data. This defendant told AlterNet, "My phone wasn't present at the time of arrest and wasn't taken." The defendant's attorney, Goldstone, said, "It's an outrageous overreach by the government to try to data-mine personal property that wasn't seized at the demonstration."

Another person arrested, a journalist swept up in the mass arrest who had his phone taken, sent AlterNet a screenshot of his Google account, showing that, once his password-protected phone was in MPD custody, there had been almost immediate activity on his Google account. George Joseph of CityLab documented similar activity in the case of an unidentified medic who was also arrested. Joseph reported on January 24, 2017 that a screenshot of Google account activity suggested that "police began mining information from the captured cellphones almost immediately after the arrests."

Lazare reported that Google, Apple, and Facebook, as well as the MPD and the US Attorney's Office, all declined to comment for AlterNet's story.

It was unclear what legal instrument law enforcement used to compel the three companies to turn over information on their customers. Different legal instruments grant various degrees of power. A National Security letter would require no court order while a 2703(d) court order allows access to metadata about communications and possibly location. The information to be turned over could range from a relatively small, targeted cache, to everything a user has in the iCloud, photos taken, and messages and emails received and sent.

This story is critically important for several reasons. Mark Goldstone has defended protesters in the Washington, DC, area for more than thirty years. He emphasized to AlterNet that he had never heard of a case in which mobile phones were seized at protests, and was unaware of previous cases in which protestors faced felony riot charges. Unlike the usual misdemeanor charge, a felony riot charge carries a penalty of up to ten years in prison and fines up to $25,000. "We're in a dangerous new world," Goldstone said. Evidence that MPD officers accessed arrested individuals' phones and Google accounts begs the question, did the police break the law? Specifically, their actions during Trump's inauguration seem to violate the Supreme Court's ruling in *Riley v. California.* In that 2014 decision, the Court ruled 9–0 that "officers must generally secure a warrant before conducting such a search." In combination, the threats of felony riot charges and cellphone seizures are likely to have a chilling effect on citizens exercising their First Amendment right to assembly.

Citizens' First and Fourth Amendment rights are further threatened as local, state, and federal law enforcement are increasingly equipped with both cellphone interception devices and cellphone extraction devices. CityLab's George Joseph has reported that the fifty largest police departments in the US have invested heavily in military-grade surveillance tools. One device, called a Dirtbox in honor of the company that produces the devices, Digital Receiver Technology (DRT), can track and receive data from almost ten thousand phones at once.

In May 2017, the *Guardian* reported that, since Trump was elected, more than twenty states have proposed bills that would "crack down" on protests and demonstrations, in ways that UN experts have described as "criminalizing peaceful protests." In March 2017, the *Guardian* reported that David Kaye and Maina Kiai, special rapporteurs on the freedom of expression and freedom of peaceful assembly, respectively, from the UN's Office of the High Commissioner for Human Rights, submitted a report to the US State Department, documenting the "worrying trend" in state legislation restricting the rights to freedom of peaceful assembly and freedom of expression in the US.[59]

12
US Quietly Established New "Anti-Propaganda" Center

Claire Bernish, "Propaganda Bill in Congress Could Give America Its Very Own Ministry of Truth," MintPress News, June 7, 2016, http://www.MintPressnews.com/propaganda-bill-congress-give-america-ministry-truth/217016/.
Sarah Lazare, "Obama Just Signed Off on a Shadowy New 'Anti-Propaganda' Center That will be Handed Over to Trump," AlterNet, December 30, 2016, http://www.alternet.org/human-rights/obama-just-signed-shadowy-new-anti-propaganda-center-will-be-handed-over-trump.
Rick Sterling, "The War Against Alternative Information," Consortium News, January 1, 2017, https://consortiumnews.com/2017/01/01/the-war-against-alternative-information/.
Lambert Strether, "Does the 'Countering Foreign Propaganda and Disinformation Act' Apply to American Independent or Alternative Media?," Naked Capitalism, January 3, 2017, http://www.nakedcapitalism.com/2017/01/100755.html.

Student Researchers: Samuel Mathias Ditlinger (Citrus College) and Tom Field (Diablo Valley College)

Faculty Evaluators: Andy Lee Roth (Citrus College) and Mickey Huff (Diablo Valley College)

On December 23, 2016, then-president Obama signed the 2017 National Defense Authorization Act (NDAA). As Sarah Lazare reported for AlterNet, the 2017 NDAA included a provision to create a new federal center with "sweeping" surveillance powers to counter foreign "propaganda and disinformation." The Global Engagement Center, Lazare wrote, will be granted "broad and ill-defined powers to surveil the 'populations most susceptible to propaganda,' compile reporting and social media messaging critical of the U.S. government and disseminate pro-American propaganda." The NDAA set aside

$160 million to be used in fighting propaganda and disinformation deemed unfavorable to US interests.

The NDAA stated, "The purpose of the Center shall be to lead, synchronize, and coordinate efforts of the Federal Government to recognize, understand, expose, and counter foreign state and non-state propaganda and disinformation efforts aimed at undermining United States national security interests." For example, the Center will be responsible for keeping track of "counterfactual narratives abroad that threaten the national security interests of the United States and United States allies and partner nations." As Lazare noted, the imprecise wording of the NDAA "could be interpreted as targeting information and communications critical of the U.S. government."

The AlterNet report quoted Michael Macleod-Ball, chief of the ACLU's Washington Legislative Office: "We have big concerns with the retention of that information and how it might be shared across agencies . . . Whether you're talking about law enforcement or intelligence officials, having the government in the business of monitoring individual communications is very troubling to us."

The NDAA specified that the president shall appoint the Global Engagement Center's director. As Lazare noted, passage of the NDAA took place at the very end of 2016, with "little debate or notice," despite its "broad implications." Ohio Republican senator Rob Portman and Connecticut Democratic senator Chris Murphy initially proposed the Global Engagement Center in separate legislation.

The NDAA authorized the Global Engagement Center to provide "grants or contracts of financial support" to "civil society groups, media content providers, nongovernmental organizations, federally funded research and development centers, private companies, or academic institutions." These groups, Rick Sterling of Consortium News wrote, would be hired to identify and investigate print and online news sources deemed to be distributing propaganda and misinformation directed at the US and its allies.

Identifying a set of "propaganda themes" that have "permeated" the coverage of Syria by Western media—including, he noted, the "generally progressive" radio and TV program *Democracy Now!*—Sterling wrote that, with establishment of the new Global Engagement Center, we should expect to see an "escalation" of the information war, including "even more aggressive and better-financed assaults" on the "few voices" that dare to challenge US media narratives on critical foreign policy issues.

In November 2016, the *Washington Post* ran a story that described the proposed program as being "aimed at foreign information sources, not ones based in the United States."[60] But independent coverage by other news sources called this claim into question. Writing for Naked Capitalism, Lambert Strether noted that ambiguity in the statute's language could indeed allow action against US-based sources. Strether compared the language in the 2017 NDAA with the wording of the Intelligence Authorization Act for 2015. Where the latter featured precise wording—"including threats from foreign countries and foreign non-state actors"—Section 1287(2) of the 2017 law applied to "foreign state and non-state propaganda and disinformation efforts." Strether noted the difference, stressing the addition of the phrase "non-state propaganda." He further noted that Snopes had attempted to debunk a "rumor" that this law could be enforced on US media, but had relied on a press release from Senator Rob Portman about the earlier proposed legislation which did not examine the actual language of the NDAA. Strether concluded that a "careful reading" of the 2017 NDAA provides "good reason to fear an impact on American independent or alternative media," because they could be categorized as "non-state actors."

MintPress News was among the only outlets that ran a story critical of the original House bill, and the 2017 NDAA and its implications for freedom of speech passed virtually without mention in the corporate press.

13

Right-Wing Money Promotes Model Legislation to Restrict Free Speech on University Campuses

Alex Kotch, "Right-Wing Billionaires are Funding a Cynical Plot to Destroy Dissent and Protest in Colleges Across the U.S.," AlterNet, March 18, 2017, http://www.alternet.org/education/right-wing-billionaires-are-funding-cynical-plot-destroy-dissent-and-protest-colleges.

Student Researchers: Dawn M. Lucier (College of Marin) and Emily von Weise (University of Vermont)

Faculty Evaluators: Susan Rahman (College of Marin) and Rob Williams (University of Vermont)

Right-wing conservatives are using money and power to influence public policy to suppress student dissent on US college and university campuses. The right-wing Goldwater Institute, which is funded by conservatives including Charles Koch and the Mercer family, has proposed model legislation that seeks to quell student dissent in favor of guest speakers who attempt to discredit climate change, oppose LGBTQ rights, and espouse hate speech, Alex Kotch reported for AlterNet in March 2017.

The stated intent of the Goldwater Institute's proposed "Campus Free Speech Act" is to "uphold free-speech principles" and to ensure "the fullest degree . . . of free expression"—but, Kotch reported, the model legislation does not consider protest or dissent to be free speech. In fact, the model legislation stated that "protests and demonstrations that infringe upon on the rights of others to engage in or listen to expressive activity shall not be permitted and shall be subject to sanction."[61] Students found to have infringed on the expressive rights of others more than one time would be "suspended for a minimum of one year, or expelled," according to the model legislation.

UnKoch My Campus is a campaign that seeks to "expose and expel undue donor influence" from institutions of higher education.[62] Kotch's AlterNet article quoted Ralph Wilson, a senior researcher with UnKoch My Campus: "These laws would create a chilling effect on students who reject the idea that white supremacists or climate deniers are simply representing an 'opposing viewpoint' that should be tolerated, and who are rightfully relying on their first amendment freedoms to stop the rise of fascism and prevent global climate catastrophe."

The Goldwater Institute's "Campus Free Speech Act" has been adapted in proposed legislation in many states. For example, states including Illinois, North Dakota, Virginia, and Tennessee have proposed bills that crack down on free speech with some elements of the model legislation. Additional states, including Colorado, Florida, and Utah, are also proposing so-called "campus free speech" bills.

The text of the proposed legislation was written by Stanley Kurtz, James Manley, and Jonathan Butcher. Kurtz is a fellow at the Ethics and Public Policy Center, a conservative think tank that applies "the Judeo-Christian moral tradition to critical issues of public policy." The Ethics and Public Policy Center, Kotch reported, has received "millions of dollars in donations" from the foundations of conservative families, as well as "hundreds of thousands" from Donors Trust and Donors Capital Fund, which serve as vehicles for wealthy right-wing donors. Between 2006 and 2015, the two groups received more than $9 million in contributions from Charles and David Koch. The Goldwater Institute's senior attorney, Manley, previously worked for the Mountain States Legal Foundation, which also received significant donations from the Donors Trust and Donors Capital Fund. Butcher, the Institute's education director, worked at the conservative Heritage Foundation—which has been heavily funded by the Kochs—from 2002 to 2006.

14

Judges across US Using Racially Biased Software to Assess Defendants' Risk of Committing Future Crimes

Julia Angwin, Jeff Larson, Surya Mattu, and Lauren Kirchner, "Machine Bias," ProPublica, May 23, 2016, https://www.propublica.org/article/machine-bias-risk-assessments-in-criminal-sentencing.

Jeff Larson, Surya Mattu, Lauren Kirchner, and Julia Angwin, "How We Analyzed the COMPAS Recidivism Algorithm," ProPublica, May 23, 2016, https://www.propublica.org/article/how-we-analyzed-the-compas-recidivism-algorithm.

Student Researcher: Hector Hernandez (Citrus College)

Faculty Evaluator: Andy Lee Roth (Citrus College)

In 2014, then–US attorney general Eric Holder warned that so-called "risk assessments" might be injecting bias into the nation's judicial system. As ProPublica reported in May 2016, courtrooms across the country use algorithmically-generated scores, known as risk assessments, to rate a defendant's risk of future crime and, in many states—including Arizona, Colorado, Delaware, Kentucky, Louisiana, Oklahoma, Virginia, Washington, and Wisconsin—to unofficially inform judges' sentencing decisions. The Justice Department's National Institute of Corrections now encourages the use of such assessments at every stage of the criminal justice process.

Although Holder called in 2014 for the US Sentencing Commission to study the use of risk scores because they might "exacerbate unwarranted and unjust disparities that are already far too common in our criminal justice system," the Sentencing Commission never did so. Julia Angwin, Jeff Larson, Surya Mattu, and Lauren Kirchner's article reported the findings of an effort by ProPublica to assess Holder's concern. As they wrote, ProPublica "obtained the risk scores assigned to more than 7,000 people arrested in Broward County, Florida, in 2013 and 2014 and checked to see how many were charged with new crimes over the next two years." The ProPublica study was specifically intended to assess whether an algorithm known as COMPAS, or Correctional Offender Management Profiling for Alternative Sanctions, produced accurate prediction results through its assessment of "criminogenic needs" that relate to the major theories of criminality, including "criminal personality," "social isolation," "substance abuse," and "residence/stability."

Judges across the country are provided with risk ratings based on the COMPAS algorithm or comparable software. Broward County, Florida—the focus of ProPublica's study—does not use risk assessments in sentencing, but it does use them in pretrial hearings, as part of its efforts to address jail overcrowding. As ProPublica reported, judges in Broward County use risk scores to determine which defendants are sufficiently low risk to be released on bail pending their trials.

Based on ProPublica's analysis of the Broward County data, Angwin, Larson, Mattu, and Kirchner reported that the risk scores produced by the algorithm "proved remarkably unreliable" in forecasting violent crime: "Only 20 percent of the people predicted to commit violent crimes actually went on to do so." In fact, the algorithm was only "somewhat more accurate" than a coin toss.

The study also found significant racial disparities, as Holder had feared. "The formula was particularly likely to falsely flag black defendants as future criminals, wrongly labeling them this way at almost twice the rate as white defendants," ProPublica reported.

Defendants' prior crimes or the types of crime for which they were arrested do not explain this disparity. After running a statistical test that controlled for the effects of criminal history, recidivism, age, and gender, black defendants were still 77 percent more likely to be identified as at higher risk of committing a future violent crime and 45 percent more likely to be predicted to commit a future crime of any kind, compared with their white counterparts.

Northpointe, the for-profit company that created COMPAS, disputed ProPublica's analysis. However, as ProPublica noted, Northpointe deems its algorithm to be proprietary, so the company will not publicly disclose the calculations that COMPAS uses to determine defendants' risk scores—making it impossible for either defendants or the public "to see what might be driving the disparity." In practice, this means that defendants rarely have opportunities to challenge their assessments.

As ProPublica reported, the increasing use of risk scores is controversial, and the topic has garnered some previous independent news media coverage, including 2015 reports by the Associated Press, The Marshall Project, and FiveThirtyEight.[63]

15
Shell Understood Climate Change as Early as 1991—and Ignored It

Jelmer Mommers, "Shell Made a Film about Climate Change in 1991 (Then Neglected to Heed Its Own Warning," De Correspondent, February 28, 2017, https://thecorrespondent.com/6285/shell-made-a-film-about-climate-change-in-1991-then-neglected-to-heed-its-own-warning/692663565-87533f6.

Jelmer Mommers and Damian Carrington, "If Shell Knew Climate Change was Dire 25 Years Ago, Why Still Business as Usual Today?," De Correspondent, February 28, 2017, https://thecorrespondent.com/6286/if-shell-knew-climate-change-was-dire-25-years-ago-why-still-business-as-usual-today/692773774-4d15b476.

Damian Carrington and Jelmer Mommers, "Shell's 1991 Warning: Climate Changing 'at Faster Rate Than at Any Time since End of Ice Age,'" Guardian, February 28, 2017, https://www.theguardian.com/environment/2017/feb/28/shell-film-warning-climate-change-rate-faster-than-end-ice-age.

Damian Carrington and Jelmer Mommers, "'Shell Knew': Oil Giant's 1991 Film Warned of Climate Change Danger," Guardian, February 28, 2017, https://www.theguardian.com/environment/2017/feb/28/shell-knew-oil-giants-1991-film-warned-climate-change-danger.

Student Researcher: Clare Charlesworth (University of Vermont)

Faculty Evaluator: Rob Williams (University of Vermont)

In 1991, Shell Oil Company produced and distributed a twenty-eight-minute documentary titled *Climate of Concern*. Asserting that climate change was taking place "at a rate faster than at any time since the end of the ice age—change too fast perhaps for life to adapt, without severe dislocation," the film addressed potentially drastic consequences of climate change including extreme weather, flooding, famines, and climate refugees. While commenting that global warming was "not yet certain," the Shell film stated, "many think that to wait for final proof would be irresponsible." The film's narrator explained that a "uniquely broad consensus of scientists" had issued a "serious warning" in a report to the United Nations at the end of 1990.[64]

Recently *Climate of Concern* resurfaced, after Jelmer Mommers obtained a copy of it, and he and Damian Carrington posted it online as part of a joint investigative report for De Correspondent and the *Guardian*. As Mommers and Carrington documented, instead of trying to combat climate change as the company's own documentary urged, Shell's actions since 1991 have often contributed to increasing the negative impact of climate change.

A former geologist who had researched shale deposits with funding from Shell and BP, Jeremy Leggett, told Mommers and Carrington, "The film shows that Shell understood that the threat was dire, potentially existential for civilization, more than a quarter of a century ago." Mommers and Carrington also quoted HSBC's former global head of oil and gas, Paul Spedding (now at the think tank Carbon Tracker), who noted that "Shell's oil production is destined to become heavier, higher cost, and higher carbon, hardly a profile that fits the outlook described in Shell's video."

Shell's documentary addressed the need for action on climate change. When asking how societies could reduce carbon emissions, the documentary identified nuclear, hydroelectric, solar, and wind power as alternative energy options. However, as Mommers and Carrington reported, Shell has consistently undermined the production of renewable energy for its own financial gain. One recent example was documented in an April 2015 *Guardian* article, which revealed that, in order to ensure that its gas investments would remain lucrative, Shell successfully lobbied to "undermine European renewable energy targets ahead of a key agreement on emissions cuts" reached by the EU in 2014.[65]

Furthermore, Mommers and Carrington wrote, until 2015 Shell was a member of the American Legislative Exchange Council (ALEC), a lobby group that denies climate change, and it remains a member of the Business Roundtable and the American Petroleum Institute, "which both fought against Barack Obama's Clean Power Plan." According to Shell officials, it has remained a member of groups that hold different views on climate action to "influence" them, but Mommers and Carrington quoted Thomas O'Neill, from the group

Influence Map, which tracks lobbying, who told them that the "trade associations and industry groups are there to say things the company cannot or does not want to say. It's deliberately that way."

Mommers and Carrington also presented a "confidential" Shell report, written in 1986, that warned about the possibility of "fast and dramatic" climate changes that "would impact on the human environment, future living standards and food supplies, and could have major social, economic, and political consequences."

The revelation that as early as 1986 Shell Oil Company had a sophisticated scientific understanding of climate change and its potentially disastrous consequences, as documented by Mommers and Carrington, echoes a July 2015 report in the *Guardian*. That report featured internal company emails revealing that ExxonMobil knew of climate change "as early as 1981 . . . seven years before it became a public issue." Despite this knowledge, the *Guardian* reported, ExxonMobil "spent millions over the next 27 years to promote climate [change] denial."[66]

16

"Resilient" Indian Communities Struggle to Cope with Impacts of Climate Change

Anuradha Sengupta, "Tired of Running from the River: Adapting to Climate Change on India's Disappearing Islands," *YES! Magazine*, June 2, 2016, http://www.yesmagazine.org/planet/tired-of-running-from-the-river-adapting-to-climate-change-on-indias-disappearing-islands-20160602.

Student Researcher: Caroline Yoss (College of Marin)

Faculty Evaluator: Susan Rahman (College of Marin)

The Sundarbans are a vast mangrove delta that connects India and Bangladesh along the coast of the Bay of Bengal. In Bengali, Sundarban means "beautiful forest," and the region is designated as a UNESCO World Heritage Site. However, as Anuradha Sengupta reported for *YES! Magazine*, residents of islands in the Sundarbans, such as Ghoramara, are "struggling to cope" with rising seas, erratic weather patterns, severe floods, heavy rainfall, and intense cyclones that are the consequences of global climate change. The Intergovernmental Panel on Climate Change (IPCC) has warned that rising sea levels mean that areas like the Sundarbans will, in Sengupta's words, "bear the brunt" of climate change, with submerged lands, farmlands damaged by increasingly saline soils, homes swept away, livelihoods destroyed, and families broken apart. "The effects of global warming," Sengupta reported, "will be most severe on those who did the least to contribute to it, and who can least afford measures to adapt or save themselves."

Residents of the Sundarbans have typically made a living by reliance upon natural resources, deriving sustenance from small-scale farming, fishing, and honey gathering. However, with climate change, rising water levels have reduced the amount of arable land and frequent intrusion of saltwater has reduced the quality of remaining farmlands, while extreme weather conditions mean fewer flowers to sustain honey harvests.

Nevertheless, Sengupta reported, the people of the Sundarbans are "resilient." While many of the region's men now leave for most of the year to work for wages in urban areas on the mainland, the women have responded by planting hardy native crops, adopting integrated farming methods, and banking seeds. Many have switched from "modern high-yield" rice seeds to native grains that are saline-resistant. A West Bengal nongovernmental development organization, the Development Research Communication and Services Centre (DRCSC), provides support to families adopting sustainable agricultural practices in the face of climate change.

However, as Sengupta acknowledged, the number of those who adopt sustainable methods is "still quite low." Aditya Ghosh, who covered the Sundarbans as a journalist between 2000 and 2004 and is now a research associate with the University of Heidelberg's South Asia Institute, told *YES! Magazine*, "Years of ineffective, unplanned, and chaotic governance have made the Sundarbans a soft target for any abrupt environmental change." In his research, Ghosh found eighty-two reported incidents of flooding, affecting more than five hundred households, between 2010 and 2015. His research also indicated that flooding and other impacts of climate change have led to a six-fold increase in marginal labor—people who work less than six months per year—from 1991 to 2012. Workers who previously had employment security have "gradually slipped into marginality," he told *YES! Magazine*.

Several islands in the Sundarbans have already been completely submerged by rising sea levels. When the island of Lohachara went under in 2006, it displaced seven thousand people. As Sengupta and other journalists have reported, if scientific predictions about rising sea levels prove accurate, in fifteen to twenty-five years as many as thirteen million residents of the Sundarbans would be left homeless, "forcing a massive exodus of climate refugees." Sengupta's *YES! Magazine* report was distinctive in emphasizing the ways that residents of the Sundarbans—and especially the region's women—are "rebuilding their lives" in the face of climate change, as well as the positive role that NGOs, such as the DRCSC, could play in helping to minimize a looming humanitarian disaster in the Bay of Bengal.

17
Young Plaintiffs Invoke Constitutional Grounds for Climate Protection

James Conca, "Federal Court Rules on Climate Change in Favor of Today's Children," *Forbes*, April 10, 2016, http://www.forbes.com/sites/jamesconca/2016/04/10/federal-court-rules-on-climate-change-in-favor-of-todays-children/#5e5973246219.

Michelle Nijhuis, "The Teen-Agers Suing Over Climate Change," *New Yorker*, December 6, 2016, http://www.newyorker.com/tech/elements/the-teen-agers-suing-over-climate-change.

Gabriela Steier, "No Ordinary Lawsuit: Juliana v. United States is a Landmark Precedent for Climate Change Legislation," JURIST, January 6, 2017, http://www.jurist.org/forum/2017/01/Gabriela-Steier-juliana-v-united-states.php.

Zahra Hirji, "Children's Climate Lawsuit Against U.S. Adds Trump as Defendant," Inside Climate News, February 9, 2017, https://insideclimatenews.org/news/09022017/climate-change-lawsuit-donald-trump-children.

Ciara O'Rourke, "The 11-Year-Old Suing Trump over Climate Change," *Atlantic*, February 9, 2017, https://www.theatlantic.com/science/archive/2017/02/trump-climate-lawsuit/516054/.

Student Researchers: Sabrina Salinas and Eric Osterberg (Citrus College)

Faculty Evaluator: Andy Lee Roth (Citrus College)

In September 2015, twenty-one plaintiffs, aged eight to nineteen, brought a lawsuit against the federal government and the fossil fuel industry to the US Federal District Court in Eugene, Oregon. The case, *Juliana v. United States*, argued that the federal government and the fossil fuel industry have knowingly endangered the plaintiffs by promoting the burning of fossil fuels, and that this violates their constitutional and public trust rights. Their complaint said that the defendants "deliberately allow[ed] atmospheric CO_2 concentrations to escalate to levels unprecedented in human history." The lead counsel for the plaintiffs in the case, Julia Olson, is executive director of Our Children's Trust, a Eugene-based group that advocates for "legally-binding, science-based climate recovery policies."[67]

In April 2016, US Magistrate Judge Thomas Coffin denied a motion to dismiss the case, ruling in favor of the plaintiffs' charge that the federal government violates constitutional and public trust rights by its ongoing promotion of fossil fuels that destabilize the earth's climate. In a report published by *Forbes*, James Conca wrote that the lawsuit was the first of its kind, examining whether the causes of climate change violate the US Constitution. By denying a motion to dismiss, the court found that the federal government is also subject to the public trust doctrine, Conca reported. Public trust doctrine, he explained, "asserts that the government is a trustee of the natural resources that we depend on for life, liberty and the pursuit of happiness."

In his ruling, Justice Coffin wrote, "The debate about climate change and its impact has been before various political bodies for some time now. Plaintiffs give this debate justiciability by asserting harms that befall or will befall them personally and to a greater extent than older segments of society . . . [T]he intractability of the debates before Congress and state legislatures and the alleged valuing of short-term economic interest despite the cost to human life, necessitates a need for the courts to evaluate the constitutional parameters of the action or inaction taken by the government."

As Conca reported, the decision "upheld the youth Plaintiffs' claims in the Fifth and Ninth Amendments 'by denying them protections afforded to previous generations and by favoring the short-term economic interests of certain citizens.'" In January 2016, three fossil fuel industry trade associations, representing nearly all of the world's largest fossil fuel companies, had called the case "a direct, substantial threat to our businesses." According to sixteen-year-old plaintiff Victoria Barrett, "Our generation will continue to be a force for the world."

In November 2016, US District Court Judge Ann Aiken affirmed Coffin's April ruling, which prepared the way for *Juliana v. United States* to proceed to trial. As Gabriela Steier reported in JURIST, Judge Aiken's opinion stated, "This is no ordinary lawsuit." Judge Aiken's opinion explained, "This action is of a different order than the typical environmental case. It alleges that defendants' actions and inactions—whether or not they violate any specific statutory duty—have so profoundly damaged our home planet that they threaten plaintiffs' fundamental constitutional rights to life and liberty."

In February 2017, the plaintiffs updated their case to list President Donald Trump as a defendant, replacing former President Barack Obama. A month later, the Trump administration filed a motion to delay trial preparation.[68] As *Censored 2018* goes to print, the plaintiffs are pursuing an effort to depose Rex Tillerson, the former ExxonMobil CEO and Trump's secretary of state, and the country's most powerful fossil fuel lobbies are seeking the judge's permission to withdraw from the lawsuit.[69] The trial might begin as early as fall of 2017.

As *Juliana v. United States* has progressed to its trial phase, the case has received increasing corporate media coverage. But it is important to note that initially corporate media ignored or marginalized the lawsuit. For instance, in a rare instance of corporate news coverage from 2015, MSNBC described the lawsuit as an "unusual case" that is "long on symbolism" but "unlikely" to win, while noting the risks associated with any decision that might diminish the fossil fuel industry's interests.[70] In November 2016, CBS News and Fox News published stories, based on an Associated Press report, that made passing reference to *Juliana v. United States* (although not by name) and focused, instead, on a related lawsuit, involving some of the same plaintiffs, in the Washington state judicial system.[71]

18
Rise in Number of Transgender People Murdered

Alex Schmider, "GLAAD Calls for Increased and Accurate Media Coverage of Transgender Murders," GLAAD, July 26, 2016, updated June 28, 2017, http://www.glaad.org/blog/glaad-calls-increased-and-accurate-media-coverage-transgender-murders.

Meredith Talusan, "Documenting Trans Homicides," Mic, December 8, 2016, https://mic.com/unerased.

Sandy E. James, Jody L. Herman, Susan Rankin, et al., "The Report of the 2015 U.S. Transgender Survey," National Center for Transgender Equality, December 2016, http://www.transequality.org/sites/default/files/docs/usts/USTS%20Full%20Report%20-%20FINAL%201.6.17.pdf.

Trudy Ring, "Virginia Woman is 27th Trans Person Murdered in 2016," *Advocate*, January 6, 2017, http://www.advocate.com/transgender/2017/1/06/virginia-woman-27th-trans-person-murdered-2016.

Student Researcher: Keira Andrews (Syracuse University)

Faculty Evaluator: Jeff Simmons (Syracuse University)

Proposing a "comprehensive look" at transgender homicides since 2010, Mic's Meredith Talusan investigated in December 2016 "how and why trans lives are not counted and what we can do to end the violence." The Mic report began with a revealing comparison of homicide figures: Among the general US population, one in 19,000 persons is murdered every year; for young adults, aged 15–34, the figure is one in 12,000. For black trans women in the same age range, the rate is one in 2,600. In 2015 FBI homicide data documented 15,696 murders. As Mic reported, "If in 2015 all Americans had the same risk of murder as young black trans women, there would have been 120,087 murders." Put another way, although the total number of transgender homicides per year may seem small, it "represents a rate of violence that far exceeds that of the general population."

And, in fact, as Talusan's report went on to document, due to underreporting and misidentification (many trans murder victims are "misgendered" by officials and news reports, and even by immediate family members who sometimes reject a relative's trans identity), the actual trans murder rate is likely "much higher." The result of the Mic investigation is what Talusan described as a "comprehensive database" of transgender Americans who have died by homicide since 2010.[72] 2010 was the first year that the National Coalition of Anti-Violence Programs (NCAVP), an organization that tracks homicides in the transgender community, began its formal count.

As of late June 2017, GLAAD had documented fourteen transgender people killed in 2017, all of whom, its website noted, were transgender women of color.[73] Between 2010 and 2016, Talusan summarized, at least 111 transgender and gender-nonconforming Americans were murdered "because of their gender identity." Under the LGBTQ umbrella, she elaborated, no group "faces more violence" than transgender people, who accounted for 67 percent of the hate-related homicides against queer people in 2015, according to the NCAVP. The US Census does not track transgender people; and, although the FBI added gender identity to its records of hate crimes in 2014, it does not track gender identity along with its homicide statistics.

"At every stage," Shannon Minter, a transgender attorney and legal director of the National Center for Lesbian Rights, told Mic, "there are bias-based obstacles" that diminish the chances that a trans person's death by murder will be accounted for publicly, "and those levels reinforce each other." People hesitate to even go to the police in some cases. Official records—from police reports and hospital records, to death certificates and obituaries—typically lack the means to represent transgender people. And even when police or coroners correctly identify a murder victim as transgender, law enforcement defer to families on releasing that information. A sergeant for the Metropolitan Police Department (MPD) in Washington, DC, who is a transgender woman and the MPD's LGBT liaison, told Mic, "I would never out anyone as trans during life or in their deaths, not coming from a police department." Media reporting on transgender homicides is improving, said the NCAVP's communications director, Sue Yacka, but "local press still has a long way to go." Yacka routinely contacts news organizations to attempt to get them to use transgender victims' names and genders. Similarly, in its report, GLAAD called on news media to "report on the brutal violence perpetrated against transgender people, particularly transgender women of color" and to "respect and use the lived identity, name, and pronoun of the victim." But fundamentally, Talusan wrote, tracking transgender homicides is problematic because "gender identity can be difficult to pin down . . . Trans people don't look or act just one way."

Cases of homicide of transgender people are not only under-counted, they are also less likely to be solved and prosecuted. Mic reported that there have been "no arrests" in connection with 39 percent of transgender murders from 2010 to 2015. Furthermore, when perpetrators are found, the legal outcomes of those cases show "clear disparities" between victims who are black trans women and those who are not. People who kill black trans women and femmes are usually convicted of lesser charges—such as manslaughter or assault—than those who kill people of other trans identities, Mic found. In the time span studied, no case of trans homicide had resulted in a hate crime conviction, according to the report.

Despite these bleak circumstances, Talusan reported that recent activism focused on transgender murders might be having a positive effect. Juries are still hesitant to convict suspects of first-degree murder for killing a transgender person, but since 2010 just one case has resulted in a jury returning a not-guilty verdict. This, Talusan wrote, may encourage future prosecutors "to be more aggressive in pursuing murder convictions rather than settling for plea bargains." Similarly, due to public pressure, police departments are responding to transgender-related violence with "greater awareness." Perhaps most significantly, improved economic conditions, which would keep transgender people from being "forced to make choices that could endanger their lives," will be fundamental to protecting them in the future. As Talusan reported, "a startling 34% of black trans people live in extreme poverty."

19

Inmates and Activists Protest Chemical Weapons in US Prisons and Jails

Daniel Moattar, "Prisons are Using Military-Grade Tear Gas to Punish People," *Nation*, April 28, 2016, https://www.thenation.com/article/prisons-are-using-military-grade-tear-gas-to-punish-inmates/.

Sarah Lazare, "The Scandal of Chemical Weapons in U.S. Prisons," AlterNet, January 11, 2017, http://www.alternet.org/activism/scandal-chemical-weapons-us-prisons.

Student Researchers: Cynthia Alvarez, Veronica Esquivez, and William Ha (Citrus College)

Faculty Evaluator: Andy Lee Roth (Citrus College)

Daniel Moattar, writing for the *Nation*, and Sarah Lazare, a journalist at AlterNet, reported how chemical weapons, including several types of tear gas, are being used against prisoners in the United States, despite the fact that the international Chemical Weapons Convention of 1997 bans their use in warfare. Despite the arms control treaty that now binds nearly two hundred nations, Lazare reported, "in prisons and jails across the United States, far from any conventional battle-field or public scrutiny, tear gas and other chemical weapons are rou-tinely used against people held captive in enclosed spaces, including solitary confinement." Tear gas is known to cause skin and respira-tory irritation, intense pain, blindness, and, in severe cases, death.

Since 2013, the War Resisters League has been documenting the use of tear gas in prisons.[74] As Moattar reported, letters from inmates sent to the War Resisters League document the use of tear gas and pepper spray against inmates—in men's and women's prisons, including maximum- and medium-security facilities—in eigh-teen states across the country. Lazare summarized inmates' reports of "burns, scars and memories of agony and suffocation." Some reported being denied treatment or even being allowed to rinse their eyes after being subject to tear gas.

As a result of inmates' letters, activists have taken action. Seeking to end the use of tear gas in US prisons and jails, activists argue that "the deployment of chemical weapons of any kind against imprisoned people constitutes militarization and torture," Lazare reported. In early January 2017, shortly before the inauguration of Donald Trump, representatives of the War Resisters League, Witness Against Torture, Black Movement Law Project, and other organizations brought their demands to the Department of Justice, where they held a press con-ference and delivered a petition with over 13,000 signatures to then–deputy attorney general Sally Q. Yates.

Tear gases and pepper sprays are lucrative commodities for those who produce them. The War Resisters League also documented com-panies—including Sabre, Combined Tactical Systems (CTS), Sage, and Safariland—that sell tear gas to prisons in forms "designed spe-cifically for 'enclosed spaces.'" As Moattar documented in his article, through private companies such as Sabre and Safariland, the US "remains the single largest manufacturer" of CS, one of the two compounds used in most forms of tear gas. "Producers of tear gas and pepper spray worry more about finding new markets than navigating the law," Moattar wrote. "Even if existing restrictions on the use of force were enforced, the direct use of pain-inducing chemicals on prisoners, including inmates restrained or in solitary, is still minimally regulated and broadly legal."

There is little corporate news coverage on chemical weapons being used against inmates in US prisons and jails. What coverage there is tends to frame incidents as local and isolated, as in a September 2016 article in the *Miami Herald* which focused on the case of a twenty-seven-year-old inmate, Randall Jordan-Aparo, who died at Franklin Correctional Institution in 2010 after corrections officers allegedly tortured, gassed, and beat him.[75]

20

Seattle Activist Group Leads First Successful Campaign to Defund Police

Melissa Hellmann, "Defunding Police—How Antiracist Organizers Got Seattle to Listen," *YES! Magazine*, March 9, 2017, http://www.yesmagazine.org/peace-justice/defunding-police-how-antiracist-organizers-got-seattle-to-listen-20170309.

Student Researcher: Katie Doke Sawatzky (University of Regina)

Faculty Evaluator: Patricia Elliott (University of Regina)

In September 2016 the Block the Bunker campaign in Seattle was the first to persuade US city officials to divest from police funding and allocate more tax dollars for community services.

In summer 2016, a coalition of antiracist grassroots organizers protested the city's plans to spend nearly $150 million on a new police station in North Seattle. In September, the mayor shelved the plans for the 2017 budget and an additional $29 million was added to the affordable housing budget. According to the Movement for Black Lives, no other organization is known to be actively working on divestment policy, and it is the first such campaign to be successful.[76]

NBC's KING5 and the *Seattle Times* covered the story in August and September 2016 but activists' voices were barely included.[77] KING5's coverage, in particular, emphasized the disruption the group caused during city council meetings.[78] No attention was given to the campaign's success in divesting from police funding and its significance for antiracism movements across the US. By contrast, in a *YES! Magazine* article, Melissa Hellmann spoke with the activists and dissected the argument that more policing makes communities safer. Palca Shibale, a recent University of Washington graduate and one of the original organizers against the proposed police station, told *YES! Magazine* that she hoped Block the Bunker would inspire others to organize and address issues of police brutality and gentrification in their own cities. "It's so important to do whatever you can do in your own spaces to fight for equity, however that looks," Shibale said. Hellmann interviewed Michelle Phelps, assistant professor of sociology at the University of Minnesota, who said there was not a lot of research on alternative strategies to reduce crime rates, but that spending more on police and less on social services puts "a strain on the relationships between communities and police."

A Seattle city council member, Kshama Sawant, said, "The only reason that this new police precinct is not going to go ahead in this year's budget is because of the Block the Bunker movement and because ordinary people, young people, and activists came and shut the city all down."

21

Fossil Fuel Industry "Colonizing" US Universities

Benjamin Franta and Geoffrey Supran, "The Fossil Fuel Industry's Invisible Colonization of Academia," *Guardian*, March 13, 2017, https://www.theguardian.com/environment/climate-consensus-97-per-cent/2017/mar/13/the-fossil-fuel-industrys-invisible-colonization-of-academia.

Student Researcher: Zeinab Benchakroun (College of Marin)

Faculty Evaluator: Susan Rahman (College of Marin)

Without the public's awareness, fossil fuel interests—representing oil, gas, and coal companies as well as utilities and investors—have "colonized nearly every nook and cranny of energy and climate policy research in American universities," two researchers at Stanford University and the Massachusetts Institute of Technology (MIT) reported in the *Guardian* in March 2017. Fossil fuel interests dominate energy and climate policy research at the nation's most prominent universities, including Harvard, MIT, Stanford, and the University of California, Berkeley. "The very experts we assume to be objective, and the very centers of research we assume to be independent," Benjamin Franta and Geoffrey Supran wrote, "are connected with the very industry the public believes they are objectively studying. Moreover, these connections are often kept hidden." The result is more than a "conflict of interest," Franta and Supran reported. These are "industry projects with the appearance of neutrality and credibility given by academia."

As an example of such "colonizing," Franta and Supran described in detail a February 2017 event, "Finding Energy's Rational Middle," hosted by Harvard Kennedy School's Belfer Center for Science and International Affairs. It was not publicly disclosed that Shell Oil Company sponsored the event. The Harvard event featured a documentary film, *The Great Transition*, produced by Shell and directed by a vice president of an oil and gas company funded by Shell. The Kennedy School has received at least $3.75 million from Shell, Franta and Supran reported.

The report also detailed how the Shell documentary provided supposedly objective scholars' assessments while failing to disclose their fossil fuel industry connections. The people shown in the documentary consistently expressed skepticism about renewable energy solutions and promoted being "realistic" about fossil fuels, while advocating natural gas as a great transition to "clean" energy—without mentioning that methane emissions have even greater impacts on global warming than carbon emissions do. Franta and Supran documented some of the film's participants' undisclosed connections to the fossil fuel industry; for example, Amy Myers Jaffe, who is identified in the film as the executive director of energy and sustainability at the University of California, Davis, is also a member of the US National Petroleum Council. In the film Jaffe says, "We need to be realistic that we're gonna use fossil fuels now, because in the end, we are." Michelle Michot Foss, identified as the chief energy economist at the University of Texas at Austin's Center for Energy Economics, is also a partner in a natural gas company, and Chevron, ExxonMobil, and the Koch Foundation, among others, fund the Center where she works.

As Franta and Supran noted, the fossil fuel industry often employs the tactic of claiming to promote a "rational middle" between total

dependence on nonrenewable energy and total independence from it, and in practice this tactic is used to undermine the shift to renewable energy sources. In this case, the report explained, Shell and allied figures were able to deploy the tactic with "Harvard's stamp of approval."

Beyond Harvard, Franta and Supran documented that the MIT Energy Initiative is "almost entirely funded" by fossil fuel companies, including Shell, ExxonMobil, and Chevron. MIT has received $185 million from David Koch, the oil billionaire and climate change denial financier, who is a life member of the university's board. ExxonMobil funds Stanford's Global Climate and Energy Project. UC Berkeley's Energy Biosciences Institute (EBI) was initiated thanks to a $500 million deal signed in 2007 with BP. BP appoints half of the voting members of EBI's Governance Board.[79]

Franta and Supran called for universities to stop ignoring the problem of climate change and confront it, either by disclosing financial funding from the fossil fuel industry in order to reduce conflicts of interest, or by prioritizing sponsors and personnel who are "less conflicted."

Corporate news coverage of how the fossil fuel industry has captured energy and climate policy research at US universities is rare, and when the topic is addressed coverage gives the impression of isolated incidents. In 2010, for example, the *Los Angeles Times* emphasized the benefits of BP's partnership with UC Berkeley.[80] After the Center for American Progress released a 2010 study that documented the fossil fuel industry's strong grip on university research, this topic received some coverage in the corporate press, including SFGate, but, as with previous coverage, these reports tended to focus on individual cases rather than systemic patterns.[81]

Greenpeace's PolluterWatch website maintains an interactive database of the Koch Foundation's funding for colleges and universities, which totaled over $144 million between 2005 and 2015.[82]

22

Lawsuit against Illinois Department of Corrections Exposes Militarization of Law Enforcement inside Prisons

Brian Dolinar, "Orange Crush: The Rise of Tactical Teams in Prison," Truthout, January 2, 2017, http://www.truth-out.org/news/item/38941-orange-crush-the-rise-of-tactical-teams-in-prison.

Student Researchers: Daniel Hayden and Nicholas Duran (Citrus College)

Faculty Evaluator: Andy Lee Roth (Citrus College)

Against a backdrop of national concern over the militarization of police, Brian Dolinar reported for Truthout that a judge has approved a 2015 lawsuit against 232 Illinois Department of Corrections officers to proceed to the discovery phase. The class-action suit, *Ross v. Gossett*, brought on behalf of prisoners at Menard, Illinois River, Big Muddy River, and Lawrence Correctional Centers, alleges that the "Orange Crush" tactical team used excessive force, including physical and sexual abuse, when it conducted mass shakedowns in the spring of 2014.[83] As Dolinar wrote, "less is known beyond prison walls about guards who regularly brutalize those incarcerated," but the Illinois lawsuit "names a list of horrific abuses that includes strip searches, beatings and mass shakedowns of cells," indicating how militarization of law enforcement has occurred inside prisons as well as in public.

Dolinar described the development and increasing use of so-called Special Operations Response Teams (SORTs), also known as tactical teams, in prisons across the US since the 1971 prison rebellion at Attica in New York. Dolinar's report focused in particular on one such group, within the Illinois Department of Corrections (IDOC), that has come to be known informally as the "Orange Crush," referencing their orange jumpsuits and extreme "horrific abuses." IDOC Orange Crush teams, Dolinar reported, first developed in 1996 when Illinois attempted to address the problem of prisons gangs, including the Vice Lords and Latin Kings, that often ran illicit operations with the cooperation of prison authorities.

The lawsuit alleges that Orange Crush teams used tear gas against prisoners and that, at some prisons, officers forced inmates to undergo what are known as "nuts to butts" searches, in which prisoners are forced to walk bent over at approximately a ninety-degree angle with no space between them. According to former inmates, if prisoners were to stand up during this procedure, they could be beaten. Documents released during discovery in the trial have revealed that dozens of inmates have required medical treatment as a result of Orange Crush searches. Officers also allegedly wore riot helmets to conceal their identities.

According to inmate statements, during cell searches some officers removed legal documents that prisoners intended to use in their trials. As Dolinar reported, "The reason why the Orange Crush conducted the sweeps is still unclear."

The lawsuit, filed by the Uptown People's Law Center and Loevy & Loevy, a Chicago-based firm, seeks to expose the Orange Crush and those who ordered raids at four separate facilities in Spring 2014. After the IDOC sought to have the suit dismissed, District Judge Staci Yandle concluded that defendants "purposely concealed their identities to evade responsibility for their actions."

Beyond Brian Dolinar's Truthout report, the alleged abuses by the IDOC Orange Crush unit and the resulting lawsuit have received limited news coverage, with reports restricted to local outlets, such as the *Belleville News-Democrat* and the *Chicago Defender*.[84]

23

Facebook Buys Sensitive User Data to Offer Marketers Targeted Advertising

Julia Angwin, Terry Parris, Jr., and Surya Mattu, "Breaking the Black Box: What Facebook Knows About You," ProPublica, September 28, 2016, https://www.propublica.org/article/breaking-the-black-box-what-facebook-knows-about-you.

Julia Angwin, Terry Parris, Jr., and Surya Mattu, "Facebook Doesn't Tell Users Everything It Really Knows About Them," ProPublica, December 27, 2016, https://www.propublica.org/article/facebook-doesnt-tell-users-everything-it-really-knows-about-them.

Student Researcher: Jonnie Zambrano (Citrus College)

Faculty Evaluator: Andy Lee Roth (Citrus College)

Julia Angwin, Terry Parris, Jr., and Surya Mattu reported that, since 2012, Facebook has been buying sensitive data about users' offline lives from data brokers and combining this information with the online data it collects in order to sell this information to advertisers who seek to target specific types of Facebook users for their products and services. Facebook, they reported in September 2016, uses a "particularly comprehensive set of dossiers" on its more than two billion members in order to "offer marketers a chance to target ads to increasingly specific groups of people." As Angwin, Parris, and Mattu described in that report, "we found Facebook offers advertisers more than 1,300 categories for ad targeting—everything from people whose property size is less than .26 acres to households with exactly seven credit cards."

Their December 2016 report quoted Jeffrey Chester, executive director of the Center for Digital Democracy. Facebook, Chester said, is "not being honest . . . Facebook is bundling a dozen different data companies to target an individual customer, and an individual should have access to that bundle as well."

Facebook collects information on users in many ways beyond users' posts and "likes." For instance, many websites include a Facebook link where a visitor to the site can like it on Facebook. In such cases, even if the website visitor does not choose to like the site on Facebook, Facebook is still able to track that the page was visited—linking back to the user. The data brokers from which Facebook buys additional information track *offline* sources, such as supermarket loyalty cards, mailing lists, and public records information (which includes records of home or car ownership).

Facebook seeks to puts users at ease by providing an opt-out option. However, as Angwin, Parris, and Mattu wrote, "Limiting commercial data brokers' distribution of your personal information is no simple matter." Even getting data brokers to share the information that they have about you (and can sell) could require sending the last four digits of your social security number, as in the case of Acxiom, one of six data brokers from which Facebook buys personal information. Reporter Julia Angwin noted that in 2013 she tried to opt out from as many data brokers as she could find. Sixty-five of the ninety-two brokers she found required her to submit some form of identification.[85] "In the end, she could not remove her data from the majority of providers," despite the fact that she had not signed up for any of these tracking services herself, the December ProPublica story reported.

One of the ways ProPublica gathered data for its report on Facebook's data collection processes was by asking Facebook users to share with ProPublica the categories of interest that the site assigned to them. ProPublica collected more than 52,000 unique attributes that Facebook had used to classify users' interests.

Although Facebook's methods of collecting data about the platform's users have received corporate coverage, this reporting has not explained the specific tactics used or the information obtained by data brokers. For instance, a 2010 *Wall Street Journal* article described how Facebook reported that "it had placed some developers on a six-month suspension from its site" because "a data broker" had "been paying application developers for identifying user information."[86] Rather than appearing as an isolated and unusual case as the *Wall Street Journal* report implied, Facebook's practice of engaging data brokers and selling user data to advertisers seems, according to ProPublica's 2016 reports, to be systemic and, apparently, entirely acceptable to Facebook.

24

Eight Use of Force Policies to Prevent Killings by Police

Kate Stringer, "We Already Know How to Reduce Police Racism and Violence," *YES! Magazine*, July 8, 2016, http://www.yesmagazine.org/people-power/cities-have-the-power-to-reduce-police-racism-and-violence.

Jamilah King, "Study: More Restrictive 'Use of Force' Policies Could Curb the Epidemic of Police Violence," Mic, September 21, 2016, https://mic.com/articles/154715/study-more-restrictive-use-of-force-policies-could-curb-the-epidemic-of-police-violence.

Alice Speri, "Here are Eight Policies That Can Prevent Police Killings," *Intercept*, September 21, 2016, https://theintercept.com/2016/09/21/here-are-eight-policies-that-can-prevent-police-killings.

Student Researcher: Malcolm Pinson (San Francisco State University)

Faculty Evaluator: Kenn Burrows (San Francisco State University)

Killings by police are not inevitable or difficult to prevent, according to a September 2016 study by Campaign Zero, a police-reform group formed in the aftermath of the Ferguson protests. The study, "Police Use of Force Policy Analysis," examined police departments in ninety-one of the nation's largest cities and found that departments with stricter use of force regulations killed significantly fewer people. Noting that many police departments fail to establish "common sense restrictions" on use of force and that police violence is "distributed disproportionally," with black people being three times more likely to be killed by police than their white counterparts, the study's authors wrote, "fundamentally changing use of force polic[i]es can dramatically reduce the number of people killed by police in America."[87] As Jamilah King reported in Mic, the study is "the first wide-scale analysis to demonstrate the connection between differing 'use of force' policies and the rate of police killings."

Campaign Zero identified the following eight guidelines, restricting when and how police officers should use force, that greatly decrease the likelihood of civilian deaths:

> ▸ Require officers to de-escalate situations before resorting to force.
> ▸ Limit the kinds of force that can be used to respond to specific forms of resistance.
> ▸ Restrict chokeholds.
> ▸ Require officers to give a verbal warning before using force.
> ▸ Prohibit officers from shooting at moving vehicles.
> ▸ Require officers to exhaust all alternatives to deadly force.

- Require officers to stop colleagues from exercising excessive force.
- Require comprehensive reporting on use of force.

Campaign Zero found that, on average, "each additional use of force policy was associated with a 15% reduction in killings," and that implementing all eight guidelines would result in a 54 percent reduction in killings for the average police department. Taking into account the number of arrests made, assaults on officers, and community demographics, Campaign Zero reported that police departments with all eight use of force policies implemented "would kill 72% fewer people than departments that have none of these policies in place."[88]

As King reported for Mic, Campaign Zero determined its findings by combining police department data on use of force policies, obtained through Freedom of Information Act requests, and records of police-involved killings dating back to 2015, as compiled by the *Guardian* and the *Washington Post*.[89]

In her coverage of the Campaign Zero study, Alice Speri of the *Intercept* noted that just thirty-four of the ninety-one police departments studied by Campaign Zero had policies requiring officers to de-escalate situations before resorting to force, and only thirty-one of the ninety-one departments required officers to exhaust all alternatives before resorting to deadly force. Just fifteen of the ninety-one departments required officers to report on all uses of force, including threatening a civilian with a firearm.

Yet, as King reported in Mic, Campaign Zero found significant differences between metropolitan police departments that had four or more of the policies in place and those that did not. For example, Washington, DC, and Miami did have four or more of the policies in place, and these cities had relatively low rates of police killings (between six police killings per million residents for Washington, DC, and ten per million for Miami). By contrast, the police departments of Orlando, Florida; Stockton, California; and Oklahoma City each implemented fewer than four of the use of force guidelines, and these cities had the nation's worst rates of police killings (between twenty-one police killings per million residents for Oklahoma City and twenty-five per million for Orlando).

Samuel Sinyangwe, one of the study's researchers and authors, told the *Intercept* that few departments have implemented all or most of these policies, partly due to "resistance from police unions that claim more restrictive policies will endanger officers." On the contrary, the Campaign Zero study showed that the numbers of officers assaulted or killed in the line of duty decreased in proportion with the number of regulations adopted by their department.[90]

Sinyangwe, the Campaign Zero researcher, told Mic, "Two years ago we didn't even have the data to know which police departments were killing people at higher rates than others and why . . . Now we can identify the key policies to prevent these killings."

Kate Stringer's *YES! Magazine* article, "We Already Know How to Reduce Police Racism and Violence," predated the publication of the Campaign Zero report, but offered insights on how cities could interrupt police violence, based on findings of previous research. Her report cited prior studies encouraging support for police reforms which included training officers against racial bias, hiring more female officers, hiring to match communities' racial diversity, opening departments to research, and using body cameras.

As of June 2017, Campaign Zero's findings appear to have been completely overlooked by the nation's major corporate news outlets.

25

Juvenile Court Fees Punish Children for Their Families' Poverty

Nika Knight, "Debtors' Prison for Kids: Poor Children Incarcerated When Families Can't Pay Juvenile Court Fees," Common Dreams, August 31, 2016, http://www.commondreams.org/news/2016/08/31/debtors-prison-kids-poor-children-incarcerated-when-families-cant-pay-juvenile-court.

Student Researcher: Raquel Guerrero (Sonoma State University)

Faculty Evaluator: Diana Grant (Sonoma State University)

Low-income children across the US are being imprisoned when they or their families cannot afford to pay court fees, Nika Knight reported in Common Dreams. Aside from court costs, low-income children also face fees for probation, health tests, care, and other services in juvenile facilities. This amounts to "punishing children for their families' poverty," Knight wrote, "and that may be unconstitutional."

Knight's article drew on a 2016 report by the Juvenile Law Center, a legal aid advocacy group, which reviewed statutes in all fifty states and the District of Columbia to assess "the legal framework for financial obligations placed on youth in the juvenile justice system and their families."[91] The Juvenile Law Center also conducted interviews with 183 people involved in the juvenile justice system—including lawyers, family members, and adults who had been incarcerated as children—across forty-one states. Noting "stark racial disparities" in the juvenile justice system generally, from arrests to diversion and detention, the study's authors wrote that costs, fines, fees, and restitution "exacerbate racial disparities in the juvenile justice system," in some cases creating what they described as "modern-day debtors' prisons." Notably, the Juvenile Law Center's report not only identified problems in the system but also highlighted solutions, including promising practices, legislative remedies, and case studies of jurisdictions that no longer impose court costs, fees, and fines in their juvenile systems.

Knight's article identified "myriad ways" that juvenile court systems levy fines on children's families "and then imprison those children when their families are too poor to pay the mounting costs." These include, for example, monthly fees on families whose children are sentenced to probation, the costs of "diversion" programs intended to keep children out of detention, and charges for court-ordered evaluations and tests (such as mental health evaluations, tests for sexually-transmitted diseases, and drug and alcohol assessments). When families cannot afford to pay these fees and fines, children may be incarcerated instead.

The Juvenile Law Center report described the fines imposed by juvenile court as "highly burdensome." For example, in Alameda County, California, the average cost of juvenile system involvement is $2,000 per case. Cost can be "significantly higher," according to the report, in cases in which young people are incarcerated for extended periods of time.

Furthermore, Knight reported, in some states parents themselves may also face imprisonment if they fail to pay fees and fines levied against their children. Incarcerating parents puts children further at risk and adds to the stresses on families already struggling with the consequences of poverty. According to the report's authors, "When parents face incarceration or mounting debt for failure to pay, they have even fewer resources to devote to educating, helping, and supporting their children."

While noting that a detailed analysis of these policies' constitutional implications went beyond its scope, the Juvenile Law Center report noted prior legal decisions in which the Supreme Court has held that courts must consider "alternative measures of punishment other than imprisonment" for poor defendants. The Supreme Court has also repeatedly held that constitutional protections must be calibrated to the unique developmental needs of adolescents.

In August 2016, the *New York Times* published a substantial article on the Juvenile Law Center's study, describing low-income juveniles—and especially racial minorities—as overburdened by fees.[92] However, the *Times* article did not mention that parents in some states were also being jailed, and the report overlooked the precedent of Supreme Court decisions upholding additional protections for adolescents.

Notes

1. Max Weber, "Science as a Vocation," *The Vocation Lectures*, eds. David Owen and Tracy B. Strong, trans. Rodney Livingstone (Indianapolis: Hackett Publishing, 2004), 1–31, 22. The German word Weber used for "science"—*Wissenschaft*—can refer more broadly to any scholarly discipline or body of knowledge. Thus, as David Owen and Tracy B. Strong noted in their introduction to Weber's lecture, Weber spoke to all those who would "dedicate themselves to a particular area of knowledge" (xxi).
2. E.g., "Kellyanne Conway Denies Trump Press Secretary Lied: 'He Offered Alternative Facts'— Video," *Meet the Press*, NBC, January 22, 2017, posted on the *Guardian*, January 22, 2017, https://www.theguardian.com/us-news/video/2017/jan/22/kellyanne-conway-trump-press-secretary-alternative-facts-video.
3. Todd: "Four of the five facts he uttered were just not true. Look, alternative facts are not facts. They're falsehoods." "Kellyanne Conway Denies," *Guardian*.
4. The Oxford Dictionaries defined "post-truth" as "relating to or denoting circumstances in which objective facts are less influential in shaping public opinion than appeals to emotion and personal belief." See Oxford Dictionaries, "Word of the Year 2016 is...," English Oxford Living Dictionaries, https://en.oxforddictionaries.com/word-of-the-year/word-of-the-year-2016.
5. Project Censored's website maintains a complete archive of each year's Top 25 story list. See "Top 25 Archive," projectcensored.org/top-25-censored-stories-of-all-time/.
6. See Howard Gardner, Mihaly Csikszentmihalyi, and William Damon, *Good Work: When Excellence and Ethics Meet* (New York: Basic Books, 2001), ix.
7. On news as propaganda, the classic statement is Edward S. Herman and Noam Chomsky's *Manufacturing Consent: The Political Economy of Mass Media* (New York: Pantheon, 2002 [1988]). For an assessment of Herman and Chomsky's "propaganda model" thirty years on, see Edward S. Herman's chapter in this volume.

8. For a sociological perspective on lumping and splitting, see Eviatar Zerubavel, "Lumping and Splitting: Notes on Social Classification," *Sociological Forum*, Vol. 11, No. 3 (September 1996), 421–33.

9. See Andy Lee Roth, "Top 25 Story Analyses: Rights, Responsibilities, and Breaking News," *Censored 2016: Media Freedom on the Line*, eds. Mickey Huff and Andy Lee Roth with Project Censored (New York: Seven Stories Press, 2015), 90–95, and "Top 25 Story Analyses: Story Categories and Historical Themes," *Censored 2015: Inspiring We the People*, eds. Andy Lee Roth and Mickey Huff with Project Censored (New York: Seven Stories Press, 2014), 88–93. The "Censored News Clusters" featured in the 2012, 2013, and 2014 *Censored* yearbooks were more ambitious efforts at this type of synthesis.

10. See "How to Support Project Censored" at the back of this volume; online, see "Project Censored in the Classroom," projectcensored.org/project-censoreds-commitment-to-independent-news-in-the-classroom/.

11. For information on how to nominate a story, see "How to Support Project Censored" at the back of this volume.

12. Validated Independent News stories are archived on the Project Censored website at projectcensored.org/category/validated-independent-news.

13. For a complete list of the national and international judges and their brief biographies, see the acknowledgments section at the back of this volume.

14. The CDC defines five micrograms per deciliter as its threshold for elevated blood lead levels in children up to age six. In 2012, the CDC lowered this threshold from ten to five micrograms to reflect medical consensus that even low levels of lead exposure can do permanent harm to children.

15. M.B. Pell and Joshua Schneyer, ed. Ronnie Greene, "Unsafe at Any Level" (series), Reuters, first article published March 9, 2016 (ongoing), http://www.reuters.com/investigates/section/usa-lead/.

16. Pell and Schneyer reported that some states' health departments did not have the data, or did not respond to records requests, while other states would not share the data they did have. The twenty-one reporting states are home to about 61 percent of the US population.

17. See, for example, "Childhood Lead Poisoning," World Health Organization, 2010, http://www.who.int/ceh/publications/leadguidance.pdf.

18. Joshua Schneyer and M.B. Pell, "U.S. Cities Move to Curb Lead Poisoning following Reuters Report," Reuters, January 19, 2017, http://www.reuters.com/article/us-usa-lead-reform-idUSKBN1531P7.

19. "Buried No Longer: Confronting America's Water Infrastructure Challenge," American Water Works Association, 2012, http://www.awwa.org/Portals/0/files/legreg/documents/BuriedNoLonger.pdf, 10.

20. Elizabeth A. Mack and Sarah Wrase, "A Burgeoning Crisis? A Nationwide Assessment of the Geography of Water Affordability in the United States," *PLOS ONE*, Vol. 12, No. 1 (January 11, 2017), http://journals.plos.org/plosone/article?id=10.1371/journal.pone.0169488, 13.

21. Ibid., 7.

22. "Flint Homeowners Face Foreclosure over Unpaid Bills for Poison Water," *Democracy Now!*, May 5, 2017, https://www.democracynow.org/2017/5/5/headlines/flint_homeowners_face_foreclosure_over_unpaid_bills_for_poison_water.

23. "Army General Fund Adjustments Not Adequately Documented or Supported," Report No. DODIG-2016-113, Inspector General U.S. Department of Defense, July 26, 2016, http://www.dodig.mil/pubs/documents/DODIG-2016-113.pdf, p. i.

24. For Project Censored's previous coverage of the Pentagon's "inauditable" budget, see "Pentagon Awash in Money Despite Serious Audit Problems," *Censored 2015*, 59–60.

25. Craig Whitlock and Bob Woodward, "Pentagon Buries Evidence of $125 Billion in Bureaucratic Waste," *Washington Post*, December 5, 2016, https://www.washingtonpost.com/investigations/pentagon-buries-evidence-of-125-billion-in-bureaucratic-waste/2016/12/05/e0668c76-9af6-11e6-a0ed-ab0774c1eaa5_story.html.

26. William Hartung, "The Pentagon's War on Accountability," Huffington Post, May 24, 2016, updated May 25, 2016, http://www.huffingtonpost.com/william-hartung/the-pentagons-war-on-accountability_b_10116176.html.

27. Section 5 of the Voting Rights Act required specific states and local governments to obtain federal preclearance before implementing any changes to their voting laws or practices. Section 4 of the Voting Rights Act established the formula to determine which state and local governments must comply with the Act's preapproval requirement.

28. "New Voting Restrictions in America," Brennan Center for Justice, March 1, 2017, http://www.brennancenter.org/voting-restrictions-first-time-2016.

29. Guy Cecil, "RE: Voter Suppression Analysis," Priorities USA, May 3, 2017, posted on Scribd, https://www.scribd.com/document/347821649/Priorities-USA-Voter-Suppression-Memo. Berman cautioned, "This study was conducted by a Democratic Party–affiliated group and has not been peer-reviewed or gone through the typical academic vetting process."

30. "Voting Laws Roundup 2017," Brennan Center for Justice, May 10, 2017, https://www.brennancenter.org/analysis/voting-laws-roundup-2017.

31. Carole Cadwalladr, "Google, Democracy and the Truth about Internet Search," *Guardian*, December 4, 2016, https://www.theguardian.com/technology/2016/dec/04/google-democracy-truth-internet-search-facebook.

32. Jonathan Albright, "The #Election2016 Micro-Propaganda Machine," Medium, November 18, 2016, https://medium.com/@d1gi/the-election2016-micro-propaganda-machine-383449cc1fba.

33. On the Heartland Institute, see also Suzanne Goldenberg, "Leak Exposes How Heartland Institute Works to Undermine Climate Science," *Guardian*, February 14, 2012, https://www.theguardian.com/environment/2012/feb/15/leak-exposes-heartland-institute-climate.

34. Mayer researched the Mercer family for her book, *Dark Money: The Hidden History of the Billionaires behind the Rise of the Radical Right* (New York: Doubleday, 2016).

35. Sascha Marchang and Natasha Hurley, "Drug Resistance through the Back Door: How the Pharmaceutical Industry is Fuelling the Rise of Superbugs through Pollution in Its Supply Chains," European Public Health Alliance, 2016, http://epha.org/wp-content/uploads/2016/08/DRUG-RESISTANCE-THROUGH-THE-BACK-DOOR_WEB.pdf.

36. Martin Khor, "Alarm Bells over Antibiotic Resistance," TripleCrisis, May 6, 2014, http://triplecrisis.com/alarm-bells-over-antibiotic-resistance/.

37. Margaret Chan, "Remarks at the G7 Health Ministers Meeting: Session on Antimicrobial Resistance: Realizing the 'One Health' Approach," World Health Organization, October 8, 2015, http://www.who.int/dg/speeches/2015/g7-antimicrobial-resistance/en/.

38. Patrick McGann, Erik Snesrud, Rosslyn Maybank, et al., "*Escherichia coli* Harboring *mcr-1* and bla_{CTX-M} on a Novel IncF Plasmid: First Report of *mcr-1* in the USA," *Antimicrobial Agents and Chemotherapy*, Vol. 60, No. 8 (August 2016), posted online May 26, 2016, http://aac.asm.org/content/early/2016/05/25/AAC.01103-16.full.pdf+html.

39. "Following are Numbers of Takes of Marine Mammal Species, in Just Four North Pacific Areas of Naval Operation," West Coast Action Alliance, posted online April 2016, http://westcoastactionalliance.org/wp-content/uploads/2016/04/Takes-by-species.pdf.

40. Ben Guarino, "Navy's Submarine Hunts are Too Disturbing for Marine Life, California Court Rules," *Washington Post*, July 20, 2016, https://www.washingtonpost.com/news/morning-mix/wp/2016/07/20/navys-submarine-hunts-are-too-disturbing-for-marine-wildlife-california-federal-appeals-court-rules/.

41. See also Marsha Walton, "Hospitals Train to Track, React to Maternal Bleeding," Women's eNews, June 23, 2015, http://womensenews.org/2015/06/hospitals-train-to-track-react-to-maternal-bleeding/.

42. Ashley Nelson, "An Unspoken Risk of Vaginal Birth," *Motherlode* blog, *New York Times*, October 24, 2012, https://parenting.blogs.nytimes.com/2012/10/24/an-unspoken-risk-of-vaginal-birth/.

43. Michael Ollove, "U.S. Maternal Death Rate is Spiking. Here's What's being Done to Change That," *Washington Post*, May 9, 2016, https://www.washingtonpost.com/

national/health-science/us-maternal-death-rate-spikes-heres-whats-being-done-to-change-that/2016/05/09/3e9c9d6e-113e-11e6-81b4-581a5c4c42df_story.html.

44. Sabrina Tavernise, "Maternal Mortality Rate in U.S. Rises, Defying Global Trend, Study Finds," *New York Times*, September 21, 2016, https://www.nytimes.com/2016/09/22/health/maternal-mortality.html.

45. See, e.g., Michael Sainato, "Debbie Wasserman Schultz Served Class Action Lawsuit for Rigging Primaries," *Observer*, June 30, 2016, http://observer.com/2016/06/debbie-wasserman-schultz-served-class-action-lawsuit-for-rigging-primaries/.

46. The relevant text of the DNC charter states: "the Chairperson shall exercise impartiality and evenhandedness as between the Presidential candidates and campaigns. The Chairperson shall be responsible for ensuring that the national officers and staff of the Democratic National Committee maintain impartiality and evenhandedness during the Democratic Party Presidential nominating process." Article V, Section 4, The Charter & The Bylaws of the Democratic Party of the United States, as Amended by the Democratic National Committee, August 28, 2015, available at https://s3.amazonaws.com/uploads.democrats.org/Downloads/DNC_Charter__Bylaws_9.17.15.pdf.

47. For one example of this perspective that is distinguished by its careful analysis of exit polls, margin of error theories, and discrepancies in absentee and early ballots, see Jessica Bernstein and Hanna J. Hoffman, "With the Clinton Coronation Underway, Did Sanders Actually Win the Primary?" Truthout, July 28, 2016, http://www.truth-out.org/speakout/item/37013-with-the-clinton-coronation-underway-did-sanders-actually-win-the-primary.

48. See, e.g., an earlier piece by Joshua Holland, "The Conspiracy Theory That the Clinton Campaign Stole Votes Makes No Sense," *Nation*, April 14, 2016, https://www.thenation.com/article/the-conspiracy-theory-that-the-clinton-campaign-stole-votes-makes-no-sense/.

49. E.g., Chris Riotta, "Was the Election Rigged Against Bernie Sanders? DNC Lawsuit Demands Repayment for Campaign Donors," *Newsweek*, May 15, 2017, http://www.newsweek.com/bernie-sanders-rigged-hillary-clinton-dnc-lawsuit-donald-trump-president-609582.

50. David Weigel, "The Seth Rich Conspiracy Shows How Fake News Still Works," *Washington Post*, May 20, 2017, https://www.washingtonpost.com/news/the-fix/wp/2017/05/20/the-seth-rich-conspiracy-shows-how-fake-news-still-works/.

51. Margaret Menge, "WaPo Claims $300 Million Class-Action Suit Against DNC 'Frivolous,'" PoliZette, May 23, 2017, http://www.lifezette.com/polizette/wapo-claims-300-million-class-action-suit-against-dnc-frivolous/. Menge further noted, "No mainstream media organization covered the April 25 hearing at the federal courthouse in Fort Lauderdale, Florida, and the media blackout of the case would be total and complete if not for the Internet and a handful of digital news outlets that initially covered the suit." See also Caitlin Johnstone, "The Media Blackout on the DNC Lawsuit Proves That It is Nuclear," Medium, May 13, 2017, https://medium.com/@caityjohnstone/the-media-blackout-on-the-dnc-lawsuit-proves-that-it-is-nuclear-32305f574f6e.

52. Darrell M. West, "Internet Shutdowns Cost Countries $2.4 Billion Last Year," Brookings Institution, October 2016, https://www.brookings.edu/wp-content/uploads/2016/10/intenet-shutdowns-v-3.pdf.

53. "The Promotion, Protection and Enjoyment of Human Rights on the Internet," United Nations General Assembly, Human Rights Council, June 27, 2016, revised June 30, 2016, https://www.article19.org/data/files/Internet_Statement_Adopted.pdf.

54. Sanja Kelly, Mai Truong, Adrian Shahbaz, et al., "Freedom on the Net 2016: Silencing the Messenger: Communication Apps Under Pressure," Freedom House, November 2016, https://freedomhouse.org/report/freedom-net/freedom-net-2016.

55. Selena Larson, "This African Country is Taking an Unprecedented Step in Internet Censorship," CNN, September 16, 2016, http://money.cnn.com/2016/09/16/technology/internet-censorship-blackouts-gabon/.

56. Dionne Searcey and Francois Essomba, "African Nations Increasingly Silence Internet to Stem Protests," *New York Times*, February 10, 2017, https://www.nytimes.com/2017/02/10/world/africa/african-nations-increasingly-silence-internet-to-stem-protests.html.

57. EFF calls this practice "evidence laundering." See Hanni Fakhoury, "DEA and NSA Team Up to Share Intelligence, Leading to Secret Use of Surveillance in Ordinary Investigations," Electronic Frontier Foundation, August 6, 2013, https://www.eff.org/deeplinks/2013/08/dea-and-nsa-team-intelligence-laundering. For Project Censored's prior coverage of "parallel construction," see "ICREACH: The NSA's Secret Search Engine," in *Censored 2016*, 78–79; online at projectcensored.org/18-icreach-the-nsas-secret-search-engine/.

58. Dave Maass, "Shareholders Demand Transparency for AT&T's Hemisphere Phone Records Spying Program," Electronic Frontier Foundation, December 7, 2016, https://www.eff.org/deeplinks/2016/12/shareholders-demand-transparency-atts-hemisphere-phone-records-spying-program; see also Pat Miguel Tomaino, "Investing in a Time of 'Resistance,'" Medium, December 5, 2016, https://medium.com/zevin-views/investing-in-a-time-of-resistance-5cceb451706f.

59. Adam Gabbatt, "Anti-Protest Bills Would 'Attack Right to Speak Out' under Donald Trump," *Guardian*, May 8, 2017, https://www.theguardian.com/world/2017/may/08/donald-trump-anti-protest-bills.

60. Craig Timberg, "Effort to Combat Foreign Propaganda Advances in Congress," *Washington Post*, November 30, 2016, https://www.washingtonpost.com/business/economy/effort-to-combat-foreign-propaganda-advances-in-congress/2016/11/30/9147e1ac-e221-47be-ab92-9f2f7e69d452_story.html.

61. Stanley Kurtz, James Manley, and Jonathan Butcher, "Campus Free Speech: A Legislative Proposal," Goldwater Institute, January 30, 2017, http://goldwaterinstitute.org/en/work/topics/constitutional-rights/free-speech/campus-free-speech-a-legislative-proposal/, quotations at 19, 20.

62. UnKoch My Campus, no date, http://www.unkochmycampus.org/.

63. Eileen Sullivan and Ronnie Greene, "States Predict Inmates' Future Crimes with Secretive Surveys," AP News, February 24, 2015, https://apnews.com/027a00d70782476eb7cd07fbcca40fc2/states-predict-inmates-future-crimes-secretive-surveys; Anna Maria Barry-Jester, Ben Casselman, and Dana Goldstein, "The New Science of Sentencing," The Marshall Project, August 4, 2015, https://www.themarshallproject.org/2015/08/04/the-new-science-of-sentencing; Anna Maria Barry-Jester, Ben Casselman, and Dana Goldstein, "Should Prison Sentences be Based on Crimes That Haven't been Committed Yet?," FiveThirtyEight, August 4, 2015, https://fivethirtyeight.com/features/prison-reform-risk-assessment/.

64. The landmark report identified in the Shell documentary was *Climate Change: The IPCC Scientific Assessment*, eds. J.T. Houghton, G.J. Jenkins, and J.J. Ephraums (Cambridge, UK and New York: Cambridge University Press, 1990), available online at Intergovernmental Panel on Climate Change as of 2010, https://www.ipcc.ch/publications_and_data/publications_ipcc_first_assessment_1990_wg1.shtml.

65. Arthur Neslen, "Shell Lobbied to Undermine EU Renewables Targets, Documents Reveal," *Guardian*, April 27, 2015, https://www.theguardian.com/environment/2015/apr/27/shell-lobbied-to-undermine-eu-renewables-targets-documents-reveal.

66. Suzanne Goldenberg, "Exxon Knew of Climate Change in 1981, Email Says—But It Funded Deniers for 27 More Years," *Guardian*, July 8, 2015, https://www.theguardian.com/environment/2015/jul/08/exxon-climate-change-1981-climate-denier-funding.

67. "Our Mission," Our Children's Trust, no date, https://www.ourchildrenstrust.org/mission-statement/.

68. Our Children's Trust, "Trump Files Motion to Delay Kids' Historic Climate Lawsuit," EcoWatch, March 9, 2017, https://www.ecowatch.com/trump-climate-change-lawsuit-2307504755.html.

69. Neela Banerjee, "Fossil Fuel Groups Want Out of Children's Climate Change Lawsuit," Inside Climate News, May 26, 2017, https://insideclimatenews.org/news/26052017/children-climate-change-lawsuit-fossil-fuel-api.

70. Tony Dokoupil, "Big Oil Joins Legal Fight against Little Kids over Climate Change," MSNBC, November 12, 2015, http://www.msnbc.com/msnbc/big-oil-joins-legal-fight-little-kids-over-climate-change.

71. "Meet the Youth Suing Their State Government over Climate Change," CBS News, November 23, 2016, http://www.cbsnews.com/news/meet-the-youth-suing-their-state-government-over-climate-change/; "Youth in Washington State Sue Government over Climate Change," Fox News, November 23, 2016, http://www.foxnews.com/us/2016/11/23/youth-in-washington-state-sue-government-over-climate-change.html.

72. "Database of Transgender Homicides, 2010–2017," Mic, no date, https://mic.com/unerased/database.

73. See Alex Schmider, "GLAAD Calls for Increased and Accurate Media Coverage of Transgender Murders," GLAAD, July 26, 2016, updated June 28, 2017, https://www.glaad.org/blog/glaad-calls-increased-and-accurate-media-coverage-transgender-murders, cited in ibid.; for previous Project Censored coverage on the media invisibility of trans homicides, see Caitlin McCoy and Susan Rahman, "Zero Media Coverage for Transgendered Murder Victims," Project Censored, April 1, 2015, projectcensored.org/zero-media-coverage-for-transgendered-murder-victims/.

74. "Facing Tear Gas in Prison," War Resisters League, no date, https://www.warresisters.org/facing-tear-gas-prison.

75. Julie K. Brown, "As Florida Inmate Begged for Help, Guards Gassed Him to Death, Suit Says," Miami Herald, September 19, 2016, http://www.miamiherald.com/news/special-reports/florida-prisons/article102773597.html.

76. "Invest-Divest," The Movement for Black Lives, no date, https://policy.m4bl.org/invest-divest.

77. Jessica Lee and Daniel Beekman, "Mayor Does About-Face, Holds Up North Precinct Police-Station Plan," Seattle Times, September 15, 2016, http://www.seattletimes.com/seattle-news/politics/mayor-does-about-face-shelves-north-precinct-police-station-plan/.

78. "Block the Bunker Protest Disrupts Council Meeting," KING5 (NBC), September 19, 2016, http://www.king5.com/news/block-the-bunker-protest-disrupts-council-meeting/321717208.

79. "Governance Board," Energy Biosciences Institute, no date, http://www.ebiweb.org/content/ebi-leadership#3.

80. Michael Hiltzik, "Campus Is Oddly Silent on BP," Los Angeles Times, August 1, 2010, B1.

81. Jennifer Washburn, "Big Oil Goes to College," Center for American Progress, October 2010, https://cdn.americanprogress.org/wp-content/uploads/issues/2010/10/pdf/big_oil_lf.pdf; Nanette Asimov, "Big Oil Money Can Influence Research, Study Claims," SFGate, October 15, 2010, http://www.sfgate.com/bayarea/article/Big-Oil-money-can-influence-research-study-claims-3249918.php.

82. "Charles Koch University Funding Database," PolluterWatch (Greenpeace), no date, http://polluterwatch.org/charles-koch-university-funding-database.

83. "Our Lawsuits," Uptown People's Law Center, no date, http://uplcchicago.org/lawsuits/.

84. George Pawlaczyk, "Lawsuit: 'Orange Crush' Guard Unit Terrorized, Humiliated Southern Illinois Inmates," Belleville News-Democrat, February 6, 2016, http://www.bnd.com/news/local/article58855968.html; Ken Hare, "Prisoners Allege Claims of Deprivation, Physical and Sexual Abuse," Chicago Defender, September 14, 2016, https://chicagodefender.com/2016/09/14/prisoners-alleges-claims-of-deprivation-physical-and-sexual-abuse/.

85. See Julia Angwin, "Privacy Tools: Opting Out from Data Brokers," ProPublica, January 30, 2014, https://www.propublica.org/article/privacy-tools-opting-out-from-data-brokers.

86. Geoffrey A. Fowler and Emily Steel, "Facebook Says User Data Sold to Broker," Wall Street Journal, October 31, 2010, https://www.wsj.com/articles/SB10001424052748704477904575586690450505642.

87. DeRay McKesson, Samuel Sinyangwe, Johnetta Elzie, and Brittany Packnett, "Police Use of Force Policy Analysis," Campaign Zero, September 20, 2016, https://static1.squarespace.com/static/56996151cbced68b170389f4/t/57e1b5cc2994ca4ac1d97700/1474409936835/Police+Use+of+Force+Report.pdf.

88. Ibid., 9.

89. For previous Project Censored coverage of efforts to track the number of police-involved killings of civilians, see "Who Dies at the Hands of US Police—and How Often," Censored 2016, 58–61; "National Database of Police Killings Aims for Accountability," Censored 2015, 69; Peter

Phillips, Diana Grant, and Greg Sewell, "Law Enforcement–Related Deaths in the US: 'Justified Homicides' and Their Impacts on Victims' Families," *Censored 2015*, 243–68.

90. McKesson, Sinyangwe, Elzie, and Packnett, "Police Use of Force Policy Analysis," 10.

91. Jessica Feierman, Naomi Goldstein, Emily Haney-Caron, and Jaymes Fairfax Columbo, "Debtors' Prison for Kids? The High Cost of Fines and Fees in the Juvenile Justice System," Juvenile Law Center, 2016, http://debtorsprison.jlc.org/documents/JLC-Debtors-Prison.pdf.

92. Erik Eckholm, "Court Costs Entrap Nonwhite, Poor Juvenile Offenders," *New York Times*, August 31, 2016, https://www.nytimes.com/2016/09/01/us/court-costs-entrap-nonwhite-poor-juvenile-offenders.html.

Post-Truth Dystopia: Fake News, Alternative Facts, and the Ongoing War on Reality

Junk Food News and News Abuse for 2016–17

Nolan Higdon and Mickey Huff, with student writers and researchers Aimee Casey, Gabriella Custodio, Elsa Denis, Thomas Field, Alisha Huajardo, Justin Lascano, Aubrey Sanchez, Edwin Sevilla, Hannah Soule, Kelly Van Boekhout, Kristen van Zyll de Jong, Michael Vega, Clark Venter, and Mark Yolangco; these students are from California State University, East Bay, California State University Maritime Academy, Chabot College, Diablo Valley College, Las Positas College, Ohlone College, San Francisco State University, and San Jose State University

Civilization, in fact, grows more and more maudlin and hysterical; especially under democracy it tends to degenerate into a mere combat of crazes; the whole aim of practical politics is to keep the populace alarmed (and hence clamorous to be led to safety) by an endless series of hobgoblins, most of them imaginary.

—H.L. Mencken, journalist/satirist, 1918[1]

EMERGING IDIOCRACY: A BRIEF RECKONING

In 1985, Neil Postman warned about an emerging threat to the US in his book *Amusing Ourselves to Death.* In his well-researched and troubling assessment, "Americans are the best entertained and quite likely the least well-informed people in the Western world."[2] Postman's powerful, provocative argument strongly suggested most in the US knew little to nothing about what mattered most. Twenty-five years later, in *Dark Ages America*, Morris Berman wrote that "a world remade in the image of Walt Disney, and driven by an increasingly sophisticated communications technology, is the total breakdown of civilization."[3] By the time Berman wrote these words he had been documenting what he saw as the decline of the US for over a decade. He believed that the US had devolved into an ignorant population obsessed with trivial matters, whose lifestyle and positions came at the expense of civilized democratic society. By 2017, the signs of democratic society in decline have become quite visible: forty years of diminishing wages for the middle and working classes, the biggest wealth gap in a century, ongoing election fraud, endless wars, massive national debt, high and rising rates of childhood obesity, as well as increasing maternal and infant mortality rates.[4] In fact, by 2017, just as Postman and Berman presciently projected, and only a decade after the unintentional predictions in Mike Judge's satirical film *Idiocracy*, US citizens had elevated a reality TV celebrity and real estate tycoon with no political experience in the public sector to the ultimate seat of power: Donald J. Trump became president of the United States.[5]

Berman's and Postman's writings demonstrate that the real threat to a civilized society is *stupidity*.[6] Individuals lacking critical thinking skills, once taught by public educational institutions, and who utilize little of the fact-based knowledge about the world around them which the free press is supposed to provide, constitute a real and growing concern. The collective result is that many Americans lack the skills and knowledge needed to understand the interconnected workings of society and to ferret out corruption. In fact, a nation of critical thinkers aware of how political and economic institutions are supposed to function in a free society is a threat to those in power. Iconic comedian and critic George Carlin once explained this concept when he noted that those in power "don't want a population of citizens capable of critical thinking. They don't want well-informed, well-educated people capable of critical thinking. They're not interested in that. That doesn't help them. That's against their interests."[7]

Carlin notes that a critically thinking and informed population would not simply react emotionally, but rather would offer real solutions to declining wages, wealth inequality, election fraud, endless war, national debt, lack of healthcare, and many other pressing but surmountable problems.

Instead of addressing these issues, however, corporate media have taken Americans on a detour, blaming marginalized groups far from the centers of power, such as immigrants, socialists, and people struggling with mental illness or addiction, for all of society's ills. This bait and switch not only deflects from the many challenges Americans face in their nascent democracy, it worsens them. The corporate press pull this bait and switch by peddling an unhealthy diet of Junk Food News and engaging in News Abuse. *Junk Food News* is a term coined by Project Censored's founder, the late Carl Jensen. It refers to how the corporate media cover trivial yet sensational stories at the expense of more newsworthy ones. Junk Food News stories, while often titillating, are distractions from issues that most impact society. Former Project Censored director Peter Phillips created the term *News Abuse*, which refers to stories that are newsworthy but are presented in a slanted, spun, partial, or trivializing manner by corporate media as a form of propaganda.

The reporting of these kinds of news stories over the past several decades has compounded problems with the democratic process in the US. A public ill-equipped with the basic knowledge of how the political and economic systems work cannot alter or change them effectively. The corporate media wittingly and unwittingly continue to exacerbate this problem. This chapter examines the phenomenon in two key areas. The first, the Junk Food News section, looks at how news consumers' attention is deflected from more significant stories by trivial matters. This year, we specifically note the continued underreporting of one of the most important stories of our time—the threat of climate change, or what investigative journalist Dahr Jamail more specifically calls "anthropogenic climate disruption."[8] It bears noting that even during last year's presidential debates, the moderators, all considered luminaries by the corporate mass media, failed to ask the candidates even one question about this crucial issue.[9] So it may not be surprising that the corporate media were also more concerned with who was or was not attending the White House Correspondents' Association Dinner, Olympic crimes and behavior, and the Best Picture Oscar snafu at the Academy Awards, to note a few lowlights. The second key area examined in this chapter, our News Abuse section, documents the explosion of so-called "fake news" and how it has been weaponized for partisan hackery to denounce anything that threatens the power or policies of the ruling class while legitimizing actual fake news.

Though these maddening trends have grown ubiquitous over the last year, it is important to keep in mind that historically they are nothing new. The media may have come to call these methods of mass distraction by new names, but anyone armed with knowledge of the past is already familiar with the most accurate term these methods go by: propaganda.

JUNK FOOD NEWS

The years passed . . . mankind became stupider at a frightening rate. Some had high hopes the genetic engineering would correct this trend in evolution, but sadly the greatest minds and resources were focused on conquering hair loss and prolonging erections.
—Narrator, *Idiocracy*, 2006[10]

A majority of people in the world believe that climate change is the biggest problem facing humanity.[11] However, for the corporate media, other stories often trump the importance of climate change research. For example, although a majority of people in the US and Europe fear the impact of climate change, even more people find ISIS to be a significant threat despite the extraordinarily low probability of being the victim of a terrorist attack.[12] In fact, people in the US are as likely to be crushed to death by their TVs or to drown in their bathtubs as die in a terror attack, yet Americans are quite enthralled by their TVs and there is no sign of an impending national "War on Personal Hygiene."[13] Simply put, many seem to be afraid of, and fixate on, the wrong things. The interests of media consumers are linked to what the corporate media fixate upon and how they present information in emotional ways, often devoid of factual or historical context. In addi-

tion to this kind of sensationalist and repetitive news coverage based on public fears, the ongoing challenge of weeding through Junk Food stories can be equally daunting, especially since many Americans don't do much weeding. Rather, they indulge as a form of escape, skipping the main course and heading straight for dessert.

During the 2016–2017 news cycles, the corporate media peddled many tales that distracted from stories that highlighted the real and growing threat of climate change. As a result, those who do not believe climate change is real, or see it as a secondary threat to the likes of ISIS, remain ignorant of how climate change affects contemporary global society. Instead of coming to grips with what is happening outside of their homes, the American public digests a heavy diet of Junk Food News in their living rooms, staring at their increasingly large televisions that resemble the flickering shadows on a wall described in Plato's Allegory of the Cave, only the images projected are as cheap and flimsy as a Play-Doh republic.

Trumping the Press: Let Them Eat Crow . . . and Cake

On February 26, 2017, CNN reported, "Trump Declines to Attend White House Correspondents' Dinner." The story focused on the backlash against Trump for refusing to attend the annual White House Correspondents' Association (WHCA) dinner. The WHCA demonstrates everything wrong with the US media, as it invites a collection of journalists reporting on the president to drink and dine with the politicians and celebrities they are supposed to be scrutinizing in the name of democracy.[14] In 2007, then–*New York Times* columnist Frank Rich argued that the dinner is "a crystallization of the press's failures in the post-9/11 era" as it "illustrates how easily a propaganda-driven White House can enlist the Washington news media in its shows."[15] In fact, the corporate media's anger over Trump not making nice with them does not indicate their willingness to speak truth to power so much as it demonstrates their frustrated eagerness to ingratiate themselves.

Trump announced his decision to skip the correspondents' dinner, which raises money for journalism scholarships, using his preferred mode of communication: Twitter. Trump publicly announced that his absence at the dinner was a statement against journalists and the media's critiques of his administration. It was another salvo in his war on the press. According to CNN, "Trump's decision is not surprising given the negative things the President has said about the media, such as suggesting they are 'the enemy of the American people.'"[16] Even before he was "electored" (chosen by the Electoral College without winning the popular vote), Trump received near-constant coverage for his Tweets, ostensibly political squibs that often entertained and amused the American public while distracting them from more newsworthy stories. CNBC covered the same correspondents' dinner story a day later. Their coverage managed to exaggerate and further increase tensions between the White House and the national media when they dramatically reported that "in recent days, a debate has erupted over whether the WHCA should altogether cancel its event, widely regarded as elbow-rubbing between Hollywood, media and political elites."[17]

The corporate media high school grudge match over Trump not attending their party distracted from more newsworthy stories, such as the widespread famine in Yemen. Fairness and Accuracy In Reporting pointed out that, while the corporate media covered Trump's refusal to party with the people responsible for holding him accountable, the independent press covered the ongoing famine and human tragedy in Yemen.[18] In fact, on February 27, a United Nations report noted that the two-year-old US-backed Saudi-led war, which left over ten thousand dead and forty thousand wounded in the region, was intensifying the crisis. The UN report stated that the prolonged conflict led to over 90 percent of Yemeni citizens experiencing famine and/or malnutrition.[19] The report warned "that another 7.1 million people are ready to fall into the emergency level of hunger if the situation does not improve. In all, 19 of the 22 governorates of Yemen are experiencing severe hunger."[20] The corporate media and Trump jockeyed for who would have the last laugh over the WHCA dinner, where the only item on the menu they all should have been eating was crow. As for the Yemenis? *Let them eat cake* seemed to be the mantra.

Olympic-Sized Hypocrisy Flooding the Airwaves

The summer of 2016 was a great one for media spectacles. Not only was Rio de Janeiro, Brazil, hosting the Summer Olympic Games, the US presidential election was in full swing. The corporate media latched on to what seemed to be a shocking story. US swimmers Ryan Lochte, Jimmy Feigen, Jack Conger, and Gunnar Bentz claimed they were robbed at gunpoint while at the games in Brazil.[21] The robbery allegedly took place after a party the four men were returning from, possibly after a night of drinking.[22] Originally, Lochte reported that they were stopped by armed men and were forced to hand over their money, but later he said they were stopped at a gas station.[23] The station attendants stated that the swimmers stopped at the gas station to use the bathroom,[24] during which time the four men broke a door and soap dispenser. A guard on duty even drew his weapon in an effort to prevent the swimmers from running away after observing their actions.[25] The only thing being robbed here was the dignity of the US Olympic team.

The incident sparked outrage in Brazil. Mario Andrada, a spokesman for Rio 2016, said in a news briefing, "Let's give these kids a break."[26] Use of the word "kids" is an indication of how Andrada intended to frame the incident as the antics of youth, not crimes committed by adults who clearly knew better. Using the term "kids" was an attempt to downplay the swimmers' role in the situation and gave their wanton destruction of property, not to mention their flat-out lies and attempted cover-up, an air of innocence. Andrada concluded more hagiographically, "Sometimes you take actions you later regret. They are magnificent athletes. Lochte is of one of the best swimmers of all time. They had fun. They made a mistake. It's part of life. Life goes on." Indeed, for many privileged white males, after committing a crime, "life goes on."[27]

While these "bad boy" celebrity Olympians mostly got to swim away with few consequences and no formal charges, another US Olympic winner, African American gymnast Gabby Douglas, was tried and convicted by the public in a vicious bullying Internet campaign for . . . lying about crimes she committed? No. For being "unpatriotic" (gasp!). During the medal ceremony when Douglas stood on the platform, she did not put her hand over her heart when the national anthem played. This apparent "traitorous" act did not sit well with vicarious "America First" viewers at home (that Douglas was a gold medalist seemed to be lost on this demographic).[28] As a result, she was branded "unpatriotic." Douglas was criticized widely across the Internet, including in racist terms, and was the subject of a massive bullying campaign that overshadowed her major accomplishments, while the white "boys will be boys" floated home.[29]

Meanwhile, the corporate media's infatuation with Olympic athlete behavior overseas distracted from the coverage of widespread natural disasters at home. On August 12, more than four trillion gallons of rain fell in Louisiana.[30] By August 17, state officials reported that the flooding was on an historic and unprecedented scale. The federal government declared it a major disaster.[31] Instead of covering the storm's implications for the larger issue of climate change and extreme weather patterns, the corporate media focused on sensational images of flooding and then turned their attention back to the Olympic fodder. Without adequate media coverage, it was hard to raise the awareness needed to increase relief efforts, which directly corresponded to how few understood the massive scale of the floods.[32]

While the damage caused was less than that of Hurricane Katrina, twenty thousand residents had to be rescued, ten thousand were placed in shelters, and several people lost their lives.[33] This momentous tragedy in Louisiana went widely underreported, robbed of coverage by Olympic-sized hubris and misdirected outrage.

Envelopegate: And the Winner Is? The Fossil Fuel Industry

The 89th Annual Academy Awards drew particularly unwelcome attention with an unplanned and anticlimactic folly of a finale. It became clear about a minute into the victory speech for Best Picture that the wrong movie was initially announced as the winner, which meant that the losers were already giving a speech for an award they did not win. The day after the Oscars, the corporate media couldn't help but rehash over and over the mix-up in which *La La Land* was mistakenly announced as winner of the Best Picture award, until *Moonlight* was revealed as the real winner during the erroneous victory speech. It was an awkward moment, to be sure, but one that was quickly righted, yet also one that sent the corporate media into a feeding frenzy speculating about some possible scandal, one they hyped but that never actually emerged. From MSNBC to CNN to ABC, the story, dubbed by Big Media as the "Best Picture Mix-Up," was more like a Big Picture Mix-Up. While the corporate media was buzzing about the wrong film being announced as the winner, the independent press was covering a story of far more significance in the bigger picture—a coalition of more than five hundred community leaders, elected officials, business moguls, health officials, and politicians calling for doubling the strength of the Regional Greenhouse Gas Initiative, a clean air and healthy climate program. A gathering of this size to enact policies to prevent further climate change is certainly worthy of major attention. But instead the American public was treated to endless punditry on who was responsible for the year's Best Picture blunder.

Five days before the Oscar flap, Common Dreams covered a release by Environment America announcing 546 leaders signing an initiative that promised to "deliver clean air and a safe, healthy climate for us all."[34] Despite this important developing story, the corporate news instead opted to report on the mix-up at the Academy Awards. NBC went so far as to release an investigative article on how exactly the mix-up occurred and interviewed the person who wrongly announced the award.[35] None of the five-hundred-plus people who signed the environmental initiative were interviewed by any major media outlets. The topic of doubling the strength of America's best climate and clean air program is clearly newsworthy because, over the last decade, it has already helped cut emissions in half while creating cleaner air and preventing "600 premature deaths, 9,000 asthma attacks, and 43,000 lost work days."[36] If people cared as much about what is happening to the climate as they did about who won the Oscars we could be living in a very different, vastly improved world.

NEWS ABUSE

I'm not going to give you a question. You are fake news!

—President-Elect Donald Trump, to CNN's Jim Acosta (who was trying to ask him a question at an official press conference), January 11, 2017[37]

An Ongoing Truth Emergency

In 2010, Project Censored's Peter Phillips and Mickey Huff argued that the US was facing a "Truth Emergency."[38] They explained that, "[i]n the United States today, the rift between reality and reporting has reached its end. There is no longer a mere credibility gap, but rather a literal Truth Emergency . . . [this] is a culmination of the failures of the fourth estate to act as a truly free press."[39] Despite living in the digital age when we are awash in a sea of information, there is a paucity of reason among the public at large to contextualize and make sense of much of it. Phillips and Huff cited the bogus WMD claims and other underreported and misreported atrocities of the US war in Iraq to demonstrate the pervasiveness of this Truth Emergency.

Sadly, through 2017 little had changed. A recent example of this ongoing Truth Emergency reminds one of the adage, "The first casualty of war is truth." This can be seen in the fog of war that blankets Syria. The corporate media, along with Republican and Democratic leaders, repeatedly touted unsubstantiated and disputed claims about Syria as a pretext for war—most notably that President Bashar al-Assad used chemical weapons on his own people during the first week of April, killing scores and injuring hundreds more, including women and children (according to UNICEF).[40] What followed was a propaganda blitz that paved the way for President Trump to order the firing of fifty-nine Tomahawk missiles on targets in Syria, which killed nine innocent people in villages, including four children. Another report claimed fifteen were killed, including nine civilians and six others on a targeted base.[41] Not only was the US strike not called out as a naked act of aggression, it was celebrated by the political establishment and corporate press in the US and beyond.

Most notably, Brian Williams (yes, the same Brian Williams who was suspended by NBC and later reassigned by MSNBC after falsely claiming he was in an aerial firefight in Iraq) used the word "beautiful" three times when describing the Tomahawk missile strike that President Trump ordered to be launched at Syrian targets. Similarly, Chuck Schumer, the Democratic Senate minority leader, proclaimed, "Making sure Assad knows that when he commits such despicable atrocities he will pay a price is the right thing to do." Democratic Senator Dick Durbin declared, "My preliminary briefing by the White House indicated that this was a measured response to the Syrian nerve gas atrocity."[42]

However, US and NATO assertions regarding Assad's involvement have been disputed by many, including veteran investigative reporter Seymour M. Hersh, and MIT professor of science, technology, and security policy Theodore A. Postol, both of whom studied the incident in detail. Postol stated that the White House intelligence account could not be true as the attacks appeared to come from the ground, not from the air as the White House claimed. Further, the Tomahawk missile retaliatory strike came before any evidence proving Assad's involvement in the gas attack was ever corroborated.[43]

This is a complicated matter, to be sure, one that even sparks vivid disagreements among the anti-imperialist and pacifist Left in the US. To question official narratives should not mean people are automatically pro-Assad—or pro-Putin, for that matter. More importantly, what does it mean to be pro-truth in a post-truth world, when the

truth can be elusive, especially in an environment addled by propaganda coming from many sides? The corporate media's engagement
in News Abuse concerning Syria, much like Iraq over a decade earlier,
appears to be part of an attempt to build public support for a full-
blown US invasion, which makes accurate reporting and publishing
of diverse perspectives all the more crucial.

There are, nonetheless, two aspects of the Syrian story that are
absolutely clear, though hardly reported: the cost of overseas aggression first and foremost in human life (e.g., the seven-hundred-plus
civilians killed since spring by US-led coalition bombings in Syria);
and second, the cost to American taxpayers. The "beautiful" ordinance
in Trump's Tomahawk missile offensive alone cost $88 million, pay-
able to Raytheon, one of the biggest players in the military-industrial
complex, whose stocks shot up 3 percent after the strikes.[44]

In Education We Trust?

A major countermeasure to News Abuse and propaganda is having
access to an education rooted in factual details, transparent sources,
and critical thinking skills. This involves moving beyond confirmation bias and developing the ability to embrace cognitive dissonance,
to be able to change one's mind in the light of new information.
This can be daunting at times, but it's part of becoming a critical
and independent thinker. Yet for some, this is so daunting that it
requires doubling down on false ideas. Case in point: take right-
wing media personality Glenn Beck and pseudo-historian David
Barton. For $375 a head, they offer training camps to teach grad-
uating high school students their revisionist, partial version of
history. Amanda Marcotte of Salon referred to their historical
narrative as "one that valorizes straight white men as humanity's
natural leaders and grants Christian fundamentalism a centrality
to American history that it does not, in reality, have."[45] Marcotte
also noted that, "[i]n Barton's history, the Founding Fathers' idea
of government was rooted in fundamentalist Christianity, instead
of Enlightenment philosophy, and the contributions of people of
color are minimized in service of centering Christian white men
as the righteous shepherds guiding everyone else."[46] Beck, who has

historically had a tenuous relationship with reality, engages in the production of educational content that is demonstrative of how this Truth Emergency is spreading, as it were, from training camps to the college classroom.

Marcotte continued, "Beck isn't subtle about his intention to give college professors headaches by filling their classrooms with fledging right-wing nuts spewing 'alternative facts' about history." According to Beck, "Your kids will be challenged to go and find the documents to make the cases that they're most likely going to have to make in college with their professors . . . I guarantee you the professors at college will have the wrong answer." However, despite such confident presumptions, much of what Barton and Beck promote contradicts established historical facts.[47]

Of course, education does not only take place in schools—or training camps, for that matter—as much of what people learn comes in one way or another from mass media. Further compounding this Truth Emergency is the lack of critical media literacy education in US schools. The education system in the US often falls short of combating the many bad influences of mass media on the public. In fact, forty years ago, as media became a larger part of citizens' lives in industrial democracies, most European and Asian nations mandated that students had to be taught media literacy in schools.[48] These courses taught basic skills, like how to verify facts and sources. In the US at the same time, other than education groups such as Project Censored, there was little offered in the way of media literacy. Instead of addressing these challenges head-on, given the large-scale problems associated with mass media propaganda in the US, the education system drifted to the same for-profit model of information dissemination as the mass media, yielding many of the same results.[49] Only this past year, in the wake of widespread alarm over so-called "fake news," have lawmakers suddenly begun to take media literacy education more seriously—though even the bills that have been proposed, in states like California and Massachusetts, are vague and will take years to implement.

Critical theory scholar Henry A. Giroux further argues that the for-profit model of education emphasizes that individuals are supposed to blame themselves for all manner of problems rather than criticize the social order and those who construct it. The market-driven discourse in higher education, including the corporatization of education that privileges administrators over faculty (who become low-paid workers while students are seen as customers), has outlawed or marginalized those faculty who do talk about critiquing the system rather than teach students to accept it and work with it.[50] As outlined by Phillips and Huff,[51] the for-profit model replaced intellectual criticism with establishment sycophancy in the corporate press decades earlier, and the education industry has followed suit. Americans have been left with a top-down managed news and education system, spread out among a cornucopia of corporate news outlets and a mirroring curriculum that teaches students to consume information like they consume products, in a use-and-dispose manner rather than a critical one. In this age of so-called "fake news" and "alternative facts," developing critical thinking skills may not be on the test, but outside of the classroom it *is* the test, and it seems many in the US are not making the grade. Ultimately, this has significantly negative societal ramifications, especially for those already facing political and economic marginalization.

Giroux concludes that a "democracy cannot exist without informed citizens and public spheres and educational apparatuses that uphold standards of truth, honesty, evidence, facts and justice. Under Trump, disinformation masquerading as news . . . has become a weapon for legitimating ignorance and civic illiteracy."[52] To combat this, he states,

> Artists, educators, young people, journalists and others need to make the virtue of truth-telling visible again. We need to connect democracy with a notion of truth-telling and consciousness that is on the side of economic and political justice, and democracy itself. If we are all going to fight for and with the most marginalized people, there must be a broader understanding of their needs. We need to create narratives and platforms in which those who have been deemed disposable can identify themselves and the conditions through which power and oppression bear down on their lives.
>
> This is not an easy task, but nothing less than justice, democracy and the planet itself are at risk.[53]

Of Fake News and Alternative Facts

Since the fall of 2016, when the former host of NBC's *The Appren-tice*, Donald Trump, was "electored" president of the United States, the term "fake news" became ensconced in the US lexicon. In fact, in the course of one week in mid-January 2017, the trend of people researching the term "fake news" on Google jumped one hundred-fold above pre-election levels.[54] Trump and his supporters denounced any critiques of him as being "fake news." For example, Trump him-self accused CNN of being a "fake news organization" because they questioned the validity of his statements, which is what journalists are supposed to do.[55] Interestingly, Trump did not weaponize this term himself, but had help from an unlikely source—the Democrats. The Democratic National Committee (DNC), aghast at their embar-rassing loss in an election they and many "experts" saw as a slam dunk for Hillary Clinton, are the ones responsible for weaponizing the term "fake news" in the first place, blaming the phenomenon for what many described as Clinton's stunning defeat. In fact, Clinton remarked after losing the election that "it's now clear that so-called fake news can have real world consequences."[56]

The partisan practice of labeling inconvenient truths as "fake news" undermined credible journalism while distracting the public from the barrage of actual fake news (i.e., propaganda) flooding our global society. One survey conducted by HuffPost/YouGov terrify-ingly concluded that people, regardless of party lines, are likely to see any news that is in opposition to their beliefs as "fake news."[57] This is also the product of confirmation bias. For decades, scholars have defined state-sponsored and corporate media propaganda posing as journalism and advertisements posing as news stories as "fake news."[58] Actual fake news is an affront to the democratic process because it is being conflated with real journalism. Weaponizing "fake news" allows for truths that might hold those in power accountable to be brushed aside instead, because they are deemed "fake news" without any explanation of what makes them fake.

The conflating of inconvenient truths with "fake news" has resulted in what some are now calling a post-truth world. Oxford Diction-aries concluded that "post-truth" was the word of the year for 2016.[59]

Oxford defines the term, an adjective, "as relating to or denoting circumstances in which objective facts are less influential in shaping public opinion than appeals to emotion and personal belief."[60] In post-truth America, an individual's proclivity becomes reality, regardless of the facts. Thus, Americans' unwillingness or inability to decipher between fact and opinion or argument and belief is dangerous, not only for the democratic process but also for the foundations of contemporary society. The Internet's promise of delivering endless information to circumvent a post-truth world has not succeeded in producing a well-informed populace. Instead, the inflation of spurious information coupled with an education system that does not teach critical media literacy to students and does not show them how to navigate and participate in the digital world has resulted in a dystopia of falsehoods that are now referred to as "alternative facts."[61]

This post-truth environment of "fake news" gave inevitable rise to this gem of a term, which refers to an outright lie that is introduced and then used as evidence to support a desired conclusion. The phrase was coined on January 22, 2017, when Trump's counselor, Kellyanne Conway, used it during a *Meet the Press* interview to defend White House Press Secretary Sean Spicer's false claims about the size of President Trump's inauguration crowd.[62] While critics and late night hosts have used the phrase "alternative facts" as fodder for ridicule, it soon became clear that these falsehoods were now part of the new, de facto, official narrative being used to construct an emerging alternate reality.[63]

The list of "alternative facts" began to stack up fast. Here is a sampling: White House Press Secretary Sean Spicer claimed three times that there was a terror attack in Atlanta, Georgia, despite the fact that it never occurred; Trump made veiled references to how deceased nineteenth-century abolitionist and intellectual Frederick Douglass was still alive, "an example of somebody who's done an amazing job and is being recognized more and more"; US Secretary of Housing and Urban Development Dr. Ben Carson, a brain surgeon, claimed without socio-economic relevancy or historical context that African American slaves were immigrants who worked hard and found success in America; US Senator Cory Gardner (R-CO) insisted without evidence that the overwhelming number of letters, emails, phone calls, and voicemails received as the Trump administration attempted to repeal and replace Obamacare was the result of "paid protesters"; Trump claimed that Sweden was being overrun by refugees; Spicer claimed that Hitler did not use "chemical weapons"; Trump said that former president Andrew Jackson opposed the Civil War despite having died fifteen years prior to its start; and last but not least, the mother of the phrase "alternative facts," Kellyanne Conway, in no less than three interviews said that Trump's travel ban was justified by citing a fictitious "massacre" in Bowling Green, Kentucky.[64] All of these claims and statements are completely false, and appear to have only been uttered to justify policies or positions of the Trump White House. What we have here is nothing short of a war on reality.

To promote an incontestable narrative fueled by alternative facts, the Trump administration has surrounded itself with media lapdogs, in both the corporate and independent press, rather than watchdogs. Propagandists, sycophants, and extremists have filled the ranks of the inner media circle to promote and justify the administration's image and agenda. For example, Alex Jones of Infowars, who was labeled by his lawyer as a "performance artist" during his 2017 divorce proceedings, has built an economically successful career based largely on lies for monetary gain, and continuously defends and preaches the dogma of President Trump as gospel, even going so far as to say that he would die for him.[65] Similarly, so-called "alt-right" extremist Lucian Wintrich was welcomed into the White House Press Briefing Room by Trump's cabinet to act as a mouthpiece despite his history of blatant discrimination and his lack of journalism experience.[66] The creation of Trump's self-sustaining media cocoon, aptly nicknamed "Trump TV," attempted to provide Trump and his staff immunity from media criticism.[67]

However, Trump also has allies in the corporate media who use alternative facts and fabricated terms to legitimize his behavior. For example, after Trump was undoubtedly exposed for lying about then-president Barack Obama's wiretapping of Trump Tower, Jeffrey Lord of CNN insisted that Trump did not lie, but rather that he just speaks "Americanese." A term similar to "alternative facts," "Americanese" works to remove the responsibility of truth-telling from officials at the highest levels of government, who are expected to be honest, transparent, and accountable.[68]

And if that's not enough, Trump's chief strategist, Steve Bannon, is former CEO of the now well-known, right-wing nationalist news site Breitbart. In May, Trump issued retroactive ethics waivers, with a blanket waiver to all Executive Office of the President appointees, including Bannon. The waiver allows all covered under it "to work with subjects they had in the private sector before joining the government." The Office of Government Ethics noted that Bannon was still restricted from talking about specific policy matters with members of his former media company, but called the development "problematic."[69]

The DNC's Own Alternative Facts: The Russians are Coming . . . with Fake News!

Although one would think that a Republican Party hedging their bets on outright falsehoods would empower the Democratic Party to use facts to their advantage, it has instead resulted in the Democrats developing and weaponizing their own "alternative facts" and "fake news." In the 2016–2017 news cycles, these included not only the idea that Hillary Clinton was electable, but also, among a long list of things, that "fake news" and Russian hackers cost her the election.

Although there were numerous outright false stories about Hillary Clinton, including Internet yarns that claimed she was involved in running a child sex ring (dubbed "Pizzagate"), one would be hard-pressed to prove that fake news was directly responsible for the outcome of the election.[70] Nonetheless, Clinton's supporters in the corporate media, largely at MSNBC and the *Washington Post*, derided "fake news" as the primary culprit for the election upset.[71] Callum Borchers and Margaret Sullivan of the *Washington Post* correctly criticized how Trump and his supporters weaponized "fake news," but did not go as far as admitting that the corporate press engaged in their own form of it, and in some cases did so in support of Hillary Clinton.[72] *The Washington Post*'s fact-checker, Glenn Kessler, claimed, "People seem to confuse reporting mistakes by established news organizations with obviously fraudulent news produced by Macedonian teenagers."[73] Such statements helped give the false impression that corporate media outlets are the only legitimate ones, while all others are "fake news." However, that type of discussion about "fake

news" distracted from the more insidious, intentionally misleading corporate media reporting during the election.

The Democrats had sought to feed pro-Clinton propaganda to the corporate media during the primaries, as Clinton's staff organized off-the-books cocktails with "influential reporters, anchors and editors" to win their support.[74] Information about this quiet collusion between Clinton's staff and the corporate media was found in an email from Jesse Ferguson, Deputy National Press Secretary for Hillary Clinton, to John Podesta, former chairman of the Clinton campaign, published by WikiLeaks. The privileged guests at the cocktail meeting included journalists from CNN, the *New York Times*, CBS, MSNBC, and the Huffington Post. WikiLeaks's introduction to the DNC's leaked emails stated that the goal of the meeting was to "[g]ive reporters their first thoughts from team HRC in advance of the announcement" and help them with "[f]raming the HRC message and framing the race."[75] While the Clinton campaign clearly did their best to stitch up the support of the corporate media, that same corporate media may have inadvertently contributed to Clinton's defeat. Trump's name appeared in twice as many headlines as Clinton's, and Trump received nearly triple the overall coverage. While some of that coverage was more critical, it still added up to $2 billion in free exposure,[76] lending credence to the adage, "there is no such thing as bad press."[77]

The Democratic Party could also be responsible for Clinton's poor showing because it actively worked with the corporate media to bury primary challenger Bernie Sanders, who was drawing large crowds and the support of millennials, currently the largest potential voting demographic in terms of sheer numbers. Furthermore, the DNC actively worked to promote Trump as the hopeful Republican nominee during the primaries, believing he would be an easier candidate for Clinton to defeat in the general election.[78] This barrage of reasons for Trump's "electored" victory should not imply that Clinton faced insurmountable odds—after all, Obama faced incredible odds and won—but rather should contribute to establishing that Clinton constituted a risk to her party.

Rather than face the shortcomings of their candidate, the DNC resurrected a Cold War–style red-baiting campaign, and the Russian hacking tale was born with the help of the corporate press. In November 2016, the *Washington Post*, a paper known to have connections with the Democratic Party, published an article boldly titled "Russian Propaganda Effort Helped Spread 'Fake News,' Experts Say."[79] The article, written by former national security editor Craig Timberg, cited an anonymous organization, PropOrNot, that created a list of some two hundred independent news outlets it dubbed "useful idiots" at best and outright Kremlin operatives at worst. PropOrNot accused these outlets, without evidence or identifiable "experts," of peddling Russian-inspired "fake news." In fact, the list included numerous independent outlets that were comprised of real journalists that had been critical of establishment figures of both major parties (e.g., CounterPunch, Truthout, and Naked Capitalism, among others from the libertarian Right to the anarchist Left). The methodology of PropOrNot was never explained by Timberg, yet the organization's list was uncritically touted as cutting edge on the matter, even though they were nontransparent in every way. After several of the organizations on the list threatened to sue the *Post*, a partial retraction was issued by the executive editor, Marty Baron, who stated,

> The Washington Post on Nov. 24 published a story on the work of four sets of researchers who have examined what they say are Russian propaganda efforts to undermine American democracy and interests. One of them was PropOrNot, a group that insists on public anonymity, which issued a report identifying more than 200 websites that, in its view, wittingly or unwittingly published or echoed Russian propaganda. A number of those sites have objected to being included on PropOrNot's list, and some of the sites, as well as others not on the list, have publicly challenged the group's methodology and conclusions. The Post, which did not name any of the sites, does not itself vouch for the validity of PropOrNot's findings regarding any individual media outlet, nor did the article purport to do so. Since publication of The Post's story, PropOrNot has removed some sites from its list.[80]

Baron neglected to mention the threats of lawsuits in PropOrNot's decision to remove some names, or that lawsuits had anything to do with the *Post*'s decision to run the partial retraction. Also, while Baron claimed the *Post* did not vouch for the validity of the list, he aggressively promoted the piece on Twitter, writing, "Russian propaganda effort helped spread fake news during election, say independent researchers," while linking to the Timberg headlined article, "Russian Propaganda Effort Helped Spread 'Fake News' during Election, Experts Say." When considered alongside the fact that Timberg's article directly linked to PropOrNot's website without a single critical murmur, it could seem as if the *Post* was promoting their own version of "fake news."[81]

Shortly thereafter, in an alarming display of hypocrisy, the *Washington Post* removed all doubt about how the corporate press generates actual fake news when it published an article titled "Russian Hackers Penetrated U.S. Electricity Grid through a Utility in Vermont, U.S. Officials Say." The article authoritatively claimed that Russians had hacked a power grid in Vermont. However, the story turned out to be demonstrably false.[82] The *Post* issued a correction eleven hours later that clarified it was only a hacked laptop, and that no one had actually contacted the power plant or verified details of the story prior to publishing. But by then, the *Washington Post*'s story had become an Internet "fake news" phenomenon in its own right.

Despite the lack of evidence linking Russian hackers to "fake news" websites or any evidence proving that these types of stories cost Clinton the election, numerous politicians, reporters, and commentators still saw Red everywhere—no matter what, facts be damned, Russia must have cost Clinton the election. *New York Times* columnist Charles M. Blow declared, "It is absolutely clear that the Russians did interfere in our election. This is not a debatable issue. This is not fake news. This is not a witch hunt. This happened."[83] Blow was not alone. By early 2017, intelligence officials and corporate news outlets repeatedly claimed, without making public any corroborating evidence, that Russians had hacked the election. Some of the most vocal proponents of the Russian hacking tale have been Louise Mensch, who has a sordid past of peddling unsubstantiated claims; Democratic Party apologist and MSNBC host Rachel Maddow; Eric Boehlert of Media Matters; Democratic Party–friendly pollster Matt McDermott; and comedian and critic Bill Maher.[84]

Rolling Stone journalist Matt Taibbi argued that the reason so many journalists touted their belief in the Russian hackers tale without evidence—a belief he called "Putin Derangement Syndrome"—is that no one wants to be the person to claim the story is false and then get proven wrong. So instead, these reporters, commentators, and politicians jump on board with the claim, knowing they won't be blamed individually if all of them turn out to be wrong.[85] Taibbi argued that the Russian story was a distraction from the problems within the Democratic Party: "If the [Democratic] party's leaders really believe that Russian intervention is anywhere in the top 100 list of reasons why some 155 million eligible voters (out of 231 million) chose not to pull a lever for Hillary Clinton last year, they're farther along down the Purity of Essence nut-hole than Mark Warner."[86] The media's ongoing demonizing of Russia, however, was successful. One NBC News/*Wall Street Journal* poll found that 55 percent of Americans were "bothered by Russian election hacking."[87] This is despite no smoking gun evidence coming to light of actual Russian hacking that demonstrably tipped the scales in Trump's favor.

The demonization concerning Russian-inspired "fake news" was not reserved for Russia alone, as social media companies like Facebook and Google were also blamed for the supposed flood of "fake news." Outlets like BuzzFeed, Fox, National Public Radio (NPR), Vox, *New York Magazine*, and MSNBC, among others, piled on.[88] The conjecture from the Huffington Post and MSNBC's Rachel Maddow went even further, arguing, without evidence, that the Russian government was behind a fake news "tsunami" that elevated both Sanders's campaign in the primary and Trump's victory in the general election.[89] The marriage of Russian hackers with "fake news," while still uncorroborated, has been extremely successful. A 2017 Harvard University poll found that millennials believed that 48.5 percent of the news they saw in their Facebook feeds was fake.[90] This resulted in members of the Democratic Party proposing legislation for the immediate retractions of incorrect statements and the elimination of "fake news."

Facebook CEO Mark Zuckerberg initially scoffed at accusations that his company peddled "fake news" that swayed the 2016 presidential election.[91] However, mounting pressure led Facebook to examine the issue of fake news on its social media platform.[92] By late 2016, Facebook had agreed to team up with the Poynter Institute's International Fact-Checking Network, a group consisting of five corporate news outlets, to develop a tool that will fact-check stories for Facebook users.[93] Their algorithmic tool, released in March 2017, claimed it would flag "fake" news (labeling it as "disputed") and promote "fact based" stories.[94] The decision by Facebook to create these algorithms was hailed by corporate outlets such as the *Washington Post*, Huffington Post, and NBC.[95] Facebook also began cracking down on "Fake News Accounts," closing over thirty thousand accounts through spring of 2017.[96] However, their approaches are far from foolproof and pose threats to free speech and expression.

One recent investigation into Facebook's algorithms and internal rules regarding the limits of hate speech and political expression yielded troubling insights. ProPublica's research into a trove of internal company documents revealed previously secret information about Facebook censors (what the company calls "content reviewers"), suggesting that, "at least in some instances, the company's hate-speech rules tend to favor elites and governments over grassroots activists and racial minorities. In so doing, they serve the business interests of the global company, which relies on national governments not to block its service to their citizens."[97] The ProPublica report further noted that "Facebook's rules constitute a legal world of their own. They stand in sharp contrast to the United States' First Amendment protections of free speech, which courts have interpreted to allow exactly the sort of speech and writing censored by the company's hate speech algorithm." Facebook's "color blind" algorithmic approach to policing content is an example of their wish to remain unaccountable while deliberately engaging in censorship. Legal scholar Danielle Citron pointed out that while an indiscriminate filter might sound egalitarian, it does not actually provide equal protection to all groups, and, in fact, it will "protect the people who least need it and take [protection] away from those who really need it."[98]

It should be noted that Facebook's rules regarding why particular content is censored are not published, so they are not specifically made known to users who have little means by which to appeal decisions that seem to be made in the dark, and with no real way to measure consistency. Further, Facebook announced that, in addition to increasing its use of algorithms, it intends to nearly double its number of hired censors to 7,500 this year.[99] These approaches to addressing issues of political speech and expression, as well as fake news concerns, however possibly well-intentioned, are not only controversial but are misguided and anti-intellectual. ProPublica's review showed how these rules were imperfectly and unequally applied, nontransparent, and paternalistic. Most of all, they go against the very fiber of the First Amendment.

CONCLUSION

Facts and the truth are not partisan. They are the bedrock of our democracy. And you are either with them, with us, with our Constitution, our history, and the future of our nation, or you are against it. Everyone must answer that question.

—Dan Rather, former anchor, *CBS Evening News*,
two days after Trump's inauguration[100]

After the numerous efforts to fight fake news and combat alternative facts, who will check the fact-checkers and what criteria will be used? Fact-checking alone can never scale to the threat posed by actual fake news, which is rightfully called propaganda. Instead of what amounts to censorship by social media sites outsourcing to fact-checking organizations and employing various algorithms, McCarthyite blacklists used by sites like PropOrNot that include entirely legitimate independent journalistic outlets as "fake news," or legislation designed to limit the effects of the "fake news" by literally banning the media from lying (good luck with that one!), the real antidote is one that Project Censored has relied upon for over forty years—critical media literacy education.

The corporate media's lauding of Facebook's act of censoring so-called "fake news" is emblematic of the problems concerning press freedom in the US. We not only need a more open media, we need one that encourages more critical thinking. People need access to education that teaches people *how* to think, not *what* to think, with a focus on how to determine information and source integrity as well as how to formulate and ask critical questions. Instead of addressing these challenges, the corporate press, which has increasingly covered more and more Junk Food News stories over the years, have now helped weaponize the real problem of fake news, often using the threat of fake news to justify censorship of information and individuals critical of establishment power and the plutocracy.

On January 20, 2017, a president who was both a symptom and a product of post-truth America moved into the White House, with hordes of the Ignorati on his coattails. Since then, the Democratic Party and the corporate media have engaged in scapegoating while rewriting their past failures, further helping to pave the way for a post-truth dystopia. Their endless infatuations with Russia, hacking, and "fake news" are examples of what H.L. Mencken described as a "combat of crazes . . . to keep the populace alarmed . . . by an endless series of hobgoblins, most of them imaginary."[101] This charade of speculation takes away from other important and very real issues— such as rising inequality, structural racism and sexism, endless wars, the impact of climate change, and more provable corrupt and criminal behaviors inside the Trump administration.

As this book goes to print, investigations into Trump and his administration are underway on several fronts. Time will tell what those may yield. But the failures of the corporate media and education system have already contributed to the current post-truth environment by creating nothing short of an epistemological crisis. This has proven to be detrimental to our democratic process and an affront to the First Amendment rights of the American people. Creating the better world we envision will not depend on rewriting recent history to suit our purposes or flatter our illusions, but rather will depend on creating an ever more democratic, diverse, and critical free press.

NOLAN HIGDON is a professor of English, communications, and history of the US and Latin America in the San Francisco Bay Area. His dissertation, "Effective Critical Media Literacy Pedagogy in Higher Education: Turning Social Justice Theory into Practice," identified effective methods for teaching critical media literacy in higher education. He sits on the boards of the Media Freedom Foundation, Sacred Heart University's Media Literacy and Digital Culture graduate program, the Union for Democratic Communications's steering committee, and the Northwest Alliance for Alternative Media and Education. Higdon is a cofounder of the Global Critical Media Literacy Project.

MICKEY HUFF is president of the Media Freedom Foundation, director of Project Censored, professor of social science and history at Diablo Valley College (where he is cochair of the History Department), and a lecturer in communications at California State University, East Bay. For a more detailed bio, see "About the Editors" at the back of this volume.

Notes

1. H.L. Mencken, *In Defense of Women* (New York: Alfred Knopf, 1926), 53. The book was first published in 1918 by Philip Goodman.
2. Neil Postman, *Amusing Ourselves to Death: Public Discourse in the Age of Show Business* (New York: Viking Penguin, 1985), 106.
3. Morris Berman, *Dark Ages America: The Final Phase of Empire* (New York: W.W. Norton & Company, 2011), 20.
4. David Vine, *Base Nation: How U.S. Military Bases Abroad Harm America and the World* (New York: Metropolitan Books, 2015); Greg Palast, "The Election was Stolen—Here's How...," GregPalast.com, November 11, 2016, www.gregpalast.com/election-stolen-heres/; Lawrence Mishel, Elise Gould, and Josh Bivens, "Wage Stagnation in Nine Charts," Economic Policy Institute, January 6, 2015, www.epi.org/publication/charting-wage-stagnation/; Hazel Sheffield, "The Charts That Show the Countries with the Worst Wealth Inequality: Some Countries are More Unequal Than Others," January 18, 2016, www.independent.co.uk/news/business/news/the-charts-that-show-the-countries-with-the-worst-wealth-inequality-a6819291.html; Alice Park, "Childhood Obesity Rates are Still Rising," *Time*, April 25, 2016, www.time.com/4306369/childhood-obesity-rates/; Texas A&M University, "Why American Infant Mortality Rates are So High," ScienceDaily, October 13, 2016, https://www.sciencedaily.com/releases/2016/10/161013103132.htm; Sabrina Tavernise, "Maternal Mortality Rate in U.S.

Rises, Defying Global Trend, Study Finds," *New York Times*, September 21, 2016, https://www. nytimes.com/2016/09/22/health/maternal-mortality.html.

5. *Idiocracy*, directed by Mike Judge (Twentieth Century Fox, 2006). According to the Internet Movie Database (IMDb), "Private Joe Bauers, the definition of 'average American,' is selected by the Pentagon to be the guinea pig for a top-secret hibernation program. Forgotten, he awakes five centuries in the future. He discovers a society so incredibly dumbed down that he's easily the most intelligent person alive." (http://www.imdb.com/title/tt0387808/) Little did Judge know it would not take five hundred years, but rather a little over a decade.

6. *Stupidity*, directed by Albert Nerenberg (Documentary Channel, 2003). Its IMDb webpage is at http://www.imdb.com/title/tt0399704/.

7. George Carlin, *Life is Worth Losing*, directed by Rocco Urbisci (HBO, 2005).

8. Janine Jackson, "All the Warning Signs are There, Loud and Clear," Fairness and Accuracy In Reporting (FAIR), October 14, 2016, http://fair.org/home/all-the-warning-signs-are-there-loud-and-clear/.

9. Adam Johnson, "The Debates are Over and No One Asked about Climate Change," Fairness and Accuracy in Reporting (FAIR), October 19, 2016, http://fair.org/home/the-debates-are-over-and-no-one-asked-about-climate-change/.

10. *Idiocracy*, directed by Mike Judge.

11. Richard Wike, "What the World Thinks About Climate Change in 7 Charts," Pew Research Center, April 18, 2016, www.pewresearch.org/fact-tank/2016/04/18/what-the-world-thinks-about-climate-change-in-7-charts/.

12. Jill Carle, "Climate Change Seen as Top Global Threat: Americans, Europeans, Middle Easterners Focus on ISIS as Greatest Danger," Pew Research Center, July 14, 2015, www.pewglobal. org/2015/07/14/climate-change-seen-as-top-global-threat/.

13. Washington's Blog, "The Terrorism Statistics Every American Needs to Hear," Global Research, May 19, 2014, reposted April 20, 2017, http://www.globalresearch.ca/the-terrorism-statistics-every-american-needs-to-hear/538281; Barry Glassner, *The Culture of Fear: Why Americans are Afraid of the Wrong Things* (New York: Basic Books, 2000).

14. A&E History Channel, "Celebrating Our Centennial—The WHCA at 100," White House Correspondents' Association, no date, http://whca.net/history.htm.

15. Frank Rich, "All the President's Press," *New York Times*, April 29, 2007, http://www.nytimes. com/2007/04/29/opinion/29rich.html.

16. Dylan Byers, "Trump Declines to Attend White House Correspondents' Dinner," CNN, February 26, 2017, http://www.cnn.com/2017/02/25/politics/trump-declines-to-attend-white-house-correspondents-dinner/.

17. Javier E. David, "Trump Says He Won't Attend White House Correspondent's Dinner Amid Testy Relations with Media," CNBC, February 25, 2017, http://www.cnbc.com/2017/02/25/trump-says-he-wont-attend-white-house-correspondents-dinner-amid-testy-relations-with-media.html.

18. Adam Johnson, "Downplaying US Contribution to Potential Yemen Famine," Fairness and Accuracy In Reporting (FAIR), February 27, 2017, www.fair.org/home/downplaying-us-contribution-to-potential-yemen-famine/. "For almost two years, the United States has backed—with weapons, logistics and political support—a Saudi-led war in Yemen that has left over 10,000 dead, 40,000 wounded, 2.5 million internally displaced, 2.2 million children suffering from malnutrition and over 90 percent of civilians in need of humanitarian aid."

19. William Lambers, "Yemen: The Forgotten Famine," Huffington Post, no date, http://www. huffingtonpost.com/william-lambers/yemen-the-forgotten-famin_b_10864754.html.

20. Ibid.

21. Simon Romero, "U.S. Swimmers' Disputed Robbery Claim Fuels Tension in Brazil," *New York Times*, August 18, 2016, https://www.nytimes.com/2016/08/19/sports/olympics/police-say-ryan-lochte-lied-about-gunpoint-assault.html.

22. Ibid.

23. Ibid.

24. Ibid.

25. Nathan Fenno, David Wharton, and Vincent Bevins, "2 U.S. Swimmers Leave Rio after Robbery Scandal; 3rd Pays $10,800; Lochte Apologizes," *Los Angeles Times*, August 19, 2016, http://www.latimes.com/sports/sportsnow/la-sp-oly-swimmer-20160819-snap-story.html.

26. Ibid.

27. Ibid.

28. Ben Axelson, "Rio 2016: Gabby Douglas Apologizes for Not Putting Hand on Heart during US Anthem," Syracuse.com, August 10, 2016, http://www.syracuse.com/olympics/index.ssf/2016/08/gabby_douglas_hand_on_heart_national_anthem_disrespect.html.

29. Jenni Miller, "Gymnast Gabby Douglas 'Heartbroken' Over Online Bullying," The Cut, August 14, 2016, http://nymag.com/thecut/2016/08/gabby-douglas-mom-online-abuse.html.

30. Skye Cooley, "The Flood of 2016: Southeast Louisiana and the Consequences of Real Community," Huffington Post, August 17, 2016, updated August 18, 2016, http://www.huffingtonpost.com/entry/the-flood-of-2016-southeast-louisiana-the   consequences_us_57b47ffae4bob3bb4bo88bcd.

31. Russell Berman, "America is Ignoring Another Natural Disaster Near the Gulf," *Atlantic*, August 17, 2016, https://www.theatlantic.com/politics/archive/2016/08/america-is-ignoring-another-natural-disaster-near-the-gulf/496355/.

32. Ibid.

33. Cooley, "The Flood of 2016."

34. Alexander Smith, "#Envelopegate: How Did PwC's 'Moonlight' Mix-Up Happen at Oscars?" NBC News, February 27, 2017, http://www.nbcnews.com/pop-culture/movies/envelopegate-how-did-pwc-s-moonlight-mix-happen-oscars-n726031; Environment America, "More Than 500 Leaders Call for Doubling Strength of America's Best Regional Climate and Clean Air Program," Common Dreams, February 22, 2017, http://www.commondreams.org/newswire/2017/02/22/more-500-leaders-call-doubling-strength-americas-best-regional-climate-and-clean.

35. Smith, "#Envelopegate."

36. Environment America, "More than 500 Leaders."

37. Rebecca Savransky, "Trump Berates CNN Reporter: 'You are Fake News,'" The Hill, January 11, 2017,   http://thehill.com/homenews/administration/313777-trump-berates-cnn-reporter-for-fake-news.

38. Peter Phillips and Mickey Huff, "Truth Emergency: Inside the Military Industrial Media Empire," Project Censored, May 3, 2010, projectcensored.org/truth-emergency-inside-the-military-industrial-media-empire/.

39. Ibid.

40. Patrick Kingsley and Anne Barnard, "Banned Nerve Agent Sarin Used in Syria Chemical Attack, Turkey Says," *New York Times*, April 6, 2017, https://www.nytimes.com/2017/04/06/world/middleeast/chemical-attack-syria.html; Nika Knight, "Corporate Media and D.C. Politicians Praise Trump's Syrian Airstrikes," Truthdig, April 7, 2017, www.truthdig.com/report/item/corporate_media_and_dc_politicians_praise_trumps_airstrikes_20170407.

41. Jason Le Miere, "Trump's Attack on Syria Killed Four Children, State News Agency Claims," *Newsweek*, April 7, 2017, http://www.newsweek.com/syria-attack-children-civilian-killed-580555; Molly Hennessy-Fiske and Nabih Bulos, "Syrians Report 15 Dead in U.S. Airstrike," *Los Angeles Times*, April 7, 2017, http://www.latimes.com/world/middleeast/la-fg-syria-airstrike-20170406-story.html.

42. "Instant View: Trump Orders Military Strikes on Syrian Air Base," Reuters, April 6, 2017, www.reuters.com/article/us-mideast-crisis-syria-instant-idUSKBN17909I.

43. Seymour M. Hersh, "Trump's Red Line," *Die Welt*, June 25, 2017, https://www.welt.de/politik/ausland/article165905578/Trump-s-Red-Line.html; Dirk Laabs, "Air Strike in Syria: The Fog of War," *Die Welt*, June 25, 2017, https://www.welt.de/politik/ausland/article165906452/The-Fog-of-War.html; Theodore A. Postol, "The Nerve Agent Attack in Khan Shaykuhn, Syria," Unz Review, April 11, 2017, updated April 12, 2017, http://www.unz.com/article/the-nerve-agent-attack-in-khan-shaykhun-syria/.

44. "Report: U.S.-Led Coalition Airstrikes Killed 700 Civilians in Raqqa, Syria," *Democracy Now!*, June 26, 2017, https://www.democracynow.org/2017/6/26/headlines/report_us_led_coalition_airstrikes_killed_700_civilians_in_raqqa_syria; "Tomahawk Maker's Stock Jumps 3% after US Strike in Syria," RT, April 7, 2017, updated April 8, 2017, https://www.rt.com/usa/383985-tomahawk-makers-stock-jumps-3percent/.

45. Amanda Marcotte, "First Fake News, Now Fake History: Glenn Beck Wants to Train Young People to Promote an Alternative History," Salon, April 14, 2017, www.salon.com/2017/04/14/first-fake-news-now-fake-history-glenn-beck-wants-to-train-an-army-of-young-people-to-promote-an-alternative-history/.

46. Ibid.

47. Ibid.

48. Chi-Kim Cheung, "Media Education across Four Asian Societies: Issues and Themes," *International Review of Education*, Vol. 55, No. 1 (January 2009): 39–58; Renee Hobbs and Richard Frost, "Measuring the Acquisition of Media-Literacy Skills," *Reading Research Quarterly*, Vol. 38, No. 3 (July–September 2003): 330–55.

49. Henry A. Giroux, *Neoliberalism's War on Higher Education* (Chicago: Haymarket Books, 2014).

50. Ibid.

51. Phillips and Huff, "Truth Emergency."

52. Henry A. Giroux, "Trump Versus Comey: The Politics of Loyalty and Lying," Truthout, June 15, 2017, http://www.truth-out.org/opinion/item/40944-trump-versus-comey-the-politics-of-loyalty-and-lying.

53. Ibid.

54. "Fake News" interest over time, search July 1, 2012–June 24, 2017, Google Trends, https://trends.google.com/trends/explore?geo=US&q=%22fake%20news%22.

55. Justin Baragona, "'You are Fake News!': Trump and CNN's Jim Acosta Get into Shouting Match at Presser," Mediaite, January 11, 2017, http://www.mediaite.com/online/you-are-fake-news-trump-and-cnns-jim-acosta-get-into-shouting-match-at-presser/.

56. Matt Vespa, "Clinton: Fake News is a Threat That Must be Addressed," Townhall, December 9, 2016, https://townhall.com/tipsheet/mattvespa/2016/12/09/clinton-fake-news-is-a-threat-that-must-be-addressed-n2257579.

57. Ariel Edwards-Levy, "New Poll Suggests 'Fake News' Has Almost No Meaning Anymore," Huffington Post, February 17, 2017, http://www.huffingtonpost.com/entry/poll-fake-news_us_58a75d5ce4b045cd34c18258.

58. "Advertising Disguised as News," TV Tropes, no date, tvtropes.org/pmwiki/pmwiki.php/Main/AdvertisingDisguisedAsNews; Noam Chomsky and Edward S. Herman, *Manufacturing Consent: The Political Economy of the Mass Media* (New York: Pantheon Books, 1988).

59. Katy Steinmetz, "Oxford's Word of the Year for 2016 is 'Post-Truth,'" *Time*, November 15, 2016, http://www.time.com/4572592/oxford-word-of-the-year-2016-post-truth/.

60. Oxford Dictionaries, "Word of the Year 2016 is...," English Oxford Living Dictionaries, https://en.oxforddictionaries.com/word-of-the-year/word-of-the-year-2016.

61. Nolan Higdon, "Effective Critical Media Literacy Pedagogy in Higher Education: Turning Social Justice Theory into Practice," San Francisco State University, Dissertation: March 22, 2017.

62. Chuck Todd, "Conway: Press Secretary Gave 'Alternative Facts,'" *Meet the Press*, NBC, January 22, 2017, http://www.nbcnews.com/meet-the-press/video/conway-press-secretary-gave-alternative-facts-860142147643; Brian Stelter, "White House Press Secretary Attacks Media for Accurately Reporting Inauguration Crowds," CNN, January 21, 2017, http://money.cnn.com/2017/01/21/media/sean-spicer-press-secretary-statement/; Jonathan Lemire, "Trump Draws Far Smaller Inaugural Crowd Than Obama," *U.S. News & World Report*, January 20, 2017, https://www.usnews.com/news/politics/articles/2017-01-20/trump-draws-far-smaller-inaugural-crowd-than-obama.

63. Eric Boehlert, "Conway's Bowling Green Massacre Claim Wasn't an 'Honest Mistake'; It's Part of a Pattern," Media Matters, February 7, 2017, https://mediamatters.org/blog/2017/02/07/conways-bowling-green-massacre-claim-wasnt-honest-mistake-its-part-pattern/215258.

64. Justin Carissimo, "Sean Spicer Cites Fake Atlanta Terror Attack Story," *Independent*, February 9, 2017, www.independent.co.uk/news/world/americas/sean-spicer-creates-fake-atlanta-terror-attack-story-a7570561.html; Jenna Johnson and Ashley Parker, "Spicer: Hitler 'Didn't Even Sink to Using Chemical Weapons,' Although He Sent Jews to 'the Holocaust Center,'" *Washington Post*, April 11, 2017, https://www.washingtonpost.com/news/post-politics/wp/2017/04/11/spicer-hitler-I-even-sink-to-using-chemical-weapons-although-he-sent-jews-to-the-holocaust-center/; Cleve R. Wootson, Jr., "Trump Implied Frederick Douglass was Alive. The Abolitionist's Family Offered a 'History Lesson,'" *Washington Post*, February 2, 2017, https://www.washingtonpost.com/news/post-nation/wp/2017/02/02/trump-implied-frederick-douglass-was-alive-the-abolitionists-family-offered-a-history-lesson/; Jessica Estepa, "Ben Carson Just Referred to Slaves as 'Immigrants,'" *USA Today*, March 6, 2017, https://www.usatoday.com/story/news/politics/onpolitics/2017/03/06/ben-carson-calls-slaves-immigrants/98816752/; Ryan Grenoble, "GOP Senator Blames 'Paid Protesters' for Deluge of Phone Calls," Huffington Post, February 2, 2017, updated February 3, 2017, http://www.huffingtonpost.com/entry/cory-gardner-paid-protesters-trump-calls_us_58937d6ee4b07595d05a5087; Anna Ringstrom and Jeff Mason, "Sweden Mocks Trump's 'Alternative Facts' on Fictional Refugee Incident," National Memo, February 19, 2017, https://www.nationalmemo.com/sweden-mocks-trump-incident/; Samantha Schmidt and Lindsey Bever, "Kellyanne Conway Cites 'Bowling Green Massacre' That Never Happened to Defend Travel Ban," *Washington Post*, February 3, 2017, https://www.washingtonpost.com/news/morning-mix/wp/2017/02/03/kellyanne-conway-cites-bowling-green-massacre-that-never-happened-to-defend-travel-ban/; Ed Mazza, "#TrumpTeachesHistory are the Lessons You Never Learned in School: '7/11. Never Forget. Sad,'" Huffington Post, May 1, 2017, updated May 2, 2017, http://www.huffingtonpost.com/entry/trump-teaches-history_us_5907e141e4b0bb2d0870c8b6.

65. Nolan Higdon, "Disinfo Wars: Alex Jones' War on Your Mind," Project Censored, September 26, 2013, projectcensored.org/disinfo-wars-alex-jones-war-mind/; Media Matters Staff, "Alex Jones: 'I'm Ready to Die for Trump,'" Media Matters, February 6, 2017, https://mediamatters.org/video/2017/02/06/alex-jones-i-m-ready-die-trump/215248; Corky Siemaszko, "InfoWars' Alex Jones is a 'Performance Artist,' His Lawyer Says in Divorce Hearing," NBC News, April 17, 2017, www.nbcnews.com/news/us-news/not-fake-news-infowars-alex-jones-performance-artist-n747491.

66. Media Matters Staff, "A Dangerous Troll is Now Reporting from the White House," Media Matters, February 13, 2017, https://mediamatters.org/blog/2017/02/13/dangerous-troll-now-reporting-white-house/215320.

67. Thomas Bishop, "'Trump TV' will be in the White House Press Briefings," Media Matters, December 6, 2016, http://mediamatters.org/blog/2016/12/06/trump-tv-will-be-white-house-press-briefings/214735; Eric Boehlert, "Michael Flynn Scandal Shatters GOP Dream of Protecting Trump in 'Alternative Fact' Cocoon," Media Matters, February 15, 2017, https://mediamatters.org/blog/2017/02/15/michael-flynn-scandal-shatters-gop-dream-protecting-trump-alternative-fact-cocoon/215351.

68. Derek Hawkins, "Trump Didn't Lie, Jeffrey Lord Says on CNN. He Just Speaks a Different Language—'Americanese,'" *Washington Post*, March 21, 2017, https://www.washingtonpost.com/news/morning-mix/wp/2017/03/21/trump-didnt-lie-jeffrey-lord-says-on-cnn-he-just-speaks-a-different-language-americanese/.

69. Allan Smith, "Office of Government Ethics Says Steve Bannon's Waiver to Speak with Breitbart is 'Problematic,'" *Business Insider*, June 14, 2017, http://www.businessinsider.com/steve-bannon-problematic-ethics-waiver-breitbart-2017-6.

70. Joshua Gillin, "How Pizzagate Went from Fake News to a Real Problem for a D.C. Business," PolitiFact, December 5, 2016, www.politifact.com/truth-o-meter/article/2016/dec/05/how-pizzagate-went-fake-news-real-problem-dc-busin/.

71. "Trump Campaign Rhetoric Aligned with Russian Propaganda," *The Rachel Maddow Show*, MSNBC, March 31, 2017, www.msnbc.com/rachel-maddow/watch/trump-campaign-rhetoric-aligned-with-russian-propaganda-911659587810; Margaret Sullivan, "It's Time to Retire the Tainted Term 'Fake News,'" *Washington Post*, January 8, 2017, https://www.washingtonpost.

com/lifestyle/style/its-time-to-retire-the-tainted-term-fake-news/2017/01/06/a5a7516c-d375-11e6-945a-76f69a399dd5_story.html.

72. Callum Borchers, "Millennials Don't Like Trump, but He Has Successfully Warped Their View of 'Fake News,'" *Washington Post*, April 25, 2017, https://www.washingtonpost.com/news/the-fix/wp/2017/04/25/millennials-dont-like-trump-but-he-has-successfully-warped-their-view-of-fake-news/.

73. Sullivan, "It's Time to Retire the Tainted Term."

74. Claire Bernish, "Red Alert: Corporate Media's War on 'Fake News' is being Used to Silence Dissent and Alt Media," The Free Thought Project, November 15, 2016, http://thefreethought-project.com/mainstream-war-dissent-fake-news/.

75. "The Podesta Emails," WikiLeaks, no date, https://wikileaks.org/podesta-emails/; Jesse Ferguson, "RE: Event Memo—Benensons OTR.docx," email dated April 9, 2015, WikiLeaks, no date, https://wikileaks.org/podesta-emails/emailid/5953; quoted material in this paragraph from Alex Pfeiffer, "Leaked Documents Reveal Which Journalists are Cozy with the Clinton Campaign," Daily Caller, October 9, 2016, http://dailycaller.com/2016/10/09/leaked-docu-ments-reveal-which-journalists-are-cozy-with-the-clinton-campaign/.

76. John Sides, "Is the Media Biased Toward Clinton or Trump? Here is Some Actual Hard Data," *Washington Post*, September 20, 2016, https://www.washingtonpost.com/news/monkey-cage/wp/2016/09/20/is-the-media-biased-toward-clinton-or-trump-heres-some-actual-hard-data/; Michael Calderone, "Donald Trump Shouldn't Have Bothered Buying Airtime. Cable News Ran His Ad 60 Times for Free," Huffington Post, January 5, 2016, http://www.huffingtonpost.com/entry/donald-trump-cable-news-airtime_us_568c0d96e4b014efe0dbe5a4.

77. Nolan Higdon, Mickey Huff, et al., "Millennial Demockracy: The Corporate Media's War on Social Justice," Global Critical Media Literacy Project, October 14, 2016, gcml.org/721-2/.

78. Ibid.

79. Craig Timberg, "Russian Propaganda Effort Helped Spread 'Fake News' during Election, Experts Say," *Washington Post*, November 24, 2016, https://www.washingtonpost.com/busi-ness/economy/russian-propaganda-effort-helped-spread-fake-news-during-election-experts-say/2016/11/24/793903b6-8a40-4ca9-b712-716af66098fe_story.html.

80. Ibid.

81. Ibid.; Ben Norton and Glenn Greenwald, "Washington Post Disgracefully Promotes a McCar-thyite Blacklist from a New, Hidden, and Very Shady Group," *Intercept*, November 26, 2016, https://theintercept.com/2016/11/26/washington-post-disgracefully-promotes-a-mccarthyite-blacklist-from-a-new-hidden-and-very-shady-group/.

82. Kalev Leetaru, "'Fake News' and How the Washington Post Rewrote Its Story on Russian Hacking of the Power Grid," *Forbes*, January 1, 2017, https://www.forbes.com/sites/kalev-leetaru/2017/01/01/fake-news-and-how-the-washington-post-rewrote-its-story-on-russian-hacking-of-the-power-grid/#573fdf57ad51.

83. Charles M. Blow, "Dwindling Odds of Coincidence," *New York Times*, April 3, 2017, https://www.nytimes.com/2017/04/03/opinion/dwindling-odds-of-coincidence.html; Robert Parry, "Mainstream Media as Arbiters of Truth," Consortium News, April 4, 2017, https://consor-tiumnews.com/2017/04/04/mainstream-media-as-arbiters-of-truth/.

84. Matt Taibbi, "Putin Derangement Syndrome Arrives: Whatever the Truth about Trump and Russia, the Speculation Surrounding It Has Become a Dangerous Case of Mass Hysteria," *Rolling Stone*, April 3, 2017, www.rollingstone.com/politics/features/taibbi-putin-derangement-syndrome-arrives-w474771; Mark Hensch, "Maddow Jabs at Tillerson, Exxon Mobil on Russia Deal," The Hill, April 19, 2017, www.thehill.com/homenews/news/329586-maddow-jabs-exxon-on-russia-deal.

85. Ibid.

86. Taibbi, "Putin Derangement Syndrome Arrives."

87. Mark Murray, "Poll: 55 Percent Concerned About Russia's Interference in Election," NBC News, http://www.nbcnews.com/politics/politics-news/poll-55-percent-concerned-about-russia-s-interference-election-n697391; Eric Bradner, "Poll: 55% of Americans Bothered by Russian Election Hacking," CNN, December 18, 2016, http://www.cnn.com/2016/12/18/politics/poll-russian-hacking/.

88. Michael Sainato, "Rachel Maddow Asserts Russian Government Incited 'Bot Attack' on Sanders Groups," *Observer*, March 22, 2017, www.observer.com/2017/03/rachel-maddow-russian-government-facebook-bernie-sanders/; Mike Isaac, "Facebook, in Cross Hairs after Election, is Said to Question Its Influence," *New York Times*, November 12, 2016, https://www.nytimes.com/2016/11/14/technology/facebook-is-said-to-question-its-influence-in-election.html; Yochi Dreazen, "Facebook is Full of Fake News Stories. On Election Day, Don't Fall for Them," Vox, November 8, 2016, www.vox.com/presidential-election/2016/11/8/13557952/facebook-election-day-trump-clinton-fake-stories-lies-fox; Sam Sanders, "Did Social Media Ruin Election 2016?" NPR, November 8, 2016, www.npr.org/2016/11/08/500686320/did-social-media-ruin-election-2016; Howard Kurtz, "Fake News and the Election: Why Facebook is Polluting the Media Environment with Garbage," Fox News, November 18, 2016, www.foxnews.com/politics/2016/11/18/fake-news-and-election-why-facebook-is-polluting-media-environment-with-garbage.html.

89. Sainato, "Rachel Maddow Asserts Russian Government Incited 'Bot Attack'"; Michael Sainato, "HuffPost Smears Sanders Supporters with Fake News about Russian Trolls: Motivated by Personal Bias, Journalists Mislead with Anecdotal Evidence," *Observer*, March 15, 2017, observer.com/2017/03/huffington-post-facebook-trolls-bernie-sanders/; Ryan Grim and Jason Cherkis, "Bernie Sanders' Campaign Faced a Fake News Tsunami. Where Did It Come From?: The Trolls Set Out to Distract and Divide the Invigorated Left," Huffington Post, March 11, 2017, updated March 13, 2017, www.huffingtonpost.com/entry/bernie-sanders-fake-news-russia_us_58c34d97e4b0ed71826cdb36.

90. Borchers, "Millennials Don't Like Trump."

91. Bernish, "Red Alert: Corporate Media's War"; Jessica Guynn, "Mark Zuckerberg: Facebook Fake News Didn't Sway Election," *USA Today*, November 10, 2016, updated November 11, 2016, http://www.usatoday.com/story/tech/news/2016/11/10/mark-zuckerberg-facebook-fake-news-didnt-sway-election/93622620/.

92. Hayley Tsukayama, "Facebook will Start Telling You When a Story may be Fake," *Washington Post*, December 15, 2016, https://www.washingtonpost.com/news/the-switch/wp/2016/12/15/facebook-will-start-telling-you-when-a-story-may-be-fake/.

93. George Gallanis, "Facebook's 'Fake News' Measures: A Move Toward Censorship," World Socialist Web Site, December 17, 2016, http://www.wsws.org/en/articles/2016/12/17/face-d17.html.

94. Ibid.; Peter Kafka, "Facebook has Started to Flag Fake News Stories," Recode, March 4, 2017, http://www.recode.net/2017/3/4/14816254/facebook-fake-news-disputed-trump-snopes-politifact-seattle-tribune.

95. Tsukayama, "Facebook will Start Telling You"; Mary Papenfuss, "Facebook Cracks Down on 30,000 Fake News Accounts Ahead of French Election: The Social Media Company is Taking Out Full-Page Newspaper Ads with Tips for Spotting Untrustworthy Sites," Huffington Post, April 14, 2017, www.huffingtonpost.com/entry/fake-facebook-french-election_us_58f168f4e4b0da2ff860febe; Alyssa Newcomb, "Facebook Just Rolled Out Its Fake News Tool," NBC News, March 6, 2017, www.nbcnews.com/tech/tech-news/facebook-just-rolled-out-its-fake-news-tool-n729616.

96. Ibid.

97. Julia Angwin and Hannes Grassegger, "Facebook's Secret Censorship Rules Protect White Men from Hate Speech but Not Black Children," ProPublica, June 28, 2017, https://www.propublica.org/article/facebook-hate-speech-censorship-internal-documents-algorithms.

98. Ibid.

99. Ibid.

100. Jennifer Calfas, "Dan Rather on Trump: 'These are Not Normal Times,'" The Hill, January 22, 2017, http://thehill.com/blogs/blog-briefing-room/news/315555-dan-rather-on-trump-these-are-not-normal-times.

101. Mencken, *In Defense of Women*, 53.

CHAPTER 3

Media Democracy in Action

Contributions by Rachael Jolley (Index on Censorship), Chase
Palmieri (Tribeworthy), Mahsood Ebrahim and Julianne Rodriguez
(Citrus College), Kevin Gosztola and Rania Khalek (Unauthorized
Disclosure), and Gennie Gebhart (Electronic Frontier Foundation);
introduction by Andy Lee Roth

*Changes in consciousness take place beneath the surface
of action. And so they're hard to measure. But every
once in a while they break out, they break through to the
surface. And only then do you realize that a change in
consciousness has taken place.*

—Howard Zinn[1]

The late historian Howard Zinn's basic concern, he once explained,
was to document "the countless small actions of unknown people"
that lie at the roots of history's "great moments."[2] His *People's History
of the United States*—first published in 1980 and now available in multiple editions and translations—epitomized that insight and provided
substantial documentary evidence for it, leading Noam Chomsky to
observe that Zinn's book "literally changed the consciousness of a
generation."[3]

First appearing in Project Censored's 2004 yearbook, the annual
Media Democracy in Action chapter can be read as an ongoing effort
to document the kind of breakthroughs described by Zinn in the epi-
graph above, with a special focus on "the surface of action" where
independent journalism and social activism intersect.

Whether it is voiced by pundits and scholars or reflected in polls of
public opinion, concern for the content and quality of news reporting
tends to focus on news that is broadcast or published by journalism's

corporate giants. The result of this narrow focus is a perspective on news media that mirrors the "great man" theory of history, which achieved prominence in the nineteenth century.[4] Thus, applied to news and journalism, the decisive players are an increasingly concentrated group of for-profit businesses, such as ABC, CBS, NBC, CNN, Fox News, and MSNBC in broadcasting; and the *New York Times*, *Washington Post*, and *USA Today*, among others, in print.

Just as Howard Zinn's *People's History* sought to show the centrality of otherwise "unknown people" and their "countless small actions" in the making of human history, we understand that there is more to the news of the world than the reporting of establishment journalism. Progressive scholars have identified and analyzed how an increasingly robust "networked fourth estate" provides both an alternative and a challenge to "legacy" media.[5] That understanding informs Project Censored's conception of "media democracy in action"—a vision of journalism as a progressive social movement, not limited to professional reporters or bound by establishment conventions of depersonalization and balance.[6]

Leading off this year's chapter is Rachael Jolley of the Index on Censorship. Established in 1972, the Index has been an inspiration, a source of crucial information, and a valued ally for Project Censored. In the first issue of the *Index on Censorship*, published in March 1972, Stephen Spender acknowledged the possibility that a publication of this sort might become "a bulletin of frustration." By contrast, he asserted, "the material by writers which is censored in Eastern Europe, Greece, South Africa and other countries is among the most exciting that is being written today."[7] That assessment applies equally to the diversity and scope of the Index's programs today, as Jolley, the journal's current editor, succinctly shows. For instance, she describes how the Index's Turkey Uncensored program is using digital technology and social networks to allow Turkish writers, artists, cartoonists, and photographers to share stories that cannot be told inside their country, and to extend the reach of these stories to a wider, global audience.

Similarly, Chase Palmieri of Tribeworthy describes how that California-based startup is harnessing the technological power of social media (and its popularity) in order to develop new ways of vetting news stories. As he describes, "crowd contested media" provide a means for members of the public to organize and identify potential problems in the news coverage of any given topic. In turn, this serves as a way to counter the top-down relationship between producers and consumers that was characteristic of legacy *mass* media. As an innovative social media platform, Tribeworthy provides new ways for the public to engage in meaningful dialogue, with one another and with news workers.

The need to hold news organizations accountable—whether they are corporate-owned or independent—is likely self-evident to anyone reading this book. What's less clear is *how* to do so with limited time and resources, as a grassroots "citizen journalist." In their article on newspaper coverage of police use of body cameras, Citrus College students Mahsood Ebrahim and Julianne Rodriguez demonstrate one simple but effective method of analyzing news sources, providing a critical understanding of the ways that "spin" can be used to shape public opinion. Their research investigates how four major national newspapers' decisions about who to feature as newsworthy sources of information and opinion provide a consequential but typically unseen frame for the public's understanding of this controversial topic. Although many of us consume news on a daily basis, as Ebrahim and Rodriguez show, we are more likely to recognize important patterns in news coverage when we engage in systematic inquiry. Notably, though, neither their research methods (content analysis) nor their data (newspaper articles) require graduate-level training or big university research grants in order to generate meaningful findings.

If Ebrahim and Rodriguez's findings serve to confirm what previous media scholars have documented about the narrow range of sources that form the basis for most establishment news reports, then Kevin Gosztola and Rania Khalek's article on their new podcast, *Unauthorized Disclosure*, epitomizes how truly independent media provide a genuine alternative. As Gosztola and Khalek describe, *Unauthorized Disclosure* originated with the goal of providing a platform for those "who speak up about corruption without asking for permission and without regard for whether it fits the script of what is acceptable to debate." With a public hungry for news that reflects a broader range of perspectives than are typically provided by establishment media, crowdfunded news, like *Unauthorized Disclosure* and MintPress News (which we featured in the Media Democracy in Action chapter of *Censored 2017*), is central to the emerging networked fourth estate and its financial sustainability.

A free press, Cory Doctorow has written, "requires access to the full range of press technologies, and that includes the Internet."[8] Few if any organizations have done more than the Electronic Frontier Foundation (EFF) to enhance and protect civil liberties as the use of digital technology grows. In the final article of this chapter, Gennie Gebhart describes a trio of online tools—Privacy Badger, HTTPS Everywhere, and Certbot—that EFF has developed, not only to empower the public to protect their privacy when they use the Internet, but also to provide people with a practical way to "join the movement toward a more private, secure Internet."

Taken together, the contributions to this year's Media Democracy in Action chapter provide a snapshot of a resurgence in journalism and media criticism that independent organizations and individuals are leading. This resurgence promises to counteract the scourge of "fake news," and to refresh the public's faith in the power of journalism to inform us about what matters and how we can organize to make a difference—in our communities, online, and around the world.

INDEX ON CENSORSHIP: "A BEACON FOR PRESENT AND FUTURE STRUGGLES"

Rachael Jolley

Index on Censorship was created in 1972 at the request of Pavel Litvinov and other dissident writers who sought a way to publish work that had been banned in their home nations. Established by a group of leading thinkers which included the poet Stephen Spender, Writers and Scholars International, the parent organization of Index, swiftly began publishing the magazine *Index on Censorship*. From the start, the magazine has provided a place to publish work that had been banned or censored, and for journalism to expose how regimes are trying to keep their citizens from being informed, from protesting, or even from discussing the past.

Index on Censorship has published the words of the famous and celebrated, from Václav Havel to Arthur Miller, as well as unsung journalists and whistleblowers. It publishes on issues as varied as propaganda and film, playwriting, rapping and homophobia, and football chants. Meanwhile, Index as an organization continues to campaign and advocate for change, working with writers, activists, and artists around the world. Through social media, letter-writing campaigns, protests, media appearances, and internationally-acclaimed awards, Index on Censorship brings global attention to any attempts at repression of the freedom of expression.

Mapping Media Freedom

Mapping Media Freedom is a crowd-sourced, Index-led project that collects data on attacks against members of the media in forty-two countries in and around Europe. The attacks documented include threats of physical violence, threats of job loss, censorship, legal action, and attacks on property. Reports are identified and submitted by staff writers, independent journalists, and members of the public. All reports are fact-checked and edited by a core team of investigators prior to publication and mapping online.

Index on Censorship operates this project—which is co-funded by the European Commission—in partnership with the European Federation of Journalists and Reporters Without Borders.

Quarterly reports compile a snapshot of the latest trends in the data. For instance, during the third quarter of 2016, MMF documented that four journalists were killed; 54 incidents of physical assault were reported; 107 media professionals were arrested; 150 were detained and released; 112 reports of intimidation, which includes psychological abuse, sexual harassment, trolling/cyberbullying, and defamation, were confirmed; journalistic work was censored or altered 29 times; and media professionals were blocked from covering a story in 89 cases.

The MMF project collates data that helps to identify trends across the region. The case studies provide examples, enabling Index and other organizations to make a stronger argument about the seriousness of media attacks. While it cannot claim to be comprehensive, the

MMF project does quickly pick up changes in patterns of behavior by governments and others who are attempting to silence the media.

Turkey Uncensored

In 2016, at a time when Turkish newspapers, magazines, and broadcasters were coming under government pressure, and many were closing, the Turkey Uncensored project was created as a platform to publish the work of writers, artists, cartoonists, and photographers who were experiencing extremely difficult working conditions. It was launched in a period when leading journalists were being arrested and forced to flee the country. By September 30, 2016, 98 journalists were arrested and charged, 133 media professionals were detained, 160 media outlets were shut down, and approximately 2,500 journalists lost their jobs, according to Al Jazeera, which collated numbers from Turkish journalism sources.[9]

The project publishes stories that are not being told inside Turkey, but also gives those under threat a chance to talk about the working and political conditions inside the country. Index's Turkey Uncensored team, led by its editor Sean Gallagher, works with Turkish translators to publish stories in English so they can reach a much wider audience globally. In its first quarter, stories from the Turkey Uncensored mini site saw 1,111,748 Twitter impressions and 45,000 page views in six months, showing an enormous interest in the stories. Index also heard from a mother of an imprisoned photojournalist who wanted to thank the organization for keeping what was happening in Turkey in the public eye.

Index is regularly approached by broadcasters to comment on the political situation in Turkey, and we have been able to highlight individual cases and personal stories to document the current state of affairs and to illustrate its personal impacts on specific members of the Turkish media. International media attention can have a significant impact on governments, and it is important to make sure that the attacks on those working in the Turkish media are not ignored internationally.

Magazine Issue: Staging Shakespearean Dissent

The spring 2016 issue of *Index on Censorship* magazine featured a themed report on plays that protest, provoke, and slip by the censors, using the 400th anniversary of Shakespeare's death to begin the discussion.

Articles were commissioned from Brazil, India, South Africa, Turkey, Hungary, the USA, and the UK. Authors were asked to look at how Shakespeare rattles and toys with audiences, confronts and provokes, and sometimes squeezes controversial subjects past authorities without their noticing. Actor and author Simon Callow wrote about how Shakespeare was banned by Stalin and (partly) embraced by the Nazis. Academic Preti Taneja looked at how theater makers in Kosovo and Serbia had put together a dual-language production of *Romeo and Juliet*, the first production to be sponsored by both governments. Playwright Elizabeth Zaza Muchemwa wrote about how Shakespeare slips by the limits of the censors in Zimbabwe.

The magazine provoked a themed debate at the prestigious Hay Festival in May 2016, and a second set of events in the USA are due this spring, in Washington, DC, and New York City. The issue's innovative cover design, which combined the Anonymous mask with a portrait of Shakespeare, was also adapted into masks on sticks which have been used as a way of engaging debate at various Index events.

This theme has proved successful at engaging a wide audience in discussions and raising awareness of censorship.

As the *Times Literary Supplement* wrote about *Index on Censorship* magazine in 2016: "When one considers the publication's back catalogue as a corpus, seen in historical context, its worth is hard to deny. It constitutes an archive of past battles won, and a beacon for present and future struggles."

RACHAEL JOLLEY is the editor of *Index on Censorship* magazine. She was awarded specialist editor of the year in the British Society of Magazine Editors awards in 2016.

TRIBEWORTHY: CROWD CONTESTED MEDIA

Chase Palmieri

We often hear the term "media ethics," but what we see in action looks more like "media metrics." A focus on metrics is understandable since the news media is largely a for-profit industry, so its organizations need a way to measure their success. This would not be a problem if some of the metrics guiding media behavior were in the public's best interest. Unfortunately, metrics such as Likes, Shares, Clicks, Views, and advertising revenues do nothing to measure the quality of journalism or the public's trust in it.

It's clear that one way to reform news media is by introducing a new metric that aligns the interests of news consumers and news producers. This new metric would be the people's measure of media success, and would therefore require input from the public. News-gathering would become more interactive as users hold journalists and news outlets accountable for bias, logical fallacies, and mistakes. We at Tribeworthy call this new approach "Crowd Contested Media."

Before explaining how Crowd Contested Media can solve the problem of news source accountability, it's important to understand a few of the other proposed solutions. Platforms such as Google and Facebook are considering the use of algorithms to decide what is true or false in journalism, and therefore what you will or will not see. This inherently leads to some form of censorship.

Facebook also recently partnered with third-party fact-checking organizations in an effort to attach disclaimers to contested articles in users' News Feeds, which is useful only when the organizations agree on an unreliable article before it spreads everywhere. But what about all the other articles they don't get to review? What about articles riddled with logical fallacies, biases, or mistakes, even if those do not amount to "fake" news? Websites such as Snopes and PolitiFact can't scale to meet the challenge because fact-checkers in their organization simply can't read and evaluate the never-ending stream of new information fast enough. Perhaps fact-checking organizations' greatest challenge is winning the public's trust amidst questions of their own bias, political agendas, and corporate ownership. Fact-checking the world's news is a nearly impossible feat to expect from any single organization, and a task we at Tribeworthy don't feel comfortable outsourcing to an algorithm.

To address any skepticism about a crowdsourced solution, consider the online platforms Rotten Tomatoes and Yelp. Rotten Tomatoes's rating does not mean someone will enjoy 89 percent of a given movie, but this serves as a benchmark that can be compared with other rated movies. The consumer can decide his or her own cut-off point. For example, perhaps a person won't spend time on a movie rated less than 75 percent unless it comes recommended from a trusted source or friend. The same applies to Yelp. Yelp is not saying people will have a five-star experience at a restaurant with that rating, it's simply showing the general experience of those who came before. Although it's not a perfect system, because everyone has his or her own tastes and preferences, we still find it useful when deciding where to eat. Believe it or not, there was a time when people would watch movies and eat at restaurants without leaving their feedback. That's where we are today with online news. When people come across an article they don't trust, often the first thing they do is exit the page. The next reader is just as vulnerable because the previous visitor did nothing to warn them. What if the previous person could have helped by alerting subsequent readers to potential problems? People tend to build trust online by seeing the un-incentivized feedback of their peers, yet no organization is currently using this phenomenon to tackle one of today's most distrusted industries—the news media.

So why is Crowd Contested Media the answer? Just as Rotten Tomatoes and Yelp serve as a feedback loop to improve their respective industries, we at Tribeworthy believe online news is the next industry in need of mass accountability. We are not a fact-checking organization, but a platform for news consumers to organize together and identify potential problems within any given article. The reviews create a trust rating for each article, author, and news outlet. By aggregating user reviews, we're able to create a rating page that serves as consumer protection for those gathering information online. The rating page shows how people have rated the article's significance as well as the top three most reviewed problems found within the article (e.g., red herring fallacy, religious bias, and misused terminology), and user explanations for each problem identified. This is a different approach to critiquing the news, and it's based upon our belief that all information should be made available and that sunlight is the best disinfectant.

More than just protecting each other as news consumers, authors and news outlets need a proper feedback mechanism to improve the quality of their work. Some authors read the comments section of their articles, but comments are usually lacking in constructive criticism. In fact, many websites are getting rid of their comments sections altogether, which means they're relying even more on the traffic metrics discussed earlier.

Until recently, the media has always been a one-way conversation. The *mass* media talked at us and we complained when they made mistakes. That's been the way it's worked for a long time, but the Internet has given each of us a voice. With *social* media, we can talk back in a dialogue with a news media that has reached record levels of distrust. When the media is unable to hold the powerful accountable, the public must hold the media accountable. Stated another way, we cannot have a reliable media until we have a liable media.

As with any crowdsourcing platform, Tribeworthy and Crowd Contested Media will live or die based on people's willingness to contribute. It's our job to arm society with the most effective and easy-to-use tool, and to make sure this tool is ready when the people decide they have had enough.

CHASE PALMIERI is a self-described news junkie who serves as CEO and cofounder of Tribeworthy.com, the home of Crowd Contested Media. Chase and his team are building trust among online news consumers by holding authors and news outlets accountable with a review system similar to Yelp and Rotten Tomatoes.

NEWSPAPER COVERAGE OF POLICE BODY-WORN CAMERAS

Mahsood Ebrahim and Julianne Rodriguez

Police use of body-worn cameras (BWCs) is on the rise.[10] With the safety of police officers and civilians constantly in question, police departments and the public alike have turned to this new technology in hopes of minimizing police use of force, reducing citizens' com-plaints, and increasing police accountability and legitimacy.[11] In this article, we report the main findings from research conducted at Citrus College in Fall 2016 on news coverage of police use of BWCs. Stories on the topic were prominent in the news during this time. These stories reflected a range of official perspectives on police use of BWCs; simultaneously, this news coverage helped set an agenda for public debate about the pros and cons of BWCs.[12]

We looked at news coverage to determine how the officials, experts, and advocates who were quoted in these reports justified support for, or opposition to, police BWCs. We identified recurring arguments made by both supporters and opponents of BWCs. We also analyzed one significant aspect of the debate that most news coverage failed to emphasize—the economic interests shaping the increasing preva-lence of BWCs in daily police department operations across the US. Who benefits financially as departments adopt this new technology? And why was this aspect of the issue so marginal in corporate news coverage?

Data and Methods

Our data consist of 111 news stories about police use of BWCs, pub-lished by the *Chicago Tribune, Los Angeles Times, New York Times*, and the *Washington Post* between May and August 2016.[13] Following work by sociologist William Gamson on *media standing*, our analysis focused on sources quoted directly by journalists.[14] With the help of classmates, we coded a total of 1,143 direct quotations. The coding procedure consisted of reading the articles and coding the quoted sources by type and by their positions on BWCs.

Findings

Two hundred and thirty-two quotations from the full data collection dealt specifically with police use of cameras or recordings, and these became the focus of our analysis. Of these quotes, one hundred and twenty-three expressed clear views in support of police use of cam-eras. By contrast, only twenty-one quotes clearly opposed their use.

(The additional eighty-eight quotations that focused on police use of cameras were either neutral or could not be coded with certainty.) The significant prevalence of quotations in support of BWCs is noteworthy: As prior research documents extensively, professional journalists tend to balance pro- and con-positions on controversial issues as one way of displaying objectivity.[15] We will return to discuss the significance of the unusual lack of balance in quoted sources, below.

Our findings are consistent with prior research that has established journalists' overwhelming preference for news sources with *official, bureaucratic* statuses.[16] In our data, 44 percent of those quoted directly were law enforcement officials; 17 percent were other government officials (e.g., city council members or mayors); 17 percent were attorneys; 7 percent were identified as experts (e.g., professors or researchers); and 4 percent were civil liberties advocates (including, for example, spokespersons for the American Civil Liberties Union). Fewer than 10 percent of those quoted were community members, relatives of a victim or suspect, or sources with other, unofficial statuses.

Qualitative content analysis of the data led us to identify *recurring arguments* for and against BWCs. Supporters of BWCs consistently argued that this new technology *promotes transparency*. Supporters argued that, with video recordings, nothing that happened could be hidden or denied. In this view, BWCs *alter behavior*. Being observed deters bad behavior.[17]

By contrast, opponents of BWCs consistently articulated one (or a combination) of five main frames: Cameras *malfunction*, they can be *incorrectly operated*, camera *footage can be manipulated*, BWCs lead to *controversy over making footage public*, and BWCs are a *waste of money*. A full discussion of these themes goes beyond the limits of this brief report. Here, by way of example, we emphasize how opponents of BWCs countered the pro-argument of transparency by emphasizing that video footage is subject to manipulation. For instance, as researchers have documented, the speed of video replay affects viewers' judgments.[18] Thus, opponents of BWCs argued that slow-motion replay gives viewers a false impression that the actor had more time to premeditate before acting.

Overall, our content analysis of who's quoted and the positions they articulated shows how news coverage serves both to reflect the spectrum of official views on the issue and, consequently, to frame the agenda for public debate about it.

What Newspaper Coverage Omitted

BWCs are touted as tools of accountability, but they are also big business. In December 2014, after the shooting death of Michael Brown in Ferguson, Missouri, President Obama pledged $75 million to help police departments across the nation purchase BWCs and train officers in their use. Taser International is best known as a manufacturer of electroshock weapons used by police departments across the US, but it is increasingly investing in and profiting from police demand for BWCs. In the first quarter of 2015, Taser, the leading US manufacturer of body cameras, announced earnings of $6.4 million—up 73 percent from its revenues of $3.7 million in the first quarter of 2014.[19] In 2016, its body-camera revenues increased another 50 percent, to $9.7 million.[20]

In April 2017, Taser rebranded itself as Axon and, at the same time, announced a program to provide free BWCs to every US police officer.[21] As industry analysts have noted, the cameras themselves are just one revenue source. Axon also profits from its proprietary digital storage service, Evidence.com, which allows police departments to host and manage body camera video. As the *Atlantic* reported in April 2015, "The appeal of its business model is that money will come from selling an ongoing subscription service (like Netflix or Spotify) rather than one-time sales of technology made of plastic and glass."[22]

Just one of the 111 newspaper articles in our data set addressed these economic interests. On July 14, 2016, David Gelles of the *New York Times* published a story titled "Company Known for Its Stun Guns Corners the Market for Police Body Cameras."[23] Gelles quoted Taser's chief executive, Patrick W. Smith, on the utility of the company's cameras in terms of transparency: "It's in everyone's interest to know what happened." Noting that demand for BWCs had increased significantly since Michael Brown was shot dead by an officer, Gelles also reported that "analysts now estimate that the market will soon be worth $1 billion a year."

The New York Times reported that Taser was "under fire for questionable business practices," including paying police chiefs to travel to Taser conferences, hiring retired police chiefs who bought Taser products to join the company as consultants, and negotiating contracts with cities without competitive bidding. In brief, Taser/Axon has parlayed its longstanding relationships with police departments who already used its stun guns into cornering the lucrative market for BWCs and video hosting services. As much as the newspaper articles that we examined conveyed a fairly robust debate on the pros and cons of police BWCs, the issue of who profits from their use was almost entirely absent from this news coverage. Readers of the *Chicago Tribune*, *Los Angeles Times*, and *Washington Post* would have had to look to other, independent sources to understand the economic interests at stake, while careful followers of the *New York Times* might have been fortunate enough to see David Gelles's excellent report.

Conclusion

A 2016 Pew Research poll indicated that 66 percent of police officers and 93 percent of the general public favor police BWCs.[24] Similarly, in our data, we found that 85 percent of the directly-quoted sources favored the new technology. Qualitative content analysis of the pro- and con-arguments in the newspaper coverage that we studied shows how advocates focused on one primary frame—transparency—while skeptics deployed a wider variety of arguments to warrant their opposition. Although some opponents argued that police BWCs were a waste of money—because officers might fail to use them correctly or video footage could be manipulated, for example—this is different from addressing BWC programs as lucrative business ventures.

Until news coverage expands to include the economic interests at stake when police departments decide whether or not to use body-worn cameras, the public will remain incompletely informed while Axon and its investors will continue to profit.

ACKNOWLEDGMENTS: We are grateful to our classmates in the Fall 2016 Honors section of Introduction to Sociology at Citrus College for their data coding and insights: Alex Bazaar, Nicolette Bernini, Kellen Chen, James Chiu, Samantha Clifton, Dylan Cline, Amanda

Duvall, Ronald Escalante, Jasmine Gutierrez, Zhari Johnson, Dailee Marquez, Hollie Pelto, Alondra Ponce, Frances Rivera, Melanie Sandoval, Celine Spathias, Josh Uchizono, and Alex Vasquez. We also thank our teacher, Andy Lee Roth, for assistance with background research and editing.

MAHSOOD EBRAHIM is an engineering student in the Honors Program at Citrus College. He is interested in mechanical engineering and plans to pursue a career in aerospace manufacturing upon completing college.

JULIANNE RODRIGUEZ is a student in the Honors Program at Citrus College pursuing a degree in anthropology with an emphasis in culture. She hopes to work as an applied anthropologist in one of the world's developing communities.

THE *UNAUTHORIZED DISCLOSURE* PODCAST: EXPANDING THE BOUNDARIES OF ACCEPTABLE DEBATE

Kevin Gosztola and Rania Khalek

Neither of us had any experience producing podcasts or radio shows. However, we had experience in independent journalism and recognized the potential for a weekly show, which we could co-host, to provide platforms to people who are typically overlooked or ignored by the corporate press.

We called the show "Unauthorized Disclosure" to reclaim a phrase used by the national security agencies and political elites to suppress those who speak up about corruption without asking for permission and without regard for whether it fits the script of what is acceptable to debate.

Our first show featured Paula Swearingen, a mother in West Virginia who was involved in relief efforts after a devastating chemical spill further polluted water in and around the Elk River. Only a few dozen people listened to it when it was posted in January 2014, but it officially marked the launch of our show.

Since then, *Unauthorized Disclosure* has grown tremendously. We have had listeners inform us that our show opened their "small southern US mind up to the misinformation," that it has taught them about "socialism and left politics." We have also had people from outside the US tell us they see our show as a part of the resistance to the malignant presidency of Donald Trump that threatens people all over the globe.

We established ourselves on Patreon and now average two to three thousand downloads per episode. We engage our listeners regularly, giving them opportunities to recommend guests and to influence how we produce the show. Our listeners show us appreciation by pledging to support us on a monthly basis, and we return the appreciation by making sure that each episode delivers sharp insights and a dash of humor, to acknowledge the absurdity of our collective moment.

In an economy with fewer and fewer stable jobs in journalism, the podcast is more than just an opportunity to elevate activists, independent journalists, and citizens with stories to tell and work that deserves greater attention. It also helps to deflect smear campaigns against our work and the work of others.

For example, Rania Khalek has traveled to the Middle East to report on conflicts in Syria, Libya, and Yemen. She traveled to Syria in 2016 with a delegation of Western journalists to attend a conference in Damascus convened by a nongovernmental organization known as the British Syrian Society, which was co-founded by Bashar al-Assad's father-in-law. Her name was added to a program as a speaker without her consent. This happened to multiple journalists, yet after the program circulated she was the only one targeted by a faction of overzealous pro-Syrian rebel advocates.

Their campaign forced Khalek to resign from the editorial board of the Electronic Intifada. She had to leave Damascus and never attended the conference. A prominent progressive media publication refused to publish her reporting. In February 2017, this faction scored another victory by having her speaking event at the University of North Carolina, which was to be hosted by Students for Justice in Palestine (SJP), canceled.

Multiple individuals, from a Turkish state media journalist to a San Francisco politics and international studies professor, endorsed a campaign to destroy a journalist's livelihood. *Unauthorized Disclosure* immediately became a valuable means for beating back this insidious campaign.

On social media platforms, it is far too easy to act as a demagogue, exaggerating and misrepresenting an issue in ways that whip one's followers into a frenzy. Many are comfortable with shaming people, by accusing them of sympathy for war criminals or support for dictators, without citing any proof—often with the intent of damaging their target's professional reputation. When asked to produce proof, they ignore requests or claim they do not need to show evidence because the so-called record is well known. This is much harder to get away with on a podcast or radio show.

Rather than make futile attempts at debate with smear artists or ideological opponents, we use the show to address baseless allegations. We explore what is at the core of these allegations. If there is a kernel of truth to any of the criticism, that kernel is confronted. We are able to deconstruct arguments, positions, and statements that people typically make from the comfort of their computer chair without ever considering whether they should be held responsible.

For example, when there are claims of Russian hacking and hysterical conspiracy theories spread by liberal pundits and Democratic Party operatives, we pause to assess what the truth is, dismissing those who allege we are trolls of the Kremlin. We brush off claims of being pro-Assad because it is far more important to question whether what is unfolding in Syria is well understood, as public understanding could prevent rash escalations of US military intervention. We laugh at those who reflexively label people "Bernie Bros" simply because they engage in principled politics against Democrats. We question campus and university culture and challenge movements not to play into the hands of Far Right forces that wish to fraudulently parade through our country as if they are heroes of free speech.

These kinds of conversations would be nearly impossible in corporate or establishment media. And that is the power of *Unauthorized Disclosure*. It makes it possible for us to defend those unfairly treated as pariahs, to offer a space for a fresh and perceptive conversation in celebration of dissent, and to fearlessly interrogate social and political norms as they are reinforced by both the right and left wing as well as the squishy mealy-mouthed center.

KEVIN GOSZTOLA is cohost of the *Unauthorized Disclosure* podcast and managing editor of Shadowproof.com. He was previously a staff columnist and reporter for

Firedoglake.com. His work has appeared at the *Guardian*, the *Nation*, Salon, AlterNet, and Common Dreams, and he has appeared on *Democracy Now!*, *CounterSpin*, *The Young Turks*, *Uprising*, *The Majority Report*, and Huffpost Live.

RANIA KHALEK is a journalist, political commentator, and cohost of the weekly podcast *Unauthorized Disclosure*. She is known for her reporting on US foreign policy, the Israel–Palestine conflict, the war in Syria, US presidential elections, and the US criminal justice system. Her work has appeared at the *Nation*, FAIR, VICE News, the *Intercept*, AlterNet, Salon, the Electronic Intifada, Al Jazeera, and the Real News.

HOW WE ARE BUILDING THE INTERNET: TOOLS FOR USERS FROM THE ELECTRONIC FRONTIER FOUNDATION

Gennie Gebhart

The Internet is what we make it, and we are facing an increasingly critical crossroads as we decide how to shape its business models and security standards. In response, the Electronic Frontier Foundation is empowering users with tools to protect themselves and join the movement toward a more private, secure Internet.

An Internet Built on Our Decisions

"The Internet commons." "Information wants to be free." "Net neutrality." The terms we use to talk about the Internet can be misleading. Make no mistake, the concepts behind these terms are all worth fighting for—but the way we talk about them is confusing at best. Unlike an ecological commons, the net is not an organic entity. Arguably, the information disseminated online is not capable of "wanting" anything in most senses of the word. And, contrary to the vision of a "neutral" net, the Internet has no natural state to which it must return.

Instead, the Internet is built on decisions—our decisions. There is nothing inevitable about the Internet we have today, or the Internet we could have tomorrow. Today, we inhabit a World Wide Web built with privacy-invasive business models that give users free content in return for surrendering their privacy to large companies and third-party trackers. And even when third parties aren't following us across the web, we often browse on unencrypted connections that make our activity available to anyone snooping on our connection, from government agencies to our Internet service providers (ISPs) to the people we share wireless connections with at Internet cafes or on airplanes.

In response, the Electronic Frontier Foundation is working toward a more responsible advertising economy and a fully encrypted web. The EFF is a member-supported nonprofit that advocates for privacy, security, and freedom of expression online. EFF's solutions to the related-but-separate problems of online tracking and unencrypted web traffic share a core value in common: they both work to increase users' security on the Internet, with the implicit assertion that personal privacy is at the foundation of that security.

Pushing for Responsible Advertising

Nonconsensual third-party tracking is perhaps the greatest threat to privacy and anonymity online. Unfortunately, it is also one of the Internet's bread-and-butter business models. EFF's Privacy Badger is designed to address this.

Third-party tracking—that is, when advertisers and websites track your browsing activity across the web without your knowledge, control, or consent—is an alarmingly widespread practice in online advertising. Privacy Badger is a browser extension for Chrome, Firefox, and Opera that spots and then blocks third-party domains that appear to be tracking a user and spying on their browsing habits.

Although Privacy Badger blocks many ads in practice, it is more a privacy tool than a strict ad blocker. Privacy Badger encourages advertisers to treat users respectfully and anonymously rather than engage in the industry status quo of online tracking. It does this by unblocking content from domains that respect EFF's Do Not Track policy, which states that the participating site will not retain personally identifiable information about users who have expressed that they do not want to be tracked.

Using Privacy Badger is a simple but robust way for individuals to promote responsible advertising—that is, advertising that does not track users without their consent—as a viable model for free web content. As of this writing, more than one million users have downloaded Privacy Badger and joined the call.

Encrypting the Web

Web pages get to your browser in one of two ways: via non-secure HTTP, or via secure HTTPS. The former has serious problems that make it vulnerable to eavesdropping, content hijacking, ad injection, and targeted censorship. On the other hand, HTTPS—which stands for Hypertext Transfer Protocol *Secure*—fixes most of these problems by encrypting web traffic between webservers and your browser.

A collaboration between EFF and the Tor Project, HTTPS Everywhere makes sure your browser uses HTTPS wherever possible. Some websites offer inconsistent support for HTTPS, use unencrypted HTTP as a default, or link from secure HTTPS pages to unencrypted HTTP pages. HTTPS Everywhere fixes these problems by rewriting requests to these sites to use HTTPS, automatically activating encryption and HTTPS protection that might otherwise slip through the cracks.

As of early 2017, half of all website traffic was encrypted with HTTPS. This means we are halfway to EFF's goal to encrypt the entire web—a web that is consistently safer from the security and privacy threats that HTTPS can protect against. To make it to an entirely encrypted web, we need help from every website owner and administrator, including those from small, independent sites.

While HTTPS Everywhere makes encrypted browsing more consistently available to users, EFF's **Certbot** makes moving to HTTPS easy and free for all website owners and administrators. This is particularly good news for advocacy groups, nonprofits, newspapers, and other organizations that want to resist censorship of their websites and surveillance of their users. Certbot is a client for the Let's Encrypt certificate authority (CA). CAs play a crucial identification and verification role in the web encryption ecosystem—and Let's Encrypt is one of the world's largest, having issued nearly forty million certificates as of this writing. Certbot fetches and deploys Let's Encrypt certificates with easy-to-follow, interactive instructions.

More Work to Do

Beyond fending off cookies or encrypting web traffic, these tools from EFF will let you raise your voice in protest. When you join virtually with other people in using these tools, you are taking a stand against how those in power are building the Internet, and you're doing something active to resist the state of web surveillance.

These tools work to put themselves out of the job. Ideally, advertising economies will one day shift away from nonconsensual third-party tracking so as to render Privacy Badger redundant. Similarly, as we move toward the goal of encrypting the entire web, users will hopefully no longer need HTTPS Everywhere to navigate inconsistent encryption. Until then, using Privacy Badger, downloading HTTPS Everywhere, or encrypting one's own website with Certbot are all ways of working toward a collective vision of how we want the web to function by default.

To download **Privacy Badger**, go to https://www.eff.org/privacybadger.

To learn more about EFF's **Do Not Track** policy, go to https://www.eff.org/issues/do-not-track.

To download **HTTPS Everywhere**, go to https://www.eff.org/https-everywhere.

To use **Certbot**, go to https://certbot.eff.org/.

GENNIE GEBHART is a researcher at the Electronic Frontier Foundation. Her work revolves around the conviction that, as access to information and communication technologies expands and becomes more complex, so too do threats to user security and privacy. She focuses primarily on consumer privacy, secure messaging, and international censorship.

Notes

1. *Project Censored The Movie: Ending the Reign of Junk Food News*, directed by Christopher Oscar and Doug Hecker (Hole in the Media Productions, 2013), DVD.
2. See, for example, Noam Chomsky, "Afterword: Howard Zinn's Legacy of Words and Action," in *Agitation with a Smile: Howard Zinn's Legacies and the Future of Activism*, eds. Stephen Bird, Adam Silver, and Joshua C. Yesnowitz (New York: Routledge, 2014), 207–13, quote at 208.
3. Noam Chomsky, "Remembering Howard Zinn," *Resist*, March/April 2010, online at https://chomsky.info/201002.
4. In this view, a few highly influential individuals have decisively shaped human history through their personal charisma, intelligence, or skills. "The History of the world is but the Biography

of great men," Thomas Carlyle, *On Heroes, Hero-Worship, and the Heroic in History* (London: James Fraser, 1841), online at https://www.gutenberg.org/files/1091/1091.txt.

5. See, for example, Yochai Benkler, "WikiLeaks and the Networked Fourth Estate," in *Beyond WikiLeaks: Implications for the Future of Communications, Journalism and Society*, eds. Benedetta Breveni, Arne Hintz, and Patrick McCurdy (New York: Palgrave Macmillan, 2013), 11–34; Andy Lee Roth and Project Censored, "Breaking the Corporate News Frame through Validated Independent News Online," in *Media Education for a Digital Generation*, eds. Julie Frechette and Rob Williams (New York and London: Routledge, 2016), 173–86.

6. Cf. "Media Democracy in Action," *Censored 2017: Fortieth Anniversary Edition*, eds. Mickey Huff and Andy Lee Roth with Project Censored (New York: Seven Stories Press, 2016), 191.

7. Stephen Spender, "With Concern for Those Not Free," *Index on Censorship*, Vol. 1 (March 1972), 11–15, quote at 13.

8. "The full spectrum of activities that compose free speech, a free press, and freedom of assembly cannot be realized without Internet access." Cory Doctorow, *Information Doesn't Want to Be Free: Laws for the Internet Age* (San Francisco: McSweeney's, 2015), 109.

9. Richard Gizbert, "Counting the Closures: Turkey's Media Shutdown," Listening Post (Al Jazeera, English), November 6, 2016, http://www.aljazeera.com/programmes/listeningpost/2016/11/counting-closures-turkey-media-shutdown-161106055258438.html.

10. See, for example, Mike Maciag, "Survey: Almost All Police Departments Plan to Use Body Cameras," Governing, January 26, 2016, http://www.governing.com/topics/public-justice-safety/gov-police-body-camera-survey.html.

11. Barak Ariel, Alex Sutherland, Darren Henstock, et al., "'Contagious Accountability': A Global Multisite Randomized Controlled Trial on the Effect of Police Body-Worn Cameras on Citizens' Complaints against the Police," *Criminal Justice and Behavior*, Vol. 44, No. 2 (February 2017), http://journals.sagepub.com/doi/pdf/10.1177/0093854816668218, 296.

12. On agenda-setting, see Maxwell E. McCombs and Donald L. Shaw, "The Agenda-Setting Function of Mass Media," *Public Opinion Quarterly*, Vol. 36, No. 2 (Summer 1972), 176–87, available online at https://www.unc.edu/~fbaum/teaching/PLSC541_Fall06/McCombs%20and%20Shaw%20POQ%201972.pdf.

13. We collected these stories using ProQuest's National Newspapers Expanded database.

14. As Gamson wrote, journalists grant *media standing* to individuals and organizations who are understood to "speak as or for serious players in any given policy domain: individuals or groups who have enough political power to make a potential difference in what happens." William Gamson, "Media and Social Movements," in *International Encyclopedia of the Social & Behavioral Sciences*, eds. Neil J. Smelser and Paul B. Baltes (Amsterdam: Elsevier Science, 2001), 9468–72, quotes at 9471.

15. See, for example, Robert M. Entman, *Democracy without Citizens: Media and the Decay of American Politics* (Oxford and New York: Oxford University Press, 1990), 30–38.

16. On journalists' preference for official sources, see, for example, Herbert J. Gans, *Deciding What's News: A Study of CBS Evening News, NBC Nightly News, Newsweek, and Time*, 25th Anniversary Edition (Evanston, IL: Northwestern University Press, 2004 [1979]) and David Croteau and William Hoynes, *By Invitation Only: How the Media Limit Political Debate* (Monroe, ME: Common Courage, 1994).

17. As Ariel, et al. write, "The entire premise of BWCs in police operations is to cause a change in behavior through the deterrent effect of being observed," "Contagious Accountability," 308.

18. Eugene M. Caruso, Zachary C. Burns, and Benjamin A. Converse, "Slow Motion Increases Perceived Intent," *Proceedings of the National Academy of Sciences (PNAS)*, Vol. 113, No. 33 (August 16, 2016), http://www.pnas.org/content/113/33/9250.full. For an earlier, insightful study of video footage in the case of the police officers accused of beating Rodney King, see Charles Goodwin, "Professional Vision," *American Anthropologist*, Vol. 96, No. 3 (September 1994), 606–33, available online at http://www.sscnet.ucla.edu/clic/cgoodwin/94prof_vis.pdf.

19. Robinson Meyer, "The Big Money in Police Body Cameras," *Atlantic*, April 30, 2015, https://www.theatlantic.com/technology/archive/2015/04/the-big-money-in-police-body-cameras/392009/.

20. Laurel Wamsley, "Taser Changes Its Name to Axon and Offers Free Body Cameras for Police," NPR, April 7, 2017, http://www.npr.org/sections/thetwo-way/2017/04/07/522878573/we-re-more-than-stun-guns-says-taser-as-it-changes-company-name.

21. Ibid.

22. Meyer, "Big Money in Police Body Cameras."

23. Published online, July 12, 2016, as "Taser International Dominates the Police Body Camera Market," https://www.nytimes.com/2016/07/13/business/taser-international-dominates-the-police-body-camera-market.html.

24. Rich Morin, Kim Parker, Renee Stepler, and Andrew Mercer, "Behind the Badge: Police Views, Public Views," Pew Research Center, January 11, 2017, http://www.pewsocialtrends.org/2017/01/11/police-views-public-views/.

CHAPTER 4

The New American Authoritarianism
How the Corporate Media Normalized Racism in 2016

Nolan Higdon and Nicholas L. Baham III

The corporate media coverage of President-elect Donald Trump introduced a national audience to the names, views, policies, and proposals associated with US racism, while simultaneously shattering the myth that the election of the first black president, Barack Obama, ushered in "a post-racial society." On television, viewers were stalked by stories of race, such as the Mall of America boycott over a black Santa Claus, a Victoria's Secret employee removing two young female customers because they were black, and the white privilege diatribe of a customer justifying her Trump vote to two black Chicago cashiers.[1] In between these stories, racist pundits and commentators such as Jeffrey Lord and Corey Lewandowski of CNN, Tomi Lahren of *The Blaze*, and conservative commentator Ann Coulter had their views treated as reasonable discourse on nightly news shows.[2] Meanwhile, US politicians continued to normalize hate and racism, with claims that Democratic House member Keith Ellison is an anti-Semite because he is a Muslim, that non-white immigrants pose a threat to the national economy and security, and that a DREAMer, an undocumented immigrant who was earning an engineering degree, should leave the US.[3]

In addition to seeing it on their television sets, US citizens also witnessed racism hiding in plain sight. There were nearly one thousand hate crimes documented by the Southern Poverty Law Center against "people of color, Muslims, gays, lesbians and others" in the month after Trump's victory.[4] These were accompanied by celebrations of white supremacy in communities nationwide, including North Carolina, where the Ku Klux Klan held a celebration parade; Washington, DC, where National Policy Institute members met to give Nazi salutes while chanting "Hail Trump! Hail our people! Hail victory!"; California, where KKK members held a "White Lives Matter" rally; and Montana, where white nationalists publicly targeted Jews.[5]

INTRODUCTION

At the center of these stories and controversies was Donald Trump, a business mogul turned television star, who became president of the United States. On the campaign trail, Trump and his staff tweeted neo-Nazi memes and messages, appeared on white nationalists' radio shows, and made anti-Semitic remarks regarding Jews and the banking industry.[6] Trump has garnered support from David Duke, the former Imperial Wizard of the Ku Klux Klan, and Richard B. Spencer, the leader of the National Policy Institute, which describes itself as "an independent organization dedicated to the heritage, identity, and future of people of European descent in the United States, and around the world."[7] Although Trump disavowed the support of many hate groups publicly, his campaign openly engaged in fascist tactics reminiscent of Benito Mussolini's Italy, Francisco Franco's Spain, and Adolf Hitler's Germany: patriotic preaching of nationalism, nonrecognition of human rights, development of scapegoats for domestic problems, megalomania of the leader, and control of mass media for propaganda purposes.[8] The scapegoats of Trump's brand of fascism were feminists, immigrants, Muslims, Arabs, Mexicans, African Americans, liberals, and the nation of China, in addition to other nations and peoples.[9] Like the fascist leaders in twentieth-century Europe, Trump tapped into people's fear and hysteria regarding economic issues and episodes of violence such as the 2015 attacks in Paris, France, and San Bernardino, California.[10] In fact, even the Philippines' fascist president, Rodrigo Duterte, praised Trump's electoral victory.[11]

Trump's victory depended on the classic elements of 1930s fascism in which racism and the central tenets of militarism, authoritarianism, censorship, and surveillance were all normalized. Teju Cole of the *New York Times Magazine* wrote after Trump's victory, "All around were the unmistakable signs of normalization in progress. So many were falling into line without being pushed. It was happening at tremendous speed, like a contagion."[12] In fact, upwards of half the US population believed that torture, a practice denounced by human rights advocates and the United Nations Universal Declaration of Human Rights, could produce actionable intelligence.[13] These proclivities were emblematic of a nation normalizing a fascist regime.[14]

After the presidential election, Trump's pivot to fascism was immediately evident. Trump filled his cabinet with hawkish generals known for their bellicose rhetoric and support of fascist ideas, as well as white supremacists and anti-Semitic advisors like Steve Bannon, Michael Flynn, and Jeff Sessions.[15] For example, Flynn's son worked on the Trump campaign while remaining active on white nationalist social media platforms.[16] Trump's decision to stockpile his cabinet with advisors and generals who revel in violence and fearmongering further underscored his fascist proclivities.[17]

How did America elect a fascist? Francis Wilkinson of *Bloomberg* and scholars Jonathan Haidt, Jonathan Jost, and John Dean have argued that the manner in which a candidate addresses voters' perceived morals matters more than actual issues in predicting how citizens will vote.[18] Similarly, Alexander Zaitchik, in his 2016 book, *The Gilded Rage: A Wild Ride through Donald Trump's America*, argues that Trump tapped into people's real anger and promised to restore a fair system to a disoriented working class fed up with both parties and narrowly focused on issues of economics and class.[19] Collectively, this research begs other questions such as: *How in the post–Civil Rights era and during the reign of the first self-identified African-American president in US history did racism become normalized?* Media scholar Robert McChesney points out that during the election the US media did not examine racism or racists critically.[20] As a result, racist discourse was normalized, which in turn further legitimated racism.

How did this happen? In the US, the press is tasked with investigating people and institutions of power, while providing voters essential information for making sound decisions in the voting booth. Democracy depends on a well-informed populace. However, in an effort to garner ratings and advertiser funds at the expense of the democratic process, the US media normalized racism by providing precious media time and space to racists.[21] As this chapter analyzes, the media normalized the racism associated with Trump's brand of fascism because:

▸ They lacked the intellectual skills and content to think critically about race;

▸ Their coverage of Trump increased their advertiser revenues;

▸ They valued access to the new administration; and

▸ They falsely believed that racist arguments would collapse under their own weight.

By having so many racist guests and commentators on their programming, racists became household names and their perspective was seen as a legitimate discourse. As the corporate media relied on Trump for coverage, he was able to dictate what the press covered. This included once-fringe elements of the Internet and radio programming becoming assimilated into mainstream discussions. In fact, just as Trump normalized the racist views from various hate groups, the corporate press normalized the news stories and figures that "informed" Trump and the various groups who supported him.

THE PRESS AND TRUMP'S BRAND OF FASCISM

The media's inability to illuminate the racist rhetoric of Trump's brand of fascism was a contemporary example of the historical relationship between the media, racism, and authoritarianism. Media elites, as cultural producers, are uniquely situated to disseminate narratives that can undermine or normalize racist rhetoric employed by an authoritarian regime. Undermining racist rhetoric can lead to media cultivating resistance to authoritarianism; conversely, normalizing racist rhetoric can empower an authoritarian candidate and their supporters. For example, the Ku Klux Klan (KKK), a traditionally Southern organization, was reinvigorated to expand throughout the North after the film *Birth of a Nation* was released in 1915. The film celebrated the KKK for saving the South from people of color. In fact,

the burning of a cross, which was added for dramatic effect by the director D.W. Griffith, was replicated and adopted by the KKK in the century since the film's release.[22]

Authoritarian regimes have historically understood the power of media and have sought to control media as a way to legitimize their power. For example, the Nazis manipulated print media and popular films by forcing media producers to repeat anti-Semitic lies and absurdities, making it difficult for reason to win.

There is a long history of the US press working with the US government and fascist regimes. For example, there was significant support for fascism in the US during the 1930s.[23] The support was so strong that Major General Smedley Butler was offered thousands of dollars by business leaders to raise an army, overthrow the president, and install a fascist regime.[24] In the 1930s, when fascism consumed Europe, US news outlets such as the *Saturday Evening Post, New York Herald Tribune,* Cleveland *Plain Dealer, Time, Chicago Tribune,* and the

New York Times offered little acknowledgment or critical perspective on the human rights abuses and toxic environment established by these governments. In fact, some of these US media outlets even hailed the rise of these governments as restoring "normalcy" in the economy and defeating political parties on the far left of the political spectrum.[25] Similarly, newly declassified documents revealed that conservative icon William Buckley and his magazine, the *National Review*, sought to legitimize the US-backed coup in Chile that established fascist and genocidal leader Augusto Pinochet as president from 1973 to 1990.[26] Buckley's articles covered up the thousands of individuals murdered in Chile under Pinochet's rule, and two others who were murdered in Washington, DC, in a car bombing that Pinochet ordered. Buckley wanted to promote the false narrative that Pinochet's right-wing assault on leftists was promoting freedom. As a result, he helped cover up a litany of human rights abuses and thousands of dead bodies.[27]

Similarly, the twenty-first-century corporate press has largely avoided calling Trump a "racist" or "fascist," despite glaring examples such as Trump's "birther" campaign, which sought to "prove" that Obama, the first self-identified black president of the US, was not a US citizen.[28] Even when news outlets mentioned the connection between Trump's campaign and "fascism," they were accompanied by declarations that "fascism died in the mid-twentieth century," which ignored the contemporary xenophobic behavior associated with Trump's campaign and neofascist groups in Europe (including ones supported by the US Department of State in the Ukrainian coup of 2014).[29] Others dismissed the connection completely. In a March 2016 *Newsweek* article, Matthew Cooper, who worked with the White House to garner support for the 2003 invasion of Iraq, argued that Trump's policies would not succeed because "Trump isn't Hitler. He isn't a fascist either . . . Trump's more likely to end up like Jimmy Carter."[30]

Rather than use the term "racist" or "fascist" to describe Trump and his supporters, the corporate press adopted the normalizing term "alt-right," which was coined by Richard Spencer.[31] A prominent figure of the "alt-right" movement, Milo Yiannopoulos, argued that the movement was made up of "young intellectuals," not "old-school racist skinheads."[32] *The Washington Post* described the alt-right as "a largely online movement of right-wing ideologies that presents itself as an alternative to mainstream conservatives."[33] However, the term "alt-right" only distinguishes Trump's fascism from traditional interpretations of US conservatism without illuminating the historical underpinnings of "fascism." This has prevented the corporate press from explaining to citizens the absurdity of Trump's contention that the US can go back to a pre–Civil Rights moment and "Make America White Again." Furthermore, without using historically grounded terms such as "fascism," the corporate press has been unable to specify that Trump's appeal was rooted in some individuals' desires to return to a state of unbridled white male supremacy. Chicana feminist Elizabeth "Betita" Martínez defines white supremacy as "an historically based, institutionally perpetuated system of exploitation and oppression of continents, nations, and peoples of color by white peoples and nations of the European continent, for the purpose of maintaining and defending a system of wealth, power, and privilege."[34]

WHY DO CORPORATE MEDIA NORMALIZE RACISM?

Media scholar Robert McChesney points out that the news media should function as a check and balance on elites and their power—in other words, the idea of the media as the Fourth Estate. However, the corporate press did not act as a check and balance on Trump's racist and xenophobic campaign, but were instead consistently critical of progressive movements such as Occupy Wall Street and Black Lives Matter for not having a digestible message and partaking in alleged violence and property damage.[35]

A crucial component of the media's normalization of racism on the Left and the Right was their ignorance about the realities of race and racism in the US. For example, CNN employed Trump supporter Jeffrey Lord, who argued, without any historical context, that the Ku Klux Klan sought to "further the progressive agenda."[36] Similarly, although they deny their racism, there were many racists in the press such as CNN's Jeffrey Lord and Fox's Bill O'Reilly who refused to denounce racism or recognize white privilege, which David Wellman defines as "a system of advantage based on race."[37] Also, there were many self-described liberals in media who denounced racism but still practiced it. For example, MSNBC denounced racism as a talking point for the Democratic Party, but covered the 2016 presidential election with an all-white pundit panel after firing African-American commentator Melissa Harris-Perry.[38] Even when people of color were invited to speak on issues of race in corporate media, they tended to be modern-day manifestations of Booker T. Washington's accommodationist philosophy, like Michael Eric Dyson, who supported the dominant "color-blind" market-driven policies of neoliberal candidates.[39]

Another factor enabling the corporate media's normalization of racism was their pursuit of advertiser funding. Advertisers base their decision to fund a news program on the average number of viewers. Trump turned out to be a ratings gold mine. In fact, Les Moonves, chairman of the board, president, and CEO of CBS, admitted that Trump coverage led to increased profits when he noted, "I've never seen anything like this, and this [is] going to be a very good year for us . . . Sorry. It's a terrible thing to say. But, bring it on, Donald. Keep going . . . [I]t may not be good for America, but it's damn good for CBS."[40] Trump was given three times the amount of airtime as Clinton and eighty-one times the coverage received by Democratic presidential primary candidate Bernie Sanders, a self-professed socialist.[41] That equates to two billion dollars in free coverage for Trump's brand of fascism.[42] CNN earned an estimated $1 billion and Fox News earned approximately $1.5 billion from their election coverage.[43] This served to reinforce Trump as a household name and to normalize his extraordinary beliefs and policies.

Tied closely to their pursuit of advertising revenue, the corporate media normalized racism at the expense of journalistic integrity in order to maintain access to the Trump administration. The Donald's trump card for controlling the press has been his threat to cut off its access to him and his staff. Once Trump's brand of fascism became mainstream, the corporate media sought to accept and normalize it rather than critically analyze it. For example, CBS's *60 Minutes* correspondent Lesley Stahl provided the first extensive interview of Trump after he was elected president. Media Matters explains that Stahl asked "softball questions, fixating on Trump's personal feelings about becoming president, and repeatedly minimizing Trump's most dangerous promises as mere campaign talk."[44] MSNBC, CNN,

Fox, and the *Atlantic* among others featured guests who argued that what Trump said on the campaign trail was irrelevant because it was just part of the campaign.[45] National Public Radio avoided a critical discussion of Breitbart's racism when it interviewed Breitbart senior-editor-at-large Joel Pollak.[46]

The apathetic approach of the press allowed Trump to use his wealth, celebrity status, and business connections to control their message. For example, Trump has been able to request and hold off-the-record meetings with the corporate press to dictate his wishes on their coverage.[47] In fact, Trump's handlers controlled the press by forcibly removing journalists who asked unfavorable questions.[48] In a grand example of the problematic cozy relationship between the press and politicians, Trump worked with the Right Side Broadcasting Network (RSBN), pejoratively known as "Trump TV," during the campaign. It sought to undermine news outlets that criticized Trump. RSBN will be able to continue its discredited work from the White House because it was one of the privileged news outlets allowed access to White House press conferences.[49]

A final factor enabling the corporate media's normalization of racism was pundits' false belief that racist arguments would collapse under their own weight. Since the 1970s, plutocrats and associated conservative organizations, such as the Heritage Foundation, the American Enterprise Institute, and the Manhattan Institute, have been frustrated by their inability to garner support for their conservative policies and views among the public. Rather than tweak their arguments to fit the evidence, they attacked the news media as being too biased or liberal for exposing the weaknesses in their conservative arguments and policies.[50] This resulted in many news commentators becoming fearful that their jobs might be in jeopardy if they appeared too liberal. In fact, Gerard Baker, the editor-in-chief of the *Wall Street Journal*—the newspaper with the second-largest circulation in the US—said his paper would not call out Trump's lies because by doing so "you run the risk that you look like you are, like you're not being objective."[51] The chilling effect of these attacks on media has resulted in a false equivalency between criticisms and biases. As a result, racists in media are treated as if their perspective is grounded in a legitimate, fact-based argument. Jean-Paul Sartre in *Anti-Semite and Jew* wrestled with these same themes of illegitimate debate in regards to anti-Semitism. Sartre urged readers:

> Never believe that the anti-Semites are completely unaware of the absurdity of their replies. They know that their remarks are frivolous, open to challenge. But they are amusing themselves, for it is their adversary who is obliged to use words responsibly, since he believes in words. The anti-Semites have the *right* to play. They even like to play with discourse for, by giving ridiculous reasons, they discredit the seriousness of the interlocutors. They delight in acting in bad faith, since they seek not to persuade by sound argument but to intimidate and disconcert.[52]

Sartre's work highlighted the impossibility of using reason against anti-Semites because their beliefs were not grounded in reason but in passion. This encapsulates the false debates that the corporate media set up between pro- and anti-Trump voices. It's impossible for the anti-Trump voices to deploy reason because Trump's supporters simply respond with lies, absurdities, and unreasoned passion. Examples of these absurd statements include the notion that Mexicans were taking good American jobs; that a wall along the US–Mexico border would solve issues associated with immigration; and that a Muslim registry would eliminate violence in the US.[53] These claims were completely false, but highlighting this falsehood will result in the messenger being labeled as biased or a liberal.

In direct opposition to Sartre's claim that anti-Semitic irrationality—and by extension, racist irrationality—prevents reason from changing one's perspective, the corporate media continued to provide "false balancing" for racists in their news broadcasts. For example, the BBC surprised a guest, writer Chimamanda Ngozi Adichie, with a debate against a Trump supporter. Adichie was infuriated that the BBC provided space for the supporter's views, a white man who tried to determine if Trump had inflamed racism.[54] Some in the corporate media have called out their industry for normalizing racism through false balancing. Margaret Sullivan, former *New York Times* ombudsman and current media columnist for the *Washington*

Post, noted her frustration: "[T]his perceived need to push for 'fairness' for Trump—as if he has been mistreated or put at a disadvantage—baffles me."[55] Although numerous individuals in the media, such as Soledad O'Brien, formerly of CNN, and Micheline Maynard of *Forbes*, have noted that false equivalency in election coverage normalized racism, the corporate media continued to make special concessions to allow Trump to break institutional practices and normalize racism. Heather Digby Parton of Salon reported that TV news organizations ". . . happily let him call in rather than appear on camera and give him hours of airtime in the hope that he'll say something newsworthy which, to be honest, he often does. His lies and reversals were so constant and so blatant that reporters seem to be almost paralyzed as he slithers and slides out of their grasp."[56]

The corporate media's efforts to "balance" anti-Trump voices with Trump supporters created a platform for the once-fringe elements of Internet and radio programming to become mainstream. It is critical to understand that Trump is emblematic of US racism, but is neither its founder nor its last remnant. Renée Graham of the *Boston Globe* notes that, "[F]or all his unrepentant xenophobia and misogyny, Trump invented none of the social afflictions that propelled him to the White House."[57] In fact, since Obama's election, the Southern Poverty Law Center has warned that white nationalist groups, "the hatemongers, the nativists and the antigovernment zealots," were expanding into the thousands, and not only advocating and lobbying, but also inflicting violence.[58] Trump was able to tap into many of these groups' concerns by espousing numerous unsubstantiated claims that cycle through the Internet and radio programming across the country: for instance, claims that Obama was not born in America, that William Ayers wrote Obama's autobiography, that Supreme Court Justice Antonin Scalia was murdered, that US Senator Ted Cruz's father was involved in the JFK assassination, that thousands of Muslims celebrated 9/11 in New Jersey, and that Syrian refugees were only sent to Republican-controlled states.[59] Trump took these ideas from, and became a darling of, figures like Alex Jones. Jones, a radio host whose program is broadcast on 140 stations, focuses on government and elite conspiracies, promoting numerous unsubstantiated stories and distorted claims that empower white supremacist groups.[60]

Jones amplifies his message through postings on his websites, Prison Planet and Infowars.[61] Jones claims that Trump converses with him, including calling him when Trump won the presidency.[62] Other examples of racist media outlets informing and supporting Trump included Breitbart News, whose former chairman, Steve Bannon, became Trump's campaign manager.[63]

Just as Trump normalized the racist views and claims from various hate groups, the corporate press normalized the news stories and figures that "inform" these groups. Victor Pickard in *Jacobin* argues that "through false equivalence and a lack of substantive policy coverage, the media elevated a far-right politics that should've been delegitimized the moment it reared its head."[64] For example, Fox News hosts such as Sean Hannity were notorious for taking Alex Jones and Breitbart News stories and using them for television fodder.[65] At the roast of actor Rob Lowe on Comedy Central, Ann Coulter treated racists connected with Trump as modern-day Archie Bunkers whose hatred and ignorance were loveable and comedic.[66] When Tomi Lahren, then host of her own show at conservative media site *The Blaze*, appeared on *The Daily Show*, host Trevor Noah rewarded her racist rant, which seeped with white privilege, with cupcakes backstage.[67] The loveable bigot concept is perceived as such a ratings booster that the TV channel A&E announced plans to produce a "reality" show titled "Generation KKK."[68]

The corporate press's capitulation to Trump's brand of fascism allowed for racism to be normalized in the US. Central to the normalization of racism was the news media's dissemination of Trump's absurd statements accompanied by dialogues with anti-Trump liberal voices that unsuccessfully attempted to use reason to counter the claims of Trump and his spokespersons and supporters. The corporate press's dependence on Trump for access and advertising revenues enabled him to dictate what the press covered. As Trump's stories filled more time and space, the false information he garnered from various Internet and radio programs, as well as those who espouse these lies, became mainstream. Their views, not grounded in reason, were disseminated by Trump and legitimized by the corporate press.

CONCLUSION: THE IMPACT OF TRUMP ON THE PRESS

Perhaps the most devastating impact of the media's false equivalence of reason and racist passion is the tacit acceptance of what comedian and social critic Stephen Colbert in 2005 called "truthiness." Ben Zimmer, writing in the *New York Times Magazine* in October 2010, noted Colbert's inspired recognition of "truthiness" in the conservative media:

> During the rehearsal, Colbert was stuck on what term to feature for the inaugural segment of "The Word," a spoof of Bill O'Reilly's "Talking Points." Originally, he and the writers selected the word *truth*, as distinguished from those pesky *facts*. But as Colbert told me in a recent interview (refreshingly, he spoke to me as the real Colbert and not his alter ego), *truth* just wasn't "dumb enough." "I wanted a silly word that would feel wrong in your mouth," he said.

What he was driving at wasn't *truth* anyway, but a mere approximation of it—something *truthish* or *truthy*, unburdened by the factual. And so, in a flash of inspiration, *truthiness* was born.[69]

Colbert could not have been more prescient. But even he could not have foreseen the role that "truthiness" would play in normalizing racism in the 2016 election. The media has now come to embrace the reality of the once-satirical concept of "truthiness," and to embrace a post-truth election, a post-truth presidency, and a post-truth press. In so doing the media has tacitly embraced racist white nationalist fervor. Nowhere was this more evident after the election than in Chuck Todd's Orwellian exchange with former Trump campaign manager Corey Lewandowski. On the December 4, 2016 broadcast of NBC's *Meet the Press*, Lewandowski's chilling critique of media literalism defeated Todd's feeble ruminations on whether Trump's words and frequent racist claims actually matter:

CHUCK TODD: So in that case, we were supposed to take him literally. The question is, after what many have dubbed the post-truth election, are we getting a look at a post-truth presidency? . . . Trump's first campaign manager argued at a campaign postmortem this week that his words don't matter.

COREY LEWANDOWSKI: This is the problem with the media. You guys took everything Donald Trump said so literally. And the problem with that is American people didn't.[70]

Indeed, since the election, NBC's *Meet the Press* has become the new Colosseum for the gladiator games pitting reason versus "truthiness." As Sarah K. Burris reported on Raw Story, Todd—ever the impotent inquirer and Charlie Brown-esque loveable loser—suggested that a Trump presidency might last sixteen years. As if in a debate with himself, in which Todd the rational reporter meets Todd the "truthiness" fascist abdicator, he made sure to contextualize and soften his remarks within the safe and heroic narrative of Trump's ability to defy expectations: "In a terrifying prophecy, MSNBC host Chuck Todd began his Friday evening show saying '16 years later we may look at Donald Trump and he's still President of the United States.' While Todd was likely popping off, he's not too far off base. As Mediaite captured, Todd showed clips of the times over the last few years that Trump has benefited from the bigotry of low expectations. Time and again he's managed to rebound when it seemed as though he was dead. 'I've also heard Donald Trump, boy, he won't even make it through the first year of the presidency,' Todd said. 'Ah, Donald Trump will get impeached. Ah, Donald Trump will quit the presidency.' Don't count on it. Todd called Trump the 'defier of expectations.'"[71]

We are now getting a view of what the world might have looked like if Nazi Reich Minister of Propaganda Joseph Goebbels possessed television and Internet media technology. Todd's tacit acceptance of a post-truth presidency, his contextualization of his own rational albeit terrifying prophecy, and indeed the widespread acceptance of the manifest reality of Colbert's "truthiness" in American political discourse are only a few examples of the media's capitulation to fascism. The corporate media's failures serve as fertile ground for the normalization of a new American authoritarian white male heterosexual nationalist awakening in the Trump era. In early 2017, signs of this new American authoritarianism have continued: Trump supported the Philippines' president and genocidal fascist Rodrigo Duterte's violent and murderous suppression of his own citizens; Trump allowed Turkey's president, Recep Tayyip Erdoğan, a known human rights abuser, to stay in Washington, DC—and, during that visit, Erdoğan's bodyguards violently subdued US citizens protesting his stay; and Trump remained silent after two men were killed trying to prevent a known white supremacist from harassing a young Muslim woman in Portland, Oregon.[72]

ACKNOWLEDGMENT: Special thanks to Project Censored intern Kristen van Zyll de Jong for help with editing and formatting.

NICHOLAS L. BAHAM III is a professor of ethnic studies at California State University, East Bay, and teaches courses in African American studies as well as genders and sexualities in communities of color. His academic research focuses on marginalized African American communities structured around nontraditional religious beliefs, sexual practices, and artistic expression. His book, *The Coltrane Church: Apostles of Sound, Agents of Social Justice,* was published in 2015 by McFarland Press. Dr. Baham is an emerging James Baldwin scholar who is currently working on an edited volume on James Baldwin's influence on West Coast black politics. He can be followed on his blog of African American politics and culture called *The Upper Room* at nicholas-baham.blogspot.com.

NOLAN HIGDON is a professor of English, communication, and history of the US and Latin America in the San Francisco Bay Area. His academic work focuses on nationalism, propaganda, and critical media literacy education. He sits on the boards of the Media Freedom Foundation, Sacred Heart University's Media Literacy and Digital Culture graduate program, the Union for Democratic Communications's steering committee, and the Northwest Alliance for Alternative Media and Education. Higdon is a cofounder of the Global Critical Media Literacy Project. He has contributed chapters to *Censored 2013–2017* as well as Stephen Lendman's *Flashpoint in Ukraine: How the US Drive for Hegemony Risks World War III* (2014).

Notes

1. Tom Boggioni, "'Santa is White. Boycott Mall of America': Online Racists are Having a Meltdown over Mall's Black Santa," Raw Story, December 3, 2016, http://www.rawstory.com/2016/12/santa-is-white-boycott-mall-of-america-online-racists-are-having-a-meltdown-over-malls-black-santa/; Travis Gettys, "'I Voted for Trump—So There': White Shopper Melts Down after Black Workers Ask Her to Pay for Bag," Raw Story, November 28, 2016, http://www.rawstory.com/2016/11/i-voted-for-trump-so-there-white-shopper-melts-down-after-black-workers-ask-her-to-pay-for-bag/; Sebastian Murdock, "Victoria's Secret Employee Fired after Telling Black Women to Leave Store," Huffington Post, December 9, 2016, http://www.huffingtonpost.com/entry/victorias-secret-kimberly-houzah_us_584add62e4b0bd9c3dfc6cc1.

2. Michael Calderone, "CNN Chief Jeff Zucker Defends Hiring Ex-Trump Campaign Manager Corey Lewandowski," Huffington Post, September 20, 2016, http://www.huffingtonpost.com/entry/jeff-zucker-donald-trump_us_57e1855ce4b0e28b2b50b454; Caroline Framke, "Trevor Noah Didn't 'Destroy' Tomi Lahren on The Daily Show. What He Did was Much Better," Vox, December 4, 2016, http://www.vox.com/culture/2016/12/4/13807584/daily-show-tomi-lahren-interview; Abigail Tracy, "Ann Coulter, High Priestess of Trumpism, Takes a Victory Lap," Vanity Fair, September 20, 2016, http://www.vanityfair.com/news/2016/09/ann-coulter-donald-trump.

3. Matthew Sheffield, "DNC Race Heats Up: Howard Dean Drops Out as Keith Ellison Battles Charges of Anti-Semitism," Salon, December 5, 2016, http://www.salon.com/2016/12/05/dnc-race-heats-up-howard-dean-drops-out-as-keith-ellison-battles-charges-of-anti-semitism; Willa Frej, "Twitter Erupts at Rick Santorum for Telling Dreamer to Leave the U.S.," Huffington Post, December 7, 2016, www.huffingtonpost.com/entry/rick-santorum-dreamers-immigration_us_58481d3ae4b0dodf1837232f.

4. Chauncey DeVega, "Forget 'Dialogue' with Donald Trump and His Supporters: They Have Empowered Hatred and Harm," Salon, December 6, 2016, www.salon.com/2016/12/06/forget-dialogue-with-donald-trump-and-his-supporters-they-have-empowered-hatred-and-harm/.

5. Tribune Media Wire, "Ku Klux Klan Announces Trump Victory Parade in North Carolina," WGN9, November 11, 2016, http://wgntv.com/2016/11/11/ku-klux-klan-announces-trump-victory-parade-in-north-carolina/; Eric Bradner, "Alt-Right Leader: 'Hail Trump! Hail Our People! Hail Victory!'," CNN, November 22, 2016, www.cnn.com/2016/11/21/politics/alt-right-gathering-donald-trump/; Liam Stack, "Two Klan Leaders are Charged in a North Carolina Stabbing," New York Times, December 7, 2016, https://www.nytimes.com/2016/12/07/

us/klan-grand-dragon-arrest-stabbing-north-carolina.html; Carimah Townes, "White Nationalists Target Jews in Small Montana Town," ThinkProgress, December 18, 2016, https://thinkprogress. org/white-nationalists-target-jews-in-small-montana-town-71f3ed16d14b.

6. Dana Milbank, "Anti-Semitism is No Longer an Undertone of Trump's Campaign. It's the Melody," *Washington Post*, November 7, 2016, https://www.washingtonpost.com/opinions/ anti-semitism-is-no-longer-an-undertone-of-trumps-campaign-its-the-melody/2016/11/07/ b1ad6e22-a50a-11e6-8042-f4d111c862d1_story.html.

7. Daniel Lombroso and Yoni Appelbaum, "'Hail Trump!': White Nationalists Salute the President-Elect," *Atlantic*, November 21, 2016, http://www.theatlantic.com/politics/ archive/2016/11/richard-spencer-speech-npi/508379/; Brendan Morrow, "David Duke Praises President-Elect Donald Trump's Cabinet Picks," Heavy, November 18, 2016, http://heavy. com/news/2016/11/david-duke-praise-donald-trump-cabinet-pick-appointment-jeff-sessions-michael-flynn-steve-bannon/.

8. Lawrence Britt, "Fourteen Defining Characteristics of Fascism," Rense, May 28, 2003, http://www.rense.com/general37/char.htm; Michael Calderone, "Trump Campaign Manager Accused of Physically Stopping Journalist from Doing Her Job," Huffington Post, March 9, 2016, http://www.huffingtonpost.com/entry/trump-breitbart-reproter-michelle-fields-corey-lewandowski_us_56dff882e4b0860f99d73b0e; "As Trump Disavows 'Alt-Right' Support, Critics Question If He Will Still Normalize White Supremacy," *Democracy Now!*, November 23, 2016, https://www.democracynow.org/2016/11/23/as_trump_disavows_alt_right_support; Ariel Edwards-Levy, "Half the Country Sees 'Fascist Undertones' in Donald Trump's Campaign: New Survey," Huffington Post, March 19, 2016, http://www.huffingtonpost.com/entry/ donald-trump-events-violence_us_56ec383ee4b084c672201de4.

9. Jeremy Diamond, "Donald Trump: Ban All Muslim Travel to US," CNN, December 8, 2015, http://www.cnn.com/2015/12/07/politics/donald-trump-muslim-ban-immigration/; Sarah Lazare, "Muslim Woman Ejected from Trump Rally as Crowd Hurls Epithets," Common Dreams, January 9, 2016, http://www.commondreams.org/news/2016/01/09/muslim-woman-ejected-trump-rally-crowd-hurls-epithets.

10. Isaac Chotiner, "Donald Trump and the Spike in Anti-Muslim Hate Crimes in the US," Slate, May 9, 2016, http://www.slate.com/blogs/the_slatest/2016/05/09/donald_trump_and_the_ rise_of_anti_muslim_hate_crimes.html.

11. Felipe Villamor, "Rodrigo Duterte Says Donald Trump Endorses His Violent Antidrug Campaign," *New York Times*, December 3, 2016, http://www.nytimes.com/2016/12/03/world/asia/ philippines-rodrigo-duterte-donald-trump.html.

12. Katy Waldman, "Why We Shouldn't Talk about 'Normalizing' Donald Trump," Slate, November 17, 2016, http://www.slate.com/blogs/lexicon_valley/2016/11/17/stop_talking_about_normalizing_ donald_trump_that_s_having_the_debate_on.html.

13. Somini Sengupta, "Torture Can be Useful, Nearly Half of Americans in Poll Say," *New York Times*, December 5, 2016, https://www.nytimes.com/2016/12/05/world/americas/torture-can-be-useful-nearly-half-of-americans-in-poll-say.html.

14. Federico Finchelstein, *Transatlantic Fascism: Ideology, Violence, and the Sacred in Argentina and Italy, 1919–1945* (Durham, North Carolina: Duke University Press, 2010).

15. David A. Graham, "All the President-Elect's Generals," *Atlantic*, December 8, 2016, https://www. theatlantic.com/politics/archive/2016/12/all-the-president-elects-generals/509873/; Brendan Morrow, "David Duke Praises President-Elect Donald Trump's Cabinet Picks," Heavy, November 18, 2016, http://heavy.com/news/2016/11/david-duke-praise-donald-trump-cabinet-pick-appointment-jeff-sessions-michael-flynn-steve-bannon/; Franco Ordoñez, "Trump Pick to Head Homeland Security Oversaw Guantánamo Prison," *Miami Herald*, December 7, 2016, http:// www.miamiherald.com/news/nation-world/world/americas/guantanamo/article119434493. html; Steve Holland and Warren Strobel, "Trump Taps Kelly for Homeland Security, Third General for Top Post," Reuters, December 8, 2016, http://www.reuters.com/article/us-usa-trump-homelandsecurity-idUSKBN13W22M.

16. Aaron Rupar, "Trump Transition Official is Active on White Nationalist Social Media Platform," ThinkProgress, December 5, 2016, https://thinkprogress.org/michael-flynn-jr-trump-transition-gab-7d747c46c5bb.

17. Graham, "All the President-Elect's Generals."

18. Paul Rosenberg, "The Moral Foundations of Fascism: Warring Psychological Theories Struggle to Make Sense of Hitler, Mussolini and You-Know-Who," Salon, December 4, 2016, http://www.salon.com/2016/12/04/the-moral-foundations-of-fascism-warring-psychological-theories-struggle-to-make-sense-of-hitler-mussolini-and-you-know-who/.

19. Alexander Zaitchik, The Gilded Rage: A Wild Ride through Donald Trump's America (New York: Hot Books, 2016).

20. Malihe Razazan, "The Political Economy of Mass Media and Journalism," Your Call (KALW), November 25, 2016, http://kalw.org/post/your-call-political-economy-mass-media-and-journalism.

21. David Edwards, "Amy Goodman Blasts CNN for Airing Trump's Empty Stage Instead of Sanders's Speech," Raw Story, March 20, 2016, http://www.rawstory.com/2016/03/amy-goodman-rips-cnn-for-airing-trumps-empty-stage-instead-of-sanders-speech/; Eric Boehlert, "ABC World News Tonight has Devoted Less Than One Minute to Bernie Sanders' Campaign This Year," Media Matters for America, December 11, 2015, http://mediamatters.org/blog/2015/12/11/abc-world-news-tonight-has-devoted-less-than-on/207428.

22. 13th, directed by Ava DuVernay (Netflix, 2016).

23. See, e.g., "American Nazi Organization Rally at Madison Square Garden, 1939," Rare Historical Photos, February 19, 2014, http://rarehistoricalphotos.com/american-nazi-organization-rally-madison-square-garden-1939/.

24. Jules Archer, The Plot to Seize the White House: The Shocking True Story of the Conspiracy to Overthrow FDR (New York: Skyhorse Publishing, 2007 [1973]).

25. John Broich, "How Journalists Covered the Rise of Mussolini and Hitler," Smithsonian, December 13, 2016, http://www.smithsonianmag.com/history/how-journalists-covered-rise-mussolini-hitler-180961407/.

26. Peter Kornbluh, The Pinochet File: A Declassified Dossier on Atrocity and Accountability (New York: New Press, 2013).

27. Jeet Heer, "When Will National Review Apologize for Cooperating with Murderous Dictator Augusto Pinochet?" New Republic, October 9, 2015, https://newrepublic.com/article/123073/national-review-should-apologize-cooperating-augusto-pinochet.

28. "Ignoring Trump's Record of Racism," Fairness and Accuracy In Reporting (FAIR), May 6, 2011, fair.org/media_criticism/ignoring-trumps-record-of-racism/.

29. Ibid.

30. Jim Naureckas, "Newsweek Says Not to Worry about Trump, Who Would 'End Up Like Jimmy Carter,'" Fairness and Accuracy In Reporting (FAIR), March 22, 2016, http://fair.org/home/newsweek-says-not-to-worry-about-trump-who-would-end-up-like-jimmy-carter/.

31. John Daniszewski, "Writing about the 'Alt-Right'," Associated Press, November, 28, 2016, https://blog.ap.org/behind-the-news/writing-about-the-alt-right.

32. Terry Nguyen, "The Alt-Right Movement: An 'Intelligently New' Form of Populist, White Supremacist Thinking," Study Breaks, December 5, 2016, http://studybreaks.com/2016/12/05/alt-right-movement-intelligently-new-form-populist-white-supremacist-thinking/.

33. Jenny Starrs, "What is the Alt-Right?" Washington Post, August 25, 2016, https://www.washingtonpost.com/video/politics/what-is-the-alt-right/2016/08/25/b275b12e-6aaf-11e6-91cb-ecb5418830e9_video.html.

34. Ben Mathis-Lilley, "Trump was Recorded in 2005 Bragging about Grabbing Women 'by the Pussy,'" Slate, October 7, 2016, http://www.slate.com/blogs/the_slatest/2016/10/07/donald_trump_2005_tape_i_grab_women_by_the_pussy.html; Elizabeth (Betita) Martínez, "Racism: The US Creation Myth and Its Premise Keepers," in Globalize Liberation: How to Uproot the System and Build a Better World, ed. David Solnit (San Francisco: City Lights, 2004), 51–60.

35. Razazan, "Political Economy of Mass Media and Journalism."

36. Nick Wing, "A Donald Trump Fanboy Tried to Whitesplain the KKK to Van Jones, and Things Got Heated," Huffington Post, March 2, 2016, http://www.huffingtonpost.com/entry/jeffrey-lord-van-jones-cnn_us_56d667cbe4b0871f60ed365a.

37. Charles M. Blow, "Bill O'Reilly and White Privilege," New York Times, August 27, 2014, https://www.nytimes.com/2014/08/28/opinion/charles-blow-bill-oreilly-and-white-privilege.html; Trey Sanchez, "Van Jones Won't Hear Jeffrey Lord's Truth Bomb on Racist Democrats," Truth Revolt, March 2, 2016, http://www.truthrevolt.org/news/van-jones-wont-hear-jeffrey-lords-truth-bomb-racist-democrats; Eric Hananoki, "CNN's Donald Trump Surrogate, 'the Most Grotesque Person on Television,' Hits a New Low," Media Matters, June 8, 2016, http://mediamatters.org/blog/2016/06/08/cnn-s-donald-trump-surrogate-most-grotesque-person-television-hits-new-low/210815; Karoli Kuns, "Gaslight Nation: Jeffrey Lord Stuns CNN Panel by Insisting Birther Movement Not Racist," Crooks and Liars, November 16, 2016, http://crooksandliars.com/2016/11/gaslight-nation-jeffrey-lord-stuns-cnn; James Banks, Encyclopedia of Diversity in Education (Thousand Oaks, CA: SAGE, 2012), 2300.

38. Nolan Higdon and Mickey Huff, "Millennial DeMockracy: The Corporate Media's War on Social Justice," Global Critical Media Literacy Project, October 14, 2016, gcml.org/721-2/.

39. Ben Norton, "Liberals' Attacks on Cornel West Expose Their Political Bankruptcy," CounterPunch, April 21, 2015, http://www.counterpunch.org/2015/04/21/liberals-attacks-on-cornel-west-expose-their-political-bankruptcy/; Amy Goodman/Democracy Now!, "Fireworks: Two Black Intellectual Heavyweights Debate Hillary, Trump, Race and Neoliberalism," AlterNet, July 30, 2016, http://www.alternet.org/election-2016/michael-eric-dyson-vs-eddie-glaude-race-hillary-clinton-and-legacy-obamas-presidency.

40. Nick Visser, "CBS Chief Les Moonves Says Trump's 'Damn Good' for Business," Huffington Post, March 1, 2016, http://www.huffingtonpost.com/entry/les-moonves-donald-trump_us_56d52ce8e4b03260bf780275.

41. Edwards, "Amy Goodman Blasts"; Boehlert, "ABC World News Tonight."

42. Michael Calderone, "Donald Trump has Received Nearly $2 Billion in Free Media Attention," Huffington Post, March 15, 2016, http://www.huffingtonpost.com/entry/donald-trump-2-billion-free-media_us_56e83410e4b065e2e3d75935.

43. Paul Farhi, "One Billion Dollars Profit? Yes, the Campaign has been a Gusher for CNN," Washington Post, October 27, 2016, https://www.washingtonpost.com/lifestyle/style/one-billion-dollars-profit-yes-the-campaign-has-been-a-gusher-for-cnn/2016/10/27/1fc879e6-9c6f-11e6-9980-50913d68eacb_story.html; Razazan, "Political Economy"; Hadas Gold and Alex Weprin, "Cable News' Election-Year Haul Could Reach $2.5 Billion," Politico, September 27, 2016, http://www.politico.com/media/story/2016/09/media-tv-numbers-004783.

44. Farhi, "One Billion Dollars Profit?"

45. Rohit Chandan, "TV Pundits Eager to Make Trump the New 'Normal,'" Fairness and Accuracy in Reporting (FAIR), November 18, 2016, http://fair.org/home/tv-pundits-eager-to-make-trump-the-new-normal/.

46. Kali Holloway, "Normalizing the Abnormal: NPR Begins Its Whitewashing of Breitbart's Racism," AlterNet, November 16, 2016, http://www.alternet.org/election-2016/normalizing-abnormal-npr-begins-its-whitewashing-breitbarts-racism.

47. Michael Calderone, "Donald Trump Met Privately with Network Executives and Anchors," Huffington Post, November 21, 2016, http://www.huffingtonpost.com/entry/donald-trump-network-anchors-meeting_us_583333f6e4b058ce7aac3fc0.

48. Calderone, "Trump Campaign Manager Accused."

49. Thomas Bishop, "'Trump TV' will be in the White House Press Briefings," Media Matters, December 6, 2016, http://mediamatters.org/blog/2016/12/06/trump-tv-will-be-white-house-press-briefings/214735.

50. Jane Mayer, Dark Money: The Hidden History of the Billionaires behind the Rise of the Radical Right (New York: Doubleday, 2016).

51. Laurel Raymond, "Editor of Nation's Second-Biggest Newspaper Says He Will Not Report Trump Lies, Even If He Lies," ThinkProgress, January 1, 2017, https://thinkprogress.org/

editor-of-nations-second-biggest-newspaper-says-he-will-not-report-trump-lies-even-if-he-lies-boe020f7fc34.

52. Jean-Paul Sartre, *Anti-Semite and Jew: An Exploration of the Etiology of Hate,* translated by George J. Becker (New York: Schocken, 1948), 20.

53. Lorne Matalon, "Mexico Gears Up for Trump's Plan to Build a Wall," KPBS, December 13, 2016, http://www.kpbs.org/news/2016/dec/13/mexico-reacts-plan-build-wall/; Alana Abramson, "What Trump has Said about a Muslim Registry," ABC News, November 18, 2016, http://abcnews.go.com/Politics/trump-muslim-registry/story?id=43639946.

54. Zeba Blay, "Chimamanda Ngozi Adichie Calls Out BBC for Trump Debate," Huffington Post, November 28, 2016, http://www.huffingtonpost.com/entry/chimamanda-ngozi-adichie-calls-out-for-bbc-trump-debate_us_583c5366e4b000af95eef13a.

55. Margaret Sullivan, "Yes, the Media Should Cover Trump Fairly—but Even Better, Hold Him Accountable," *Washington Post,* June 5, 2016, https://www.washingtonpost.com/lifestyle/style/yes-cover-trump-fairly-even-better-hold-him-accountable/2016/06/02/bfe80fe2-282d-11e6-b989-4e5479715b54_story.html.

56. Zeba Blay, "Soledad O'Brien Calls Out Media for 'Normalizing White Supremacy,'" Huffington Post, September 7, 2016, http://www.huffingtonpost.com/entry/soledad-obrien-calls-out-media-for-normalizing-white-supremacy_us_57d01d63e4b03d2d459776f9; Micheline Maynard, "Normalizing Trump: Why the Washington Media Must Break the Fluff Cycle," *Forbes,* November 12, 2016, https://www.forbes.com/sites/michelinemaynard/2016/11/12/normalizing-trump-why-the-washington-media-must-break-the-fluff-cycle/; Heather Digby Parton, "Normalizing Trump, Demonizing Hillary: The Media's Shameful Strategy for the 2016 Election," Salon, June 7, 2016, http://www.salon.com/2016/06/07/normalizing_trump_demonizing_hillary_the_medias_shameful_strategy_for_the_2016_election/.

57. Renée Graham, "By Normalizing Hatred, We've Already Normalized Trump," *Boston Globe,* November 15, 2016, https://www.bostonglobe.com/opinion/2016/11/15/normalizing-hatred-already-normalized-trump/fqMGI8JAEcjq4uXbpD2O0K/story.html.

58. Mark Potok, "The Year in Hate & Extremism, 2010," Southern Poverty Law Center (SPLC), February 23, 2011, https://www.splcenter.org/fighting-hate/intelligence-report/2011/year-hate-extremism-2010.

59. Brian Tashman, "58 Donald Trump Conspiracy Theories (and Counting!): The Definitive Trump Conspiracy Guide," AlterNet, May 30, 2016, http://www.alternet.org/right-wing/58-donald-trump-conspiracy-theories-and-counting-definitive-trump-conspiracy-guide.

60. Nolan Higdon, "Disinfo Wars: Alex Jones' War on Your Mind," Project Censored, September 26, 2013, projectcensored.org/disinfo-wars-alex-jones-war-mind/.

61. Ibid.

62. David Folkenflik, "Radio Conspiracy Theorist Claims Ear of Trump, Pushes 'Pizzagate' Fictions," National Public Radio (NPR), December 6, 2016, http://www.npr.org/2016/12/06/504590375/radio-conspiracy-theorist-claims-ear-of-trump-pushes-pizzagate-fictions; Aaron Bandler, "Alex Jones, the Guy Trump Called Post-Election, Says Hillary Personally Murdered Children," Daily Wire, December 7, 2016, http://www.dailywire.com/news/11418/alex-jones-guy-trump-called-post-election-says-aaron-bandler.

63. Sarah Posner, "How Donald Trump's New Campaign Chief Created an Online Haven for White Nationalists," *Mother Jones,* August 22, 2016, http://www.motherjones.com/politics/2016/08/stephen-bannon-donald-trump-alt-right-breitbart-news.

64. Victor Pickard, "Yellow Journalism, Orange President," *Jacobin,* November 25, 2016, https://www.jacobinmag.com/2016/11/media-advertising-news-radio-trump-tv/.

65. Higdon, "Disinfo Wars."

66. Meera Jagannathan and Nicole Bitette, "Comedy Central's 'Roast of Rob Lowe' Writers Reveal the Jokes Ann Coulter Rejected," *New York Daily News,* September 6, 2016, http://www.nydailynews.com/entertainment/tv/roast-rob-lowe-writers-reveal-rejected-jokes-ann-coulter-rejected-article-1.2780089; Framke, "Trevor Noah Didn't 'Destroy' Tomi Lahren."

67. Michael Darer, "Trevor Noah's Interview with Tomi Lahren is a Perfect Example of Why the White Liberal 'Discourse' Fetish is So Damn Absurd," Huffington Post, December 3, 2016,

updated December 9, 2016, http://www.huffingtonpost.com/entry/trevor-noahs-interview-with-tomi-lahren-is-a-perfect_us_58425f75e4b0b93e10f8e231; Yesha Callahan, "If You're a 'Pretty' Racist, You Can Get Cupcakes from Trevor Noah," *The Grapevine* blog, The Root, December 7, 2016, http://www.theroot.com/blog/the-grapevine/if-youre-a-pretty-racist-you-can-get-cupcakes-from-trevor-noah/.

68. Melanie McFarland, "This is Not Normal: A&E Announces New Series 'Generation KKK.'" Salon, December 20, 2016, http://www.salon.com/2016/12/20/this-is-not-normal-ae-announces-new-series-generation-k-k-k/.

69. Ben Zimmer, "Truthiness," *New York Times Magazine*, October 13, 2010, http://www.nytimes.com/2010/10/17/magazine/17FOB-onlanguage-t.html.

70. *Meet the Press*, "Meet the Press 12/04/16" (program transcript), December 4, 2016, NBC News, http://www.nbcnews.com/meet-the-press/meet-press-12-04-16-n691726.

71. Sarah K. Burris, "Chuck Todd Scares Viewers with Claim 16 Years from Now Trump Might Actually Still be President," Raw Story, December 23, 2016, http://www.rawstory.com/2016/12/chuck-todd-scares-viewers-with-claim-16-years-from-now-trump-might-actually-still-be-president/.

72. Mallory Shelbourne, "Turkish President's Bodyguards Beat Up DC Protestors: Report," The Hill, May 17, 2017, thehill.com/homenews/news/333841-nbc-erdogans-bodyguards-beat-up-dc-protestors; Joshua Berlinger and Elise Labott, "Trump Praises Duterte's Deadly Drug War in Leaked Transcript," CNN, May 24, 2017, http://www.cnn.com/2017/05/24/politics/donald-trump-rodrigo-duterte-phone-call-transcript/; Rebecca Shapiro, "Trump Had Over 20 Chances to Address the Portland Attack on Twitter before He Did So," Huffington Post, May 29, 2017, http://www.huffingtonpost.com/entry/trump-had-at-least-15-chances-to-address-the-portland-attack-on-twitter-he-didnt_us_592b8d3ee4b053f2d2ad461d.

CHAPTER 5

Trump Universe

words by Adam Bessie and pictures by Peter Glanting

Hyperbole is the native tongue of Trump Universe...

Especially since Trump seems right out of the pages of a science-fiction comic book.

Indeed, The Simpsons even predicted a President Trump.

Science-fiction seems a particularly apt form of hyperbole...

...a language of the fantastic made real.

But is it hyperbole? Or real?

To find answers, readers are turning to science fiction.

Dystopia is trending. Sales of classic books are on fire.

Philip K Dick's classic Man in the High Castle — an alternate history of World War II — is a hit on Amazon.

And as readers have found, dystopia feels a little too real.

The line is blurring...

It's tempting to think we are living in a literary dystopia...

...and, thus, are #TheResistance.

It's thrilling to feel that we've crossed the threshold into this alternate world...

...we are Winston...

...fighting against a great totalitarian evil...

...in an epic narrative...

...trapped in the past tense.

Trump's Universe is not composed of science fiction, but of lies — and this line matters.

Trump's lies are designed to maximize his administration's power, its gravity, its ability to shape us to its very real will.

Trump wants us to conflate fact and fake...

...to make them indistinguishable so that nobody knows what's real or not...

..and at a certain point, we get too tired to even care, or try.

A fiction fatigue.

INSPIRATIONS!

SELF DEFENSE

The Twilight Zone

Black Mirror

They Live

COMIC COLLECTOR

Scott McCloud.
Understanding Comics

Nick Sousanis.
Unflattening

X RAY GLASSES ONLY $1.50

Jack Kirby.
"Galactus and Dr. Doom"

Matt Groening.
Homer Simpson

Al Feldstein.
"Judgment Day!" Weird Fantasy #18

R. Sikoryak.
"The Unquotable Trump"

Comic Book Legal Defense Fund

MUSCLES? In 7 days

Ursula K. Le Guin.
Introduction to the novel *The Left Hand of Darkness*

Ursula K. Le Guin.
The Oregonian Letter to the editor, Feb 1. 2017

Jean Baudrillard.
"The Precession of Simulacra"

George Lakoff and Mark Johnson.
Metaphors We Live By

Neil Postman.
Amusing Ourselves to Death

Timothy Snyder.
On Tyranny

EVERY ITEM Only 88¢ EACH

George Orwell.
1984

Aldous Huxley.
Brave New World

Philip K. Dick.
The Man in the High Castle

M. T. Anderson.
Feed

Margaret Atwood.
The Handmaid's Tale

Sinclair Lewis.
It Can't Happen Here

Octavia Butler.
Parable of the Sower

ADAM BESSIE

Adam Bessie writes cartoons and non-fiction graphic essays which have been featured in many national outlets, including The Atlantic, The Boston Globe, The Los Angeles Times, and Truthout. Adam is a Professor of English at a San Francisco Bay Area Community College.

PETER GLANTING

Peter Glanting is a cartoonist and illustrator. Pete holds a B.A. in English from the University of California at Davis, and an M.F.A. in Comics from the California College of the Arts. He lives and works in Portland, Oregon.

WRITE RIGHT NOW!

Reality Management Representatives, Inc.
17 Simulacra Street
Desert of the Real, CA 101001

CHAPTER 6

Defamation as Censorship in the Social-Media Era
Who Counts as a Media Defendant?

Elizabeth Blakey

Does it make sense to discriminate against a blogger, a YouTuber, or a Tweet writer—by having the courts apply a different First Amendment standard, one that creates a higher likelihood of liability in defamation lawsuits—just because those social-media speakers are not traditional journalists?

This article will address the censorship that arises when courts define who counts as a *media defendant* in defamation cases. Originally, when the law of defamation was first constitutionalized, courts started to use the category of *media defendant* to provide additional privileges to mass-media actors, in order to support democratic actions in the public sphere. Nowadays, however, the category of *media defendant* is fast becoming a vehicle for censorship of social-media publishers, because the law is failing to keep up with the innovations in communications technology that ushered in the social-media era.

As a general principle, the First Amendment guarantees the freedom of speech to all speakers, without regard to a speaker's status as a member of the traditional press or the general public. Yet in many jurisdictions in the United States, the courts are creating and maintaining a hierarchy of speakers, based on whether a defendant in a defamation case is a member of the institutional media or merely a member of the general public. Originally the idea was to give a preference to media defendants because of their role as representatives of the public, gathering and disseminating news. Yet this distinction also means that there is a hierarchy of speakers. If a speaker is found to be a media defendant, the courts provide additional First

Amendment protections, but if found to be a nonmedia defendant, the speaker faces a higher likelihood of liability, depending on the state where the case is filed.[1]

The hierarchy of speakers—essentially two classes, the media and the nonmedia—does not take into account the realities of the social-media era. The hierarchy is only being pursued in a minority of US jurisdictions. The eleven states that discriminate against nonmedia speakers are Delaware, Idaho, Iowa, Kansas, Kentucky, Minnesota, Mississippi, New Jersey, Oregon, Texas, and Wisconsin. Yet the First Amendment law regarding the media/nonmedia distinction remains unclear in another thirteen states. This means that in twenty-four states, or about half of the US, speakers can experience government censorship as a matter of law, based on their status as members of the public rather than as legacy-media actors (e.g., newspaper journalists or TV stations). The Appendix, below, summarizes the case law by jurisdiction on the status of media/nonmedia defendants in libel lawsuits.

For defamation lawsuits filed in these twenty-four states, there is an existing First Amendment crisis, likely to come to a head in the social-media era, because the liberty of speech is being applied unevenly across the fabric of US jurisdictions. Some speakers, who are clearly acting in the public sphere via social media platforms or other technologies, are being afforded a lower standard of freedom because they are not members of the traditional press.

This is a problematic "censorship by law," because, in the social-media era, members of the general public are able to publish to mass audiences and contribute to democratic action in the mediated public sphere. The distinction between media and nonmedia defendants is obsolete in the social-media era. Ordinary people now have the ability to contribute to debates in the mediated public sphere via social media, even if they are not members of the legacy media. Yet courts continue to assert a distinction regarding who counts as a *media defendant*. This keeps the door open for the censorship of speakers, based on their status as social-media speakers, rather than legacy media or traditional journalists. This censorship by law is likely to harm public discourse, because the nonmedia defendant cases fail to keep pace with technological advances.

REGULATING SPEECH IN THE SOCIAL–MEDIA ERA

Communications technologies have accelerated over the last forty years, from the invention of email in 1972,[2] to the use of electronic bulletin boards in the early 1980s,[3] to the development of the public Internet in the 1990s,[4] and the explosion of social-media platforms in the twenty-first century. The last ten years saw remarkable growth in social media, with use of social-media platforms jumping tenfold between 2005 and 2015 for US adults.[5] A historic threshold was crossed in 2016 when for the first time a majority of US adults—62 percent of US adults—obtained news via social media.[6] As of January 2017, nearly 70 percent of US adults use social media regularly, with that number hitting nearly 90 percent in the 18-to-29-year-old age bracket.[7]

The regulation of social media has been so uneven, however, that experts are asking if social media will splinter into a heavily patrolled and regulated "safe space," entirely separate from a free-for-all zone.[8] The predictions tend to suggest that the fractured—partially government censored, and partially unregulated—online landscape will have chilling effects on the free exchange of ideas in the public sphere.[9] Of course, the regulation or management of social media is not entirely in the hands of government actors, as seen in controversies being handled by the social-media leader, Facebook,[10] over fake news stories intentionally posted on its site during the 2016 presidential election cycle.[11]

Communications technologies change quickly, but the law changes slowly by design. Law is designed to change slowly to maintain social stability, especially in the area of constitutional libel law.[12] When and how can a publisher be sued for injury to another's reputation? The judicial answers to this question in recent libel law cases have not kept up with how publishing actually occurs on the Internet and via social media.

In the legacy-media era of the 1990s and earlier, it was relatively clear who counted as a *media defendant*: either a defendant company owned a city newspaper or it owned a broadcast television station, making the defendant clearly a media defendant. In contrast, in the social-media era, there are a wide variety of media outlets that can be hit with a libel lawsuit, including online news sites, podcasts, video-sharing websites, self-published e-books, blogs, and micro-blogging sites, such as Twitter. The law in some jurisdictions of the US has not kept pace with the realities of social-media publishing. Individual bloggers, YouTubers, and Tweet publishers now are being sued for libel occurring in the public sphere, but the courts are still struggling to determine who counts as a media defendant. The media defendant classification was supposed to provide advantages to media defendants, but now is being used to disadvantage "nonmedia defendants" who are nevertheless speaking in the public sphere, not in purely private settings.

The upshot is that some US jurisdictions are using antiquated understandings of news production and publishing and, in defamation cases, are creating an unconstitutional classification of speakers. Social-media speakers in this schema may or may not be afforded full First Amendment protection for their speech, even though the speech takes place in the public, not private, sphere. That is to say, these jurisdictions are using definitions of who counts as a *media defendant* based on social constructs from before the social-media era, to limit public discourse reaching mass audiences, often in the same way that mass-media producers such as newspapers and broadcast stations did in the past.

The judicial outcomes tend to censor a group of speakers, by disadvantaging them as against speakers who act more like traditional media from the legacy-media era. This is because the older theories about who counts as the media, and who is *not* the media, fail to consider the dynamics of social-media publishing. But this censorship by law could well be used to target and restrict speech by some speakers, for political or other reasons, based on the content of speech, under the guise of protecting the media more than supposedly nonmedia or private speech.

LEGAL REALISM AND SOCIAL MEDIA

The censorship of defendants deemed to be nonmedia is fast becoming a problem of "law on the books, law in action." This is a jurisprudential concept from the Legal Realism school of thought.[13]

"Law on the books, law in action" is the idea that the rules written in law books are, more often than not, insufficient to resolve social problems.[14] The written rule of law alone cannot determine what would be the just or right outcome, because the variety of all possible situations cannot be anticipated by law.

In other words, judges would do well to interpret the law on the books by considering the real-world consequences of "law in action." The courts that apply the written law alone, without considering the social world, may make inadequate decisions. Deciding cases based on the formal application of rules, without regard for social consequences, is called *mechanical jurisprudence*, i.e., interpretations that consider only law on the books and not law in action.[15]

More critically and specifically, the uncertainty over who counts as a *media defendant* in libel law cases in the social-media era has been used to determine whose First Amendment rights are protected and whose are not. When the law can be interpreted "on the books" against certain speakers based on their status (in this case, determined by whether they own a legacy-media company), the effect of the "law in action" is political censorship. Publishers in the social-media era are likely to be censored, via outdated libel laws and conceptions about who has the status of media defendant, based on the legacy-media era. These outdated laws—primarily court opinions from the 1990s or earlier—are being enforced in the social-media era, without regard to the real-world dynamics of twenty-first-century publishing and journalism.

WE ARE ALL MASS MEDIA NOW

The thesis of this article is that, in social media and Internet publishing, the use of an outdated definition of the *media defendant* by judges leaves open the door for a new form of censorship by law. Interestingly, the definition of a *media defendant* originally arose in court opinions in which judges were interpreting in order to give additional advantages to mass-media publishers, on the theory that mass-media publishers are purportedly acting in the public interest.[16] Now, however, there are so many forms of mass-media publishing that the distinction between mass-media and self-publishing, or private publishing, simply doesn't exist. In the social-media era, newspapers and TV stations are no longer the only mass-media actors.

With the advent of new communication technologies and platforms, publishing is not limited to the traditional, gatekeeper companies, who produce and distribute content on the basis of one-to-many publishing (for example, one TV station broadcasting to a mass audience). Now, individuals and small groups are able to publish content to mass audiences on the basis of many-to-many publishing (for example, social media users posting and interacting with other social media users).

Yet, in some jurisdictions, the courts are still pondering whether blogging and tweeting should be considered media activities, for the purpose of granting First Amendment privileges to media defendants in libel cases—or withholding those privileges from nonmedia defendants, on the assumption that nonmedia defendants are necessarily acting in the private sphere. The laws on the books that still distinguish between media defendants and nonmedia defendants are causing an uneven and unconstitutional hierarchy between speakers who are all acting in the public sphere. This new type of censorship by law may have arisen unintentionally, due to lags in the law as it moves more slowly than technology.

Nevertheless, this censorship by law gives some speakers more privileges and liberties than others. The hierarchy of speakers created in this area of defamation law is based on the idea that speakers who are not affiliated with the traditional media must not be contributing to the public conversation (i.e., are private speakers). The social dynamics of the gatekeeper and legacy media cleanly divided speakers into mass-media or public speakers, and nonmedia or private speakers. But these lines are blurred in the social-media era.

The takeaway message is that, in an era transformed by social media, outdated defamation laws are fast becoming a dangerous form of censorship by law. Who will be silenced as a result?

UNINTENTIONAL YET UNCONSTITUTIONAL CENSORSHIP

The jurisprudence that regulates who counts as a media defendant in the social-media era does not give breathing room to publishers.

Who is not the media in the era of social media? Distinctions in the case law between who counts as a media defendant, and who does not count, could easily be used to reach political results in lawsuits that should be decided on their legal merits.

Interestingly, the media/nonmedia distinction has been rejected in comments made at the Supreme Court level, but it is still accepted in many of the lower courts.[17] The distinction causes an uneven hierarchy between speakers, some with more privileges and liberties than others, which is contrary to First Amendment guarantees. Although the interpretation of defamation law that creates unconstitutional classifications appears to be unintentional, the censorship problems it creates do not bode well for the future of public speaking via social media.

ELIZABETH BLAKEY is an assistant professor of journalism at California State University, Northridge. She earned her PhD from the University of Notre Dame in 2011. Blakey's dissertation, "A Sociology of the First Amendment," examined the dynamics of free speech in the public sphere and historical changes in civil liberties over time. Blakey also holds a JD from Loyola Law School, Los Angeles, and is an active member of the California State Bar.

APPENDIX:

US Jurisdictions and the Distinction between
Media/Nonmedia Defendants in Libel Lawsuits

Jurisdiction	Nonmedia Distinction	Case and Year
U.S. Supreme Court	Not directly addressed in majority ruling	*Dun & Bradstreet v. Greenmoss Builders* (dissent) (1985); *Philadelphia Newspapers v. Hepps* (1986); *Milkovich v. Lorain Journal Co.* (dissent) (1990)
1st Circuit Court of Appeals	No	*Piccone v. Bartels* (2014)
2nd Circuit Court of Appeals	No	*Flamm v. Am. Association of University Women* (2000); *Konikoff v. Prudential Ins. Co. of America* (2000)
3rd Circuit Court of Appeals	No	*Avins v. White* (1980); *Medico v. Time* (1981); *U.S. Healthcare v. Blue Cross of Greater Phila.* (1990)
4th Circuit Court of Appeals	No	*Snyder v. Phelps* (2009); *Mayfield v. National Assoc. for Stock Car Auto Racing* (2012)

5th Circuit Court of Appeals	Unclear	*Snead v. Redland Aggregates* (1993)
6th Circuit Court of Appeals	Unclear	*Orr v. Argus-Press Co.* (1978) (no distinction in dictum)
7th Circuit Court of Appeals	No	*Underwager v. Salter* (1994)
8th Circuit Court of Appeals	No	*In re IBP Confidential Bus. Documents Litig.* (1986); *Deupree v. Iliff* (1988)
9th Circuit Court of Appeals	No	*Obsidian Finance Group, LLC v. Cox* (2014)
10th Circuit Court of Appeals	No	*Garcia v. Bd. of Edu. of Socorro Consol. Sch. Dist.* (1985); *Jefferson County School District v. Moody's Investor Services* (1999)
11th Circuit Court of Appeals	Unclear	*Straw v. Chase Revel* (1987); *Log Creek, LLC v. Kessler* (N.D. Fla. 2010); *Intihar v. Citizens Information Associates, LLC* (M.D. Fla. 2014)
D.C. Circuit Court of Appeals	Unclear	*Davis v. Schuchat* (1975); *Pearce v. E.F. Hutton Group* (D.D.C. 1987); *White v. Fraternal Order of Police* (1990); *Vereen v. Clayborne* (1993); *Novecon v. Bulgarian-American Enterprise Fund* (D.D.C. 1997)
Alabama	No	*Beneficial Mgmt. Corp. v. Evans* (1982)
Alaska	No	*Schneider v. Pay 'N Save Corp.* (1986); *Rybachek v. Sutton* (1988)
Arizona	No	*Nelson v. Cail* (1978); *Sewell v. Brookbank* (1978); *Rosales v. City of Eloy* (1979)
Arkansas	No	*United Insur. Co. of America v. Murphy* (1998); *Gibson v. Regions Fin. Corp.* (2008)
California	No	*Miller v. Nestande* (1987)
Colorado	No	*Rowe v. Metz* (1978); *Sky Fun 1 v. Schuttloffel* (2001)
Connecticut	Unclear	No reported cases (as of 2014)
Delaware	Yes	*Kanaga v. Gannett Co.* (1996)
District of Columbia	No	*Moss v. Stockyard* (1990); *Ayala v. Washington* (1996); *Bannum v. Citizens for a Safe Ward Five* (2005)
Florida	No	*Nodar v. Galbreath* (1984); *Perry v. Cosgrove* (1985)
Georgia	No	*Triangle Publications v. Chumley* (1984); *Diamond v. American Family Corp.* (1988)
Hawaii	No	*Rodriguez v. Nishiki* (1982); *Mehau v. Gannett Pacific Corp.* (1983)
Idaho	Yes	*Student Loan Fund of Idaho v. Duerner* (1997); *Steele v. Spokesman-Review* (2002); *Clark v. Spokesman-Review* (2007)

Illinois	No	*Millsaps v. Bankers Life Co.* (1976); *Colson v. Stieg* (1982); *Gravatt v. Columbia Univ.* (1986); *Dubinsky v. United Airlines Master Exec. Council* (1999); *Missner v. Clifford* (2009); *Huon v. Breaking Media* (2014); *Doctor's Data v. Barrett* (2016)
Indiana	No	*Patten v. Smith* (1977); *Near E. Side Cmty. Org. v. Hair* (1990); *Conwell v. Beatty* (1996)
Iowa	Yes	*Anderson v. Low Rent Housing Comm.* (1981) (no distinction); *Vinson v. Linn-Mar Cmty. Sch. Dist.* (1984) (distinction); *Bierman v. Weier, Author Solutions* (2013), reversed by *Bierman v. Weier, Author Solutions* (9th Cir. 2014).
Kansas	Yes/No	*Hanrahan v. Horn* (1983) (distinction); *Knudsen v. Kansas Gas and Electric Co.* (1991) (no distinction)
Kentucky	Yes	*Columbia Sussex Corp. v. Hay* (1981); *Hill v. Petrotech Resources Corp.* (2010)
Louisiana	No	*Bussie v. Larson* (1980); *Kennedy v. Sheriff of East Baton Rouge Parish* (2006)
Maine	No	*Michaud v. Inhabitants of Town of Livermore Falls* (1978)
Maryland	No	*Jacron Sales Co. v. Sindorf* (1976); *Seley-Radtke v. Hosmane* (2016); *Hanlon v. Davis* (1988)
Massachusetts	No	*McMann v. Doe* (2006)
Michigan	Unclear	*Hodgkins Kennels v. Durbin* (1988) (distinction in dictum); *Rouch v. Enquirer & News of Battle Creek, Michigan* (1992) (unclear)
Minnesota	Yes	*Jadwin v. Minneapolis Star & Tribune Co.* (1985); *McDevitt v. Tilson* (1990); *Britton v. Koep* (1991); *Stokes v. CBS* (1998); *Bahr v. Boise Cascade Corp.* (2009); *Nexus v. Swift* (2010)
Mississippi	Yes	*Sartain v. White* (1991); *Eselin-Bullock & Assoc. Ins. Agency v. National Gen. Ins. Co.* (1992)
Missouri	No	*Ramacciotti v. Zinn* (1977); *Snodgrass v. Headco Indus.* (1982); *Henry v. Halliburton* (1985)
Montana	Unclear	No reported cases (as of 2014)
Nebraska	Unclear	No reported cases (as of 2014)
Nevada	Unclear	No reported cases on media/nonmedia defendants as of 2014, but media defendants held to negligence standard in private plaintiff/private concern cases: *Schwartz v. Estate of Greenspun* (1994)
New Hampshire	Unclear	No reported cases (as of 2014)

New Jersey	Yes	*Dairy Stores v. Sentinel Publishing Co.* (1986); *Bainhaur v. Manoukian* (1987); *Turf Lawnmower Repair v. Bergen Record Corp.* (1994); *DeAngelis v. Hill* (2004); *Senna v. Florimont* (2008); *Berkery v. Estate of Stuart* (2010); *W.J.A. v. D.A.* (2012); *Roberts & Abrams v. Mintz* (2016)
New Mexico	Unclear	No reported cases (as of 2014)
New York	Unclear	*Don King Prod. v. Douglas* (1990); but see *Banco Nacional de México, S.A. v. Menéndez-Rodriguez, Al Giordano, and Narco News Bulletin* (2001); and compare *Rupert v. Sellers* (1978) (strict liability for nonmedia defendant) and *Gaeta v. New York News* (1983) (negligence standard for media defendant)
North Carolina	No	*Gaunt v. Pittaway* (1999)
North Dakota	Unclear	No reported cases (as of 2014)
Ohio	No	*Wampler v. Higgins* (2001); *Davis v. Jacobs* (1998)
Oklahoma	No	*Hennessee v. Mathis* (1987); but see *Bird Construction Co. v. Oklahoma City Housing Authority* (2004)
Oregon	Yes	*Wheeler v. Green* (1979); *Adams v. State Farm Mutual Automobile Insurance Co.* (1978); *Obsidian Finance Group, LLC v. Cox* (2011), affirmed in part, reversed in part, *Obsidian Finance Group, LLC v. Cox* (2014)
Pennsylvania	Unclear	No reported cases (as of 2014)
Rhode Island	No	*DeCarvalho v. daSilva* (1980)
South Carolina	Unclear	*Holtzscheiter v. Thomson Newspapers* (1991) (unresolved); *Erickson v. Jones Street Publishers, LLC* (2006)
South Dakota	Unclear	No reported cases (as of 2014)
Tennessee	No	*Selby v. Ilabaca* (1996)
Texas	Yes	*Mitre v. Brooks Fashion Stores* (1992); *Hancock v. Variyam* (2013); *Young v. Parent* (2017)
Utah	No	*Cox v. Hatch* (1988)
Vermont	No	*Ryan v. Herald Association* (1989)
Virginia	No	*Gazette v. Harris* (1985); *Great Coastal Express v. Ellington* (1985); but see *Kincaid v. Anderson* (2016)
Washington	No	*Caruso v. Local 690, International Bhd. of Teamsters* (1983); *Bender v. City of Seattle* (1983); *LaMon v. Butler and Daily World* (1989)
West Virginia	No	*Long v. Egnor* (1985)
Wisconsin	Yes	*Denny v. Mertz* (1982)
Wyoming	Unclear	No reported cases (as of 2014)

Notes

1. The increased likelihood of liability is based on differences in the standards of proof regarding the legal issues of false statements, the levels of required fault by the publisher, and presumed damages. These three elements of defamation cases (falsity, fault, and damages) can vary by jurisdiction, depending on the status of the speaker (media/nonmedia).

2. Internet Society, "Internet History: Timeline," Internet Hall of Fame, no date, http://internethalloffame.org/internet-history/timeline.

3. Scott Gilbertson, "Feb. 16, 1978: Bulletin Board Goes Electronic," *Wired*, February 16, 2010, https://www.wired.com/2010/02/0216cbbs-first-bbs-bulletin-board/; see also "About," The Well, no date, https://www.well.com/aboutwell.html.

4. Barry M. Leiner, Vinton G. Cerf, David D. Clark, et al., "Brief History of the Internet," Internet Society, no date, http://www.internetsociety.org/internet/what-internet/history-internet/brief-history-internet#Transition.

5. Andrew Perrin, "Social Media Usage: 2005–2015," Pew Research Center, October 8, 2015, http://www.pewinternet.org/2015/10/08/social-networking-usage-2005-2015/.

6. Jeffrey Gottfried and Elisa Shearer, "News Use Across Social Media Platforms 2016," Pew Research Center, May 26, 2016, http://www.journalism.org/2016/05/26/news-use-across-social-media-platforms-2016/.

7. "Social Media Fact Sheet," Pew Research Center, January 12, 2017, http://www.pewinternet.org/fact-sheet/social-media/.

8. Lee Rainie, Janna Anderson, and Jonathan Albright, "The Future of Free Speech, Trolls, Anonymity and Fake News Online," Pew Research Center, March 29, 2017, http://www.pewinternet.org/2017/03/29/the-future-of-free-speech-trolls-anonymity-and-fake-news-online/.

9. Ibid.

10. Facebook is the most used of the top five social-media platforms, followed by Instagram, Twitter, LinkedIn, and Pinterest. Shannon Greenwood, Andrew Perrin, and Maeve Duggan, "Social Media Update 2016," Pew Research Center, November 11, 2016, http://www.pewinternet.org/2016/11/11/social-media-update-2016/.

11. Alexander Smith and Vladimir Banic, "Fake News: How a Partying Macedonian Teen Earns Thousands Publishing Lies," NBC News, December 9, 2016, http://www.nbcnews.com/news/world/fake-news-how-partying-macedonian-teen-earns-thousands-publishing-lies-n692451; Craig Silverman and Lawrence Alexander, "How Teens in the Balkans are Duping Trump Supporters with Fake News," BuzzFeed, November 3, 2016, https://www.buzzfeed.com/craigsilverman/how-macedonia-became-a-global-hub-for-pro-trump-misinfo.

12. Judicial decisions are bound to precedent and incrementalism in order to prevent sudden or fundamental shifts in policy, in contrast to decisions made in the political (i.e., legislative and executive) branches of government. Suzanna Sherry, "Politics and Judgment," *Missouri Law Review*, Vol. 70, No. 4 (Fall 2005), 973–87, 982; http://scholarship.law.missouri.edu/cgi/viewcontent.cgi?article=3671&context=mlr.

13. "Legal Realism," Legal Information Institute, Cornell Law School, no date, https://www.law.cornell.edu/wex/legal_realism. Legal realism can be contrasted with *legal formalism*, the jurisprudential position that law is based on abstract rules that can be applied apart from any political or social considerations.

14. Bill Clune, "Law in Action and Law on the Books: A Primer," *New Legal Realism Conversations*, June 12, 2013, https://newlegalrealism.wordpress.com/2013/06/12/law-in-action-and-law-on-the-books-a-primer/; see also Roscoe Pound, "Law on the Books, Law in Action," *American Law Review*, Vol. 44 (1910), 12–36.

15. Roscoe Pound, "Mechanical Jurisprudence," *Columbia Law Review*, Vol. 8 (December 1908), 605–23.

16. But see Edward S. Herman and Noam Chomsky, *Manufacturing Consent: The Political Economy of the Mass Media* (New York: Pantheon, 1988).

17. In *Philadelphia Newspapers v. Hepps* (1986), the dissent by Justice Brennan, in which Justice Blackmun joined, argued that the media/nonmedia distinction cannot be reconciled with the guarantees of the First Amendment; see also *Citizens United v. FEC* (2010), in which the Court stated that the First Amendment does not allow for the division of corporations into media and nonmedia classes; *Milkovich v. Lorain Journal* (1990), an opinion about media defendants that reserved judgment as to nonmedia defendants; and *Dun & Bradstreet v. Greenmoss Builders* (1985), an opinion from the legacy-media era that discussed publications that are purely private as opposed to public.

CHAPTER 7

Still Manufacturing Consent
The Propaganda Model at Thirty

Edward S. Herman

The propaganda model (PM) is the theoretical core of *Manufacturing Consent: The Political Economy of the Mass Media*, the book that Noam Chomsky and I published in 1988. We updated the work with a new introduction in 2002 and then with an afterword in 2008, but we left the rest of the book intact, comprising the presentation of the model (chapter 1), five chapters with lengthy case studies, and three appendices. It has held up quite well in its applicability, as illustrated by the additions in 2002 and 2008, and in the following updates.

The unique feature of the PM is that it offers a radical analysis and critique of the dominant, mainly commercial and advertising-based, mainstream media (MSM), locating their regular behavior and performance in their elite-dominated corporate structures and relationships, not in journalists' news-gathering practices or any supposed role as an independent watchdog serving the general public interest. The model was thus power-based, finding behavior and performance to originate from five sources related to institutional power. These five sources are (1) the ownership and profit orientation of the control group; (2) the impact of financial dependence on advertising and advertisers; (3) the sourcing of news, with power accruing to dominant sources like the Pentagon, the State Department, or Apple's headquarters, to which the media gravitate for credible and low-cost news; (4) flak, the negative feedback which is most important and influential when coming from agents of power; and (5) ideology, which also derives from individuals and institutions with economic or political power. In the 1988 edition we named "anticommunism" as the most relevant ideology. In later editions we added "free market ideology" while acknowledging that there was some variability in this factor; e.g., the occasional prioritizing of "antiterrorism."

We argued that the five elements in the model serve as filters, with news flows depending on the extent to which potential news events attract, and pass muster with, the underlying power sources that constitute the filters. For example, in a chapter titled "Worthy and Unworthy Victims," we showed that the state murder of a priest in Communist Poland in 1984 was very attractive to the media and faced no filter obstacle. By contrast, the murders of one hundred religious workers in US client states in Latin America in the years after World War II, including eight who were US citizens, were unattractive, as attention given to these murders interfered with US policy support for the killer regimes, hence their failure to make it through the filters. The filtering process is built into the media structures and requires no top-down orders or conspiracy.

We found it very useful to make comparisons like that of the "worthy" and "unworthy" victims in Poland and Latin America because of the clarity with which they demonstrate systematic bias. In our chapter on the media's treatment of Third World elections, we showed that the MSM were able to approve US-supported elections in El Salvador, while finding Nicaragua's US-disapproved election a sham, by using different criteria and focusing on different kinds of facts, thereby serving a clear but completely misleading propaganda function. This same kind of deceptive double standard has been applied in the MSM's designation of cases of alleged "aggression" and "genocide." They have used the word "aggression" frequently in discussing Russia's casualty-free takeover of Crimea in 2014, but have not been able to bring themselves to use it at all in dealing with the casualty-rich US invasion and occupation of Iraq that began in 2003. Similarly, the word "genocide" was used lavishly in the MSM to describe Bosnian Serb killings of a claimed eight thousand Bosnian Muslim "men and boys" in the "Srebrenica massacre" of July 1995, but the deaths of an estimated five hundred thousand children resulting from the US-sponsored "sanctions of mass destruction" applied to Iraq in the years 1990–2003 were never called genocide in the US MSM.[1] The Srebrenica deaths were carried out by a group targeted by the US and hence fitted the category of "worthy victims";

the Iraqi children's deaths were inflicted by this country's actions, were declared "worth it" on national TV in 1996 by US Secretary of State Madeleine Albright, and the victims were therefore treated as unworthy in the MSM (i.e., with silence).

Manufacturing Consent and the Propaganda Model were not welcomed and treated kindly by the MSM, or by most of the academic specialists on the media and communications. This was to be expected, and we predicted that the book and model would be mainly either ignored or treated harshly. After all, it is a radical analysis and critique that traces poor media performance to media structures and relationships that won't be correctable by exhortation or superficial reforms. This makes mainstream participants and liberal critics, who find the system essentially sound even if needing a little tweaking, uncomfortable and hostile. In the most extensive analysis of treatment of the PM by media and communications journals, Michael Mullen found that in ten European and North American journals between 1988 and 2007 only 79 of 3,053 articles (2.6 percent) even mentioned the PM, a majority of these only citing it without discussion.[2]

Much of the criticism of the PM has been extremely superficial and has failed to come to grips with its actual focus and claims. It is a framework of analysis that identifies major forces affecting media behavior and performance; it is not a model of effects, although media behavior and performance are surely likely to influence public opinion and actions (i.e., have effects). But these effects may vary widely, and even strenuous propaganda campaigns may fail, or at least fall short of the campaign managers' aims. We recognized this and pointed out that divisions among elites as well as the level of public knowledge and interest in an issue would impact public opinion. We did note, however, that in which elites were unified and felt strongly about an issue, the MSM would also present a united front, although even in this case media effects might be limited. This has been true, for example, in the case of trade-investment-rule campaigns such as those for the North American Free Trade Agreement (NAFTA) in 1993–1994 and the Trans-Pacific Partnership (TPP) more recently, where the strong pro-NAFTA/TPP position of the corporate elite and MSM failed to produce polling majorities for these legislative proposals.

But even in these cases where virtually unified MSM-supported propaganda campaigns failed to produce support from a majority of the public, they may have reduced the size and vigor of public opposition and helped make these proposals more viable. This was also true in the case of the wars in Central America carried out during the Reagan years (1980–1988). Polls showed that the public did not support these wars, but the Reagan administration pursued them relentlessly, supporting them with a strong covert propaganda campaign plus, of course, a flood of ordinary propaganda (selectively and sometimes literally fake news).[3] They also attacked dissident media and journalists. In one important case, after Raymond Bonner of the *New York Times* accurately reported on a major massacre in El Salvador by US-trained soldiers, attacks by the *Wall Street Journal* on Bonner led to his being removed from his post.[4] With Bonner out of the way, the *Times* resumed its usual role as a dispenser of the official line on Central America.

In *Manufacturing Consent*'s chapter on Third World election coverage, we tabulated how, in reporting on the US-sponsored El Salvador election of 1984, the *Times* simply ignored all the matters bearing on fundamental electoral conditions, including freedom of speech and press, organizational freedom, and the absence of state terror—the type of democratic safeguards the military-dominated government actively opposed. By contrast, we showed how, in reporting Nicaragua's 1984 election, which the Reaganites wanted to discredit, the *New York Times* attended to each of these electoral conditions as much as possible (and with suitable misrepresentations). In a genuinely Orwellian process, although the basic electoral conditions in 1984 were far more favorable in Nicaragua than in El Salvador, with the help of the newspaper's thoroughgoing news bias, the editors felt able to conclude that the Nicaraguan election was "a sham" whereas the one in El Salvador was legitimate. We noted also that the Latin American Studies Association (LASA) sent an experienced observer team to Nicaragua in 1984, which produced a report with a depth unmatched by any other news or foreign observer analysis of the election. The report found that the Nicaraguan election was "a model of probity and fairness" by Latin American standards. Needless to say, the *New York Times* failed to mention the LASA report, but then no other major media source picked it up either.

The reviews and critiques of the PM have in most cases acknowledged that the case studies we provided were impressive, and very few of them offered critiques applicable to those studies. One partial exception was the assessment by media scholar Daniel Hallin, who claimed that the PM failed to explain media coverage of the Central American wars of the 1980s, when there was considerable domestic hostility to Reagan's policies. Hallin suggested that this durable public hostility contradicted the model.[5] Another exception was historian Walter LaFeber's review, which also rested heavily on the continued opposition to these wars.[6] But, again, the PM is not an effects model, so the failure of the Reagan administration and MSM to produce a pro-war majority doesn't refute the model at all; but the continued support of the wars by the MSM in the face of widespread public opposition does show *their* failure to represent that public while continuing their service as a virtual propaganda arm of the state during those wars. Hallin himself admitted that, during these wars, "coherent statements of alternative visions of the world order and of US policy rarely appeared in the news."[7] There were hundreds of US reporters in El Salvador during its Reagan-era elections. If, as Hallin claimed, MSM journalism was steadily improving with increasing "professionalism," how is it that the "news" on Central American elections and wars so rarely reflected the perspectives of the majority? The PM can explain this. Hallin could not.

Another academic media scholar, Michael Schudson, cited Hallin's analysis of the alleged weakness of the PM in covering the Central American wars as an important part of his own denigration of the PM. He claimed that we were "not so careful," as we failed to note that there had been a diminution of bias over time in covering elections, from Vietnam in the 1960s and 1970s to El Salvador and Nicaragua in the 1980s.[8] His claim of our carelessness was not based on any independent study of his own but relied on Hallin's claim of MSM progress. Hallin never examined election coverage over time in detail and seems to have simply generalized from the greater public opposition to the wars in the 1980s as compared with the 1960s. This is a weak argument from unproven effects, and hence not a meaningful criticism of the PM.

Schudson had a later statement on the PM that was also neither careful nor responsible criticism. He described the PM as a "rigid view that sees the media organizations working hand-in-glove with other large corporations to stifle dissent or promote a lethargic public acceptance of the existing distribution of power." This perspective, Schudson asserted, "is inconsistent with what most journalists in democratic societies commonly believe they are doing. It also fails to explain a great deal of news content, especially news critical of corporate power . . . or news of corporate scandals, conflicts, illegalities and failures."[9] But the PM is in no way "rigid," as it only attempts to provide a broad framework of analysis, and its authors have often stated that it does not purport to explain everything and that its effects will depend on a variety of factors, including the level of elite agreement as well as public understanding of the issues. We contended that the market-based system in which the MSM operate is largely uncoordinated, not one characterized by elites engaged as a joint management team that works toward "stifling" ends. We stated clearly that corporate abuses and scandals are real but outside our broader purview. We also explained that journalists can do their work with complete integrity while still following party lines and ideologies imposed by the institutional structures within which they work. Schudson apparently couldn't imagine structural-institutional impacts that become built-in.[10]

Other media analysts have also criticized the PM as too "deterministic," while still others have criticized it for not giving weights to the filters, i.e., not being sufficiently deterministic. But any scientific model or theory has to be deterministic to some degree in fixing its explanatory factors, and the PM is a broad framework of analysis, not a model or theory designed to give precise results. It works well in the numerous cases in which we can compare media treatment of similar events which are differently regarded by a powerful agent— e.g., "worthy" and "unworthy" victims, the Reagan-era elections in El Salvador and Nicaragua, and the Russian elections in 1996 (the Yeltsin era) and 2012 (the Putin era) as seen by US officials.[11] The PM also works well where we can see conflicts of interest between important parties, like governments and corporations wishing to carry out certain policies despite public interest groups or the broad public remaining skeptical of, or hostile to, such policies. This was the case with struggles over NAFTA and TPP, in which the MSM's alignment with the government and pro-NAFTA and pro-TPP forces was impressive.[12] The same has been true of the struggle between the chemical industry and public health spokespersons over the regulation of chemicals, "junk science" on chemicals, and "scares" about chemical threats. The chemical industry has wanted freedom of action and minimal regulation, whereas many public health experts have sought—unsuccessfully—the installation of a "precautionary principle" rule that would require proof of safety before approval of new chemicals. The MSM have never pressed for precaution, have underplayed the environmental threat of weak regulation, have derided "scares" that were real, and have allowed the term "junk science" to be applied to critics of the chemical industry rather than to the industry itself, where it belongs.[13]

What is the status of the PM thirty years after publication? We can answer this by considering, first, the structural changes that have taken place since 1988 and their impact on the relevance of the PM; and, second, by testing the model in application to the contemporary performance of the MSM.

The main structural change that has affected the MSM has been the growth of the Internet, with a rapid concentration process there and a huge drain of advertising revenue from the legacy media to the leading firms providing search information access and social media, i.e., Google, Facebook, Yahoo, Microsoft, and Twitter.[14] Newspapers have been particularly hard hit, with a 60 percent drop in the workforce from 1990 to 2016,[15] and a precipitous drop in advertising revenue from $65.8 billion in 2000 to $18 billion in 2014.[16] As newspapers' advertising revenues have collapsed, Google and Facebook have experienced spectacular windfalls: In 2015, for example, Google and Facebook earned an estimated $30 billion and $8 billion, respectively, in digital advertising revenues.[17] Google's total revenues grew from $1.5 billion in 2003 to $74.5 billion in 2015.[18] By 2016, Alphabet, Google's holding company, was the largest media company in the world, with revenues 166 percent greater than Walt Disney's, its nearest rival.[19]

Although Internet optimists had forecast that we were entering a new era of media democratization, with thousands, or millions, of bloggers and other news sources, it turns out that the power and pull of advertising, the networking effect of increasing size and outreach, and government policies, have rapidly led to levels of concentration in communication on Internet sites greater than those attained earlier by the legacy media—with Google attaining an 88 percent market share in online searches and search advertising and Facebook a 77 percent market share in mobile social media.[20] These two giants have used micro-technology to identify and sell to advertisers full dossiers on the personal habits, relationships, and tastes of the vast number of people using Google's powerful search engine and posting their "likes" along with other personal information on Facebook.[21]

These Internet giants are in the surveillance-marketing ("spying and selling") business, not in the business of creating news or other content. But users of Google and especially Facebook want news, so Facebook has become a platform through which news created elsewhere flows and is consumed and redirected. Postings on Facebook have become a major news source for ordinary Facebook users and for other online services like Huffington Post and BuzzFeed, and Facebook officials, partly in response to charges of allowing and passing along "fake news," have been driven to manage the flow of news. This has included developing and utilizing algorithms that can automatically prune out materials that violate moral or other standards. But Facebook officials have also engaged in negotiations with reputable news sources that seek access to the Facebook platform and want to participate in Facebook's rulemaking on access. As Jonathan Taplin asks, "How long before Facebook becomes the controlling force in the online journalism business?"[22]

How did this structural transformation affect the workings of the filters identified by the PM? The for-profit sector of the media has certainly not diminished in relative size, and the revenue losses of the legacy media have intensified the MSM's search for advertising and made for greater dependence on powerful primary sources for news. The desire to avoid flak from the powerful and the unwillingness to challenge prevailing ideologies has also probably risen. The new Internet giants—not themselves in the journalism business but with significant power over news choices via their increasing role as news platforms—make for considerable uncertainty. They are likely to reflect in part the news choices determined by actual journalists, but the latter may be influenced by what produces traffic and advertising on the large new platforms.

The news performance of the MSM in recent decades has strongly confirmed the continued applicability of the PM. The Iraq War itself provides a plethora of evidence supportive of the PM. The intense war propaganda of the Bush administration succeeded in convincing a majority of US citizens that Saddam Hussein possessed weapons of mass destruction (WMD), but even as late as February 2003 (the attack began on March 20) a majority of the US public wanted further investigations by the UN inspection teams before the launch of any attack.[23] On February 15 and 16, 2003, there were mass antiwar protests with probably over one million people on the streets in dozens of US cities (and many millions in six hundred cities globally), a unique event since a war had yet to begin. But this massive demonstration of public opposition hardly moved the war-makers, and the MSM did not give the protests sympathetic coverage or diminish their own service as war facilitators.

The Bush administration aimed at regime change in Iraq. But as this was too conspicuous a violation of the UN Charter and international law, the officially declared aim was to remove Saddam Hussein's WMD. The Bush–Blair axis wanted to attack immediately, but a majority of the Security Council wanted to allow UN inspection teams to verify Bush's claims that Iraq possessed such weapons and, in the event that the weapons existed, to perhaps allow the inspection teams to remove them. Such inspections had, in fact, been in process for a decade. And there was already substantial evidence that such weapons had been entirely or almost entirely eliminated. Scott Ritter, a top inspector from 1991 to 1998, claimed that 90–95 percent of those weapons had been "verifiably eliminated" and that the residual was old and unusable.[24] Even more important, Hussein Kamel, Saddam Hussein's son-in-law and long in charge of Iraq's weapons program, defected in 1995, and in information he supplied to the CIA he claimed that Saddam's entire stock of chemical and biological WMD had been destroyed.[25]

Furthermore, under UN auspices there were two inspection teams at work, a United Nations Monitoring, Verification and Inspection

Commission (UNMOVIC), headed by Hans Blix; and an International Atomic Energy Agency (IAEA), headed by Mohamed ElBaradei. Both of these operations worked hard at inspections, found the Iraqi government quite cooperative, and continued to find nothing. This was exceedingly annoying to the Bush administration, which wanted a quick "favorable" finding and therefore assailed the inspectors' lack of speed and strove to discredit and bypass them. The MSM cooperated, treating the inspections as ineffective and largely ignoring their findings, thus helping set the stage for denying their authority and going to war.

The media's cooperation in this drive to war went far. There was the further demonization of Saddam Hussein and suppression of the news of his cooperation with inspections. Ignoring the credible negative findings from the on-the-scene inspectors, the MSM allowed the Bush team, their apologists, and their usually anonymous Iraqi sources to dominate the flow of purported information. Bush and company claimed that Iraq had an active nuclear weapons program as well as hidden chemical and biological weapons. The inspector chiefs denied this. The inspectors' evidence and Hussein Kamel's 1995 testimony had to be kept out of the public domain, and the MSM saw to this.

Bush, Cheney, and other officials had cited Kamel as authoritative, and in his notorious presentation to the UN Security Council on February 5, 2003, Secretary of State Colin Powell also cited Kamel as acknowledging Iraqi production of four tons of nerve gas, but he failed to mention that Kamel had said this had all been completely destroyed. Although the *Times* and other media had reported earlier on some of Hussein Kamel's evidence, his statement about destroyed WMD was suppressed except for one very late article published in *Newsweek* under the elusive title, "The Defector's Secrets."[26] Colin Powell's February 5 performance rested heavily on the claims of an Iraqi defector, Rafid Ahmed Alwan al-Janabi, also known as "Curveball," whose detailed claims of Iraq's biological warfare program were later admitted to have been entirely fraudulent. Curveball resided in Germany and the BND, Germany's Federal Intelligence Service, had warned US officials that his testimony was dubious. But his claims were obviously preferable to those of Hussein Kamel. The MSM

treated Powell's extensively disinforming Security Council performance as compelling.

MSM news flowed from Bush administration leaders, CIA and
Pentagon sources, and a steady stream of Iraqi defectors, many supplied to the media by Ahmed Chalabi, an Iraqi expatriate and head
of the Iraqi National Congress. Chalabi's organization was given
millions by the CIA, and he served the Bush program well.[27] Judith
Miller, the principal *New York Times* reporter on the Iraq War campaign, acknowledged depending heavily on Chalabi and his supply
of informants.[28] She wrote dozens of articles featured in the *Times*,
sourced entirely from Bush officials and Iraqi defectors.

The coordination with the war-makers' propaganda needs was
exemplary. Best known, and perhaps most revealing, was Miller's
article, written with Michael Gordon, published on September 8,
2002, "Threats and Responses: The Iraqis; U.S. Says Hussein Intensifies Quest for A-Bomb Parts."[29] The information was false. The aluminum tubes that Iraq was acquiring were not designed for bomb
use, as was disclosed later with less fanfare: The article was based on
a leak of classified information fed to the authors by Lewis Scooter
Libby, Vice President Dick Cheney's chief of staff.[30] The same day
Cheney cited Gordon and Miller's article on *Meet the Press* in support
of his claim that Saddam was aggressively seeking to enrich uranium,
as evidenced by his buying aluminum tubes. Other Bush officials also
quickly cited the same article as indication of the acute menace. This
was an exemplary case of government officials using a cooperative
media source for rapid propaganda service.

In its opinion columns also, the *New York Times* served the war
party well. The *Times* not only paid no attention to the evidence of
Scott Ritter, who had been a top UN Special Commission inspector
and was outspoken on the errors and dangers of Bush's Iraq policy,
it actually published an article in its *Magazine* devoted to discrediting
him.[31] The *Times* much preferred Kenneth Pollack, author of the 2002
book, *The Threatening Storm: The Case for Invading Iraq*, who had four
pro-war op-ed columns in the paper in 2002–2003. The editorial
page supported Pollack's false claims that Iraq possessed WMD and
pursued a nuclear weapons program.[32] In both its opinion columns
and news reporting on Iraq, the "Newspaper of Record" transmitted

fabricated propaganda claims flowing from the CIA, the Pentagon, and Ahmed Chalabi, an Iraqi funded by the CIA.

In sum, the performance of the *Times* and the MSM, before and during the invasion and occupation of Iraq, was as good a fit to the PM as any of the case studies presented in *Manufacturing Consent*. MSM coverage was built on Bush administration lies that were quickly exposed with the failed search for WMD. The *Times* and *Washington Post* both issued quasi-apologies for their performance in servicing the Iraq war-makers, but the responsible editors were not fired, and were almost immediately engaged in a similar performance on the next main target, Iran.

In fact, an enlightening comparison can be made of the media's treatment of the 2009 elections in Iran with elections in Honduras, also in 2009, following a coup there in the same year. A regime that the US had long targeted for destabilization and regime change carried out the Iranian election. The Honduran election took place after a democratically-elected liberal government, which had been disliked by both the domestic elite and the US-supported military establishment, had been overthrown by force on June 28. It took many weeks before the Obama government would use the word "coup" to describe what had happened in Honduras. And the United States stood pretty isolated as it tried to get other North and South American states to accept, alongside Obama and Clinton, the regime established by the coup.

With Washington opposing the Iranian government, it was a foregone conclusion that its election, like Nicaragua's in 1984, would be declared a sham, even though it was a contested election, with dissident Mir-Hossein Mousavi running against the demonized (by Western powers) incumbent Mahmoud Ahmadinejad. In the November 2009 Honduran election, there were no dissidents running, only two members of the elite, both of whom had supported the coup, and repression was almost certainly more severe than in Iran. Nevertheless, an analysis of US newspaper coverage found that derogatory terms such as "fraud" and "rigged" were used to describe the election in Honduras just 28 times, compared with 2,139 such uses in coverage of Iran's election.[33]

Another revealing difference can be seen in the treatment of the deaths of dissidents in the two countries.[34] On June 20, 2009, twenty-six-year-old Neda Agha-Soltan was shot to death in Iran while participating in a peaceful demonstration in Tehran. Her death became a "galvanizing symbol, both within Iran and increasingly around the world," Rachel Maddow said on MSNBC.[35] Video images of her plight circled the globe. That same day Roger Cohen denounced the killing on the editorial page of the *New York Times*. Only fifteen days later, nineteen-year-old Isis Obed Murillo was shot dead by the Honduran military during a peaceful protest in Honduras. Like Agha-Soltan's, his death was recorded in video images that circulated on the Internet. The differential media interest in US newspaper coverage was 736–8 in favor of Agha-Soltan; the TV differential was 231–1 in favor of Agha-Soltan.[36] The dramatic video images of Murillo's killing never caught hold in the world beyond Honduras. The social media, which had displayed such potential for organizing protest in Iran, failed to come to life in Honduras.

The agenda-setting capability of the powerful, and the resultant double standard, so obvious in the comparison of elections in El Salvador and Nicaragua in 1984, showed itself to be just as strong in the elections held in Iran and Honduras in 2009. The PM fits both of these pairings very comfortably.

The Propaganda Model is as strong and applicable as it was thirty years ago. The structural conditions have, if anything, given it more salience, with greater media concentration but still more competition for advertising revenue, enhanced power and reach of advertisers, and little if any diminution in the effects of the other three filters. What is more, the performance of the MSM in treating the run-up to the Iraq War, the conflict with Iran, and Russia's alleged election "meddling" and "aggression" in Ukraine and Crimea, offer case studies of biases as dramatic as those offered in the 1988 edition of *Manufacturing Consent*. The Propaganda Model lives on.

EDWARD S. HERMAN is an economist and an analyst of politics and media. Among his publication are three editions of *Manufacturing Consent: The Political Economy of the Mass Media* (1988, 2002, 2008), coauthored with Noam Chomsky; and the two-volume set, *The Political Economy of Human Rights* (1979), also with Chomsky. His most recent books, with David Peterson, are *The Politics of Genocide* (2010) and *Enduring Lies: The Rwandan Genocide in the Propaganda System, 20 Years Later* (2014).

Notes

1. There were few if any "boys" killed at Srebrenica; most of the eight thousand were soldiers killed in combat, not executed. See Edward S. Herman, ed., *The Srebrenica Massacre: Evidence, Context, Politics* (Evergreen Park, Illinois: Alphabet Soup, 2011).

2. Andrew Mullen, "Twenty Years On: The Second-Order Prediction of the Herman–Chomsky Propaganda Model," *Media, Culture & Society*, Vol. 32, No. 4 (July 2010), 673–90.

3. One illustration of fake news: the Reagan administration claimed that Soviet MiGs were being imported into Nicaragua in the midst of their election preparations, a false and negative distraction from the election reality. See Edward S. Herman and Noam Chomsky, *Manufacturing Consent: The Political Economy of the Mass Media* (New York: Pantheon, 2002), 137–39.

4. Raymond Bonner, *Weakness and Deceit: U.S. Policy and El Salvador* (New York: Times Books, 1984). See also Edward S. Herman, "The *Journal*'s War on the Media," in Herman, *The Myth of the Liberal Media: An Edward Herman Reader* (New York: Peter Lang, 1999), 111–13.

5. Daniel Hallin, *We Keep America on Top of the World: Television Journalism and the Public Sphere* (Milton Park, Abingdon: Routledge, 1994), 11–12.

6. Walter LaFeber, "Whose News?" *New York Times*, November 6, 1988, http://www.nytimes.com/1988/11/06/books/whose-news.html.

7. Hallin, *We Keep America on Top of the World*, 67.

8. Michael Schudson, "The Sociology of News Production," *Media, Culture & Society*, Vol. 11, No. 3 (July 1989), 263–82, 269.

9. Michael Schudson, "Four Approaches to the Sociology of News," in James Curran, ed., *Media and Society* (London and New York: Bloomsbury, 2010), 164–85, 168.

10. For a detailed analysis of Schudson's critique, see Yigal Godler, "Why Anti-Realist Views Persist in Communication Research: A Political Economic Reflection on Relativism's Prominence," *Critical Sociology*, May 16, 2016, 1–19, doi: 10.1177/0896920516645935.

11. For analysis of media performance in the Yeltsin and Putin eras, see Edward S. Herman, "Fake News on Russia and Other Official Enemies: The *New York Times*, 1917–2017," *Monthly Review*, Vol. 69, No. 3 (July–August 2017), 98–112.

12. Edward S. Herman, "NAFTA, Mexican Meltdown, and the Propaganda System," in Herman, *Myth of the Liberal Media*, 181–95.

13. Edward S. Herman, "Corporate Junk Science in the Media," in Herman, *Myth of the Liberal Media*, 231–56.

14. See "State of the News Media 2016," Pew Research Center, June 15, 2016, 56; available for download at http://www.journalism.org/files/2016/06/State-of-the-News-Media-Report-2016-FINAL.pdf.

15. Roy Greenslade, "Almost 60% of US Newspaper Jobs Vanish in 26 Years," *Guardian*, June 6, 2016, https://www.theguardian.com/media/greenslade/2016/jun/06/almost-60-of-us-newspaper-jobs-vanish-in-26-years.

16. Jonathan Taplin, *Move Fast and Break Things: How Facebook, Google, and Amazon Cornered Culture and Undermined Democracy* (New York: Little, Brown and Company, 2017), 7.

17. Mathew Ingram, "How Google and Facebook Have Taken Over the Digital Ad Industry," *Fortune*, January 4, 2017, http://fortune.com/2017/01/04/google-facebook-ad-industry/.

18. Taplin, *Move Fast and Break Things*, 7.

19. Lauren Johnson, "Google Now Controls 12 Percent of All Global Media Spend," *Adweek*, May 26, 2016, http://www.adweek.com/digital/google-now-controls-12-percent-all-global-media-spend-171701/.

20. Taplin, *Move Fast and Break Things*, 21.

21. See, for example, "Facebook Buys Sensitive User Data to Offer Marketers Targeted Advertising," story #23 in Chapter 1 of this volume.

22. Taplin, *Move Fast and Break Things*, 93.

23. E.g., "Americans on Iraq and the UN Inspections," World Public Opinion, February 21, 2003, http://worldpublicopinion.net/americans-on-iraq-and-the-un-inspections/.

24. Scott Ritter and William Rivers Pitt, *War on Iraq: What Team Bush Doesn't Want You to Know* (Sydney: Allen & Unwin, 2002), 28.
25. John Barry, "The Defector's Secrets," *Newsweek*, March 2, 2003, http://www.newsweek.com/exclusive-defectors-secrets-132803.
26. Ibid.
27. E.g., Sewell Chan, "Ahmad Chalabi, Iraqi Politician Who Pushed for U.S. Invasion, Dies at 71," *New York Times*, November 3, 2015, https://www.nytimes.com/2015/11/04/world/middleeast/ahmad-chalabi-iraq-dead.html.
28. Miller acknowledged that Chalabi "has provided most of the front-page exclusives on WMD to our paper." Quoted in Howard Friel and Richard Falk, *The Record of the Paper: How the* New York Times *Misreports US Foreign Policy* (London: Verso, 2004), 11.
29. Michael R. Gordon and Judith Miller, "Threats and Responses; The Iraqis; U.S. Says Hussein Intensifies Quest for A-Bomb Parts," *New York Times*, September 8, 2002, http://www.nytimes.com/2002/09/08/world/threats-responses-iraqis-us-says-hussein-intensifies-quest-for-bomb-parts.html.
30. David E. Sanger and David Barstow, "Iraq Findings Leaked by Aide were Disputed," *New York Times*, April 9, 2006, http://www.nytimes.com/2006/04/09/washington/us/iraq-findings-leaked-by-aide-were-disputed.html.
31. Barry Bearak, "Scott Ritter's Iraq Complex," *New York Times Magazine*, November 24, 2002, http://www.nytimes.com/2002/11/24/magazine/scott-ritter-s-iraq-complex.html.
32. For a good discussion of Pollack and his role in the *Times*'s war apologetics, see Friel and Falk, *The Record of the Paper*, 42–50.
33. For a full analysis of the two elections, see David Peterson and Edward S. Herman, "Iran and Honduras in the Propaganda System: Part 2, The 2009 Iranian and Honduran Elections," MROnline, October 24, 2010, https://mronline.org/2010/10/24/iran-and-honduras-in-the-propaganda-system-part-2-the-2009-iranian-and-honduran-elections/.
34. David Peterson and Edward S. Herman, "Iran and Honduras in the Propaganda System: Part 1, Neda Agha-Soltan versus Isis Obed Murillo," MROnline, October 5, 2010, https://mronline.org/2010/10/05/iran-and-honduras-in-the-propaganda-system-part-1-neda-agha-soltan-versus-isis-obed-murillo/.
35. *The Rachel Maddow Show*, MSNBC, June 22, 2009, http://www.msnbc.com/transcripts/rachel-maddow-show/2009-06-22.
36. Peterson and Herman, "Iran and Honduras in the Propaganda System: Part 1."

CHAPTER 8

Breaking Through Power
Mass Media Blacks Out the Super Bowl of Citizen Action

Ralph Nader

AN UNPRECEDENTED CIVIC MOBILIZATION

On the occasion of the fiftieth anniversary of my book, *Unsafe at Any Speed*, my colleagues suggested that there should be a celebratory dinner, since the movement the book ignited for safer, more fuel-efficient and less polluting motor vehicles led to the creation of numerous successful consumer, environmental, and other citizen-advocacy organizations. However, instead of looking at past achievements, I thought a more galvanizing proposal would be to organize the "Super Bowl of Citizen Action" at the historic Constitution Hall in Washington, DC. We set about planning what we hoped would be an unprecedented civic mobilization.

The eight-day program was called Breaking Through Power. All sixty-four hours of presentations were livestreamed by The Real News Network (see www.breakingthroughpower.org). The enthusiastic responses by invited speakers from around the country resulted in over 180 speakers participating in 140 presentations. These eight days featured the greatest number of civic advocates, thinkers, innovators, and whistleblowers ever brought together for civic mobilization in American history.

Many of the groups and their leaders had been driven into defensive positions by the ever-worsening corporate state to which both political parties had contributed in varying degrees. We believed that the Breaking Through Power conference, sponsored by the Center for Study of Responsive Law, would result in a major show of civic presence in the nation's capital and demonstrate that the interconnected whole of grassroots action in the United States is greater than the sum of its parts.

At the same time, the 2016 presidential election period—so dominated by the mass media's fascination with Donald J. Trump and his outrages—was producing higher ratings in a circular dance of free publicity for him and big profits for the media corporations. CBS CEO Leslie Moonves told an audience at a Morgan Stanley investors' conference, "It may not be good for America, but it's damn good for CBS." One reason the obsession with candidate Trump was not good for America is that it led to producers, editors, and reporters shutting out the policy criticisms of the candidates as well as widely supported reforms by the civil society—the roots and branches of our democracy.

The voices of civic leaders were largely silenced in the presidential election season. The two political parties and their entourages, together with the mass commercial media, diluted civil discourse in pursuit of their own goals—namely, to forge a political subculture beholden to campaign professionals and corporate interests rather than one responsive to average Americans. The range of debate narrowed to a handful of issues, which were often deceptively or superficially presented. The price for such misguided priorities is a starved, often rancid, public dialogue, which prioritizes spectacle over substance and causes many voters to feel cynical or indifferent to the political process. This in turn makes it easier for corporate super PACs to shape the political debate. Letting in citizen groups for interviews, presentations, op-eds, and civically-organized debates can broaden and enrich the content of electioneering, elevate expectations, diminish unchecked false statements, and attract the interest and participation of otherwise disenfranchised voters.

Most of the major concerns that a democratic election process should embrace are regularly taken off the table by the Republican and Democratic parties and their candidates. These concerns include prosecuting corporate crime, protecting pensions, fighting to prevent occupational disease and injuries, reducing fatalities associated with medical malpractice, cutting the bloated military budget, closing corporate tax loopholes, advocating for a living wage, defending union organizing laws, championing full Medicare for all, removing big-money from politics and strengthening democratic institutions, securing ballot access and other reforms for a competitive process that gives more voices and choices to voters, controlling the vast commons of public lands, public airwaves, and other public assets we already own, addressing the insane allocation of public budgets which often ignore the needs of everyday Americans, and confronting the boomeranging behavior of America's destructive, empire-building foreign policy, to name just a few.

The civic leaders who presented at and attended Breaking Through Power were accomplished experts and activists on these and other critical subjects. Unfortunately, their reports and actions have been increasingly ignored by the national news media. In the run-up to last year's presidential, congressional, and state elections, they were rarely interviewed or even quoted on the candidates' positions, and they were kept off the Sunday morning network shows, marginalized from the op-ed pages, and largely absent from the endless hours that the cable shows devoted to repetitive political gossip and speculation.

National Public Radio (NPR) and the Public Broadcasting Service (PBS) spent time interviewing other members of the media for comment and speculation rather than the experienced leaders of citizen groups, who in past years have changed our country for the better. Their information base for proposals that can be described as fair, prudent, and achievable were not solicited. For example, on tax proposals by the major candidates, Judy Woodruff of the *PBS News Hour* went to her usual reporter list rather than interview Robert McIntyre of Citizens for Tax Justice as her predecessors used to do. This selective censorship is troubling in any case, but is especially disheartening when perpetrated by public media institutions, as they do a disservice to their mission of informing the public by ignoring the civic community.

A REMARKABLE MASS-MEDIA BLACKOUT

We thought the critical mass of the citizen organizations at Constitution Hall might break through both the exclusion by the mass media and the indifference shown by the political candidates. After all, many of these civic leaders had been around long enough, with myriad breakthrough books, reports, legislative testimony, and lawsuits, to have received some coverage in past decades on network shows, such as the nightly news and the *Phil Donahue Show*, and in print media. They were not anonymous persons. But that was then and we had to deal with now.

We developed an elaborate media outreach plan, meeting reporters and editors in person, using social media, email, postal mailings, and news releases. I met with the bureau chief of the *New York Times* and the national news editor and managing editor of the *Washington Post*, called top editors and news directors, reporters, and columnists of other major newspapers and magazines, and even consulted with the supervising editor of NPR's DC station and the national NPR and PBS ombudsmen. These efforts were followed by news releases pertaining to each day's program, with additional focus on specialized media for the various subjects, speakers, and panelists. Thanks to the generous support of one donor, we were even able to take out a full-page ad in the *New York Times* to promote the conference. Similar full-page ads were placed in Washington's leading neighborhood newspaper, *The Current*.

Since the same media consistently cover "conservative" conventions such as the Conservative Political Action Conference (CPAC), the American Israel Public Affairs Committee (AIPAC), and other right-wing gatherings, we hoped that the media would also cover this first across-the-board mobilization to take existing civic groups to higher levels of effectiveness and to secure long-overdue democratic solutions, many appealing to liberals and conservatives alike. We strove to create a new muscular civic nexus between local communities and their counterparts in Washington, DC. Without the major media's reach and impact, this is undoubtedly a more difficult task.

It turned out to be the most remarkable blackout we've ever experienced in over fifty years of working the justice beat in Washington, DC. As the conference programs show, there was ample material for the mass media to select from on each day of the conference. They could have reported major themes of the presentations or chosen one civic innovator for a human-interest profile. I directed their attention, for example, to Ralf Hotchkiss, founder of the nonprofit Whirlwind Wheelchair, who designs wheelchairs for lower cost and greater durability, having earlier laid the groundwork in the 1980s for breaking the grip of the Everest & Jennings Corporation's domination of the market with their high-priced, low-quality wheelchairs. As a paraplegic (from a bicycle crash while in high school) he proceeded to travel by himself to many less-developed countries, showing locals, mostly women, how to build sturdy wheelchairs made from local materials. The feedback he received led to more refinements for ever more adaptable chairs crucial to the very lives of immobile, impoverished residents. Years ago, *Parade* profiled Ralf, and he received a MacArthur "Genius" Award in 1989. In more recent years he has been ignored while the media continues their infatuation with utterly trivial pursuits.

On the Constitution Hall stage Ralf tried in vain to break his wheelchair by going over a ramp and coming down hard, demonstrating the remarkable strength of his Whirlwind Wheelchair design. This was a story with contemporary relevance and appeal—some sixty million people living in less-developed countries need wheelchairs, not drones, missiles, and grenades from the American Empire. However, for the *Times*, *Post*, *Time*, and television stations, Hotchkiss was not newsworthy enough, not scatological, militaristic, or Kardashian enough.

The Breaking Through Power conference featured nine major themes germane to reporting, feature-writing, and editorializing. The speakers were among the most accomplished in their fields. The theme for the first day of the May program was "Breaking Through Power: How It's Done"; day two's featured theme was "Breaking Through Media"; day three covered "Breaking Through War"; and day four dealt with "Breaking Through Congress and Advancing a New Citizen Agenda."

Before the commencement of the May events, the *Washington Times* and the *Washington Monthly* ran small pieces and three local television stations allowed me brief interviews. During the proceedings, all the speakers were available for interviews before and after their presentations. Although Scott Wilson, the national news editor of the *Washington Post*, and several other prominent editors and reporters expressed interest in covering Breaking Through Power, they were conspicuously absent from Constitution Hall. Our sign-in list for the press did not include any of the expected journalists. *The*

New York Times, the *Wall Street Journal*, and the Associated Press were not there either. Their collective absence, and what it demonstrated about their lack of commitment to providing serious content from the civil society for their readers, was a story in itself.

Remarkably, the indie or progressive press also failed to cover this event, except for the *Washington Spectator*. When you realize how rarely the engrossing topics from Breaking Through Power are given any attention by media so consistently preoccupied by fluff and empty punditry, it is permissible to shout, "Censored!" After all, many of the Breaking Through Power participants would qualify for induction into a Citizen Hall of Fame—were there one in our country. Most of their positions would also garner majority support from the American people.

The absence of beat reporters and the specialized media, whose job it is specifically to cover many of the topics presented in-depth by the speakers, did not go unnoticed. Print and electronic media critics did not show up to hear what former commissioners of the FCC, Phil Donahue, Patti Smith, Mark Green, progressive media reporters and commentators, a prize-winning filmmaker, Eugene Jarecki, a Pulitzer Prize–winning editorial cartoonist, Matt Wuerker, Jim Hightower, Jeff Chester, or NSA-officials-turned-whistleblowers William Binney and Kirk Wiebe had to say. Nor did Mickey Huff, director of Project Censored, talking about decades of censorship, invite their curiosity.

One of my appeals was a historical one, made directly to the *New York Times*'s Washington bureau chief and two of her colleagues, and to the *Washington Post*'s managing editor. When I came to Washington in the early 1960s to pursue regulation of the auto industry, I had neither campaign money nor access to the decision-makers. What I did have was some knowledge, determination, and a sense of what it would take to break through—namely, the attention of key committee chairs and their staff in Congress, a White House chief assistant to the president, and a group of reporters committed to following the unfolding story in congressional hearings. Reporters for the major media, led by the *Washington Post*, United Press International (UPI), and the *New York Times*, started covering the auto safety regulatory story—not just doing one feature and leaving it there, as they so often do today.

For a number of years, reporters regularly covered the unfolding stories of the consumer, environmental, and occupational health and safety movements, freedom of information news, events involving whistleblowers and their protections, and related litigation conferences and marches. This coverage galvanized Congress and the White House to enact important legislation regarding motor vehicles, food, household products, gas pipelines, air and water pollution, drinking water and toxic chemicals, and the historic amendments to the Freedom of Information Act of 1974—among others. Our country became safer as a result, and the example set by such legislation prodded other countries to follow America's leadership.

"Isn't that what the free media should be about?" I asked them. "Wasn't that a shining period in the history of the mass media?" Why then, in subsequent decades, haven't the media continued to advance these noble causes and give people what they need to know, in spite of advertising revenue, company stock prices, and the rest of the more commercialized media's concerns? They weren't ready to concede my point. They alluded to so many other media outlets these days, so many of their own self-generated features, the changing economics of their business, a diminishing pool of reporters, and the pervasive implication that I was pushing my agenda. On hearing the latter observation, my reply was simply that these issues and revelations and their advocates ought to be judged for their newsworthiness and accuracy in that they offer compelling human stories and clearly serve the public interest. I usually offered some examples of important stories in that regard that were not covered at all, year after year.

Unfortunately, they remained unpersuaded. The mass media are experiencing pressure on their bottom line that convinces them, wrongly I believe, to cut back on coverage of regulatory issues that affect their readers' safety and access to necessities. The media have also come to cover much more extensively those efforts tied to existing power centers and to ignore endeavors seeking to reform or overcome the abuses of power. So, for example, if instead of publicly proposing and picketing for a higher minimum wage, I had held a joint press conference with Nancy Pelosi when she was Speaker of the House, the mass media would have covered me with her. That choice creates a vicious circle for those seeking to break through power with information, values, and presence, and it would have forced civic leaders to take a backseat in their own movements and instead attempt to persuade a reluctant Speaker Pelosi to lead. Only covering initiatives when they are endorsed by contemporary power actors is a formula for only covering the status quo power centers. This attitude toward what is "news" has stalled the upgrading of the federal minimum wage for the past decade.

Why can't the mass media have a higher estimate of its own significance and provide the kind of informed coverage that is so central to a healthy democracy? It's almost as if citizens who want to draw attention to such important issues as advocating arms control or cyber warfare control treaties, waging peace over war, auditing the Pentagon budget, or taxing Wall Street trading, require endorsements by high government officials or a very unlikely press conference by a half dozen big company CEOs to make the evening news. Those are rare occurrences. Reforms in our country usually come from the bottom up. It gets done because civic efforts persist, are given media coverage to reach more people, and eventually reach the decision-makers for enactment. That we cannot even use our own property, the public airwaves, to reach one another through our own radio, TV, and audience networks day after day, illustrates still more structural obstacles to having a people's media.

With all these experiences from the four days in May, we resolved to forge ahead, hoping for adequate media coverage for the second portion of the conference in September. Because these themes were appealing to different constituencies with different reporters covering them, we thought maybe our luck would change. The first day of the September portion of the conference devoted eight hours to "Building Civic Skills and Breaking Through Apathy." Day two examined the little-covered but vast commons in the United States under the title of "Controlling What We Own, Shifting Power." The speakers on those days focused on what they were doing to correct the huge imbalances of power between the few and the many, including empowering shareholders and savers, placing control of the commons back in the hands of the people (by definition, the rightful owners of the commons), and creating public banking institutions like the state bank that has long operated so successfully in North Dakota.

The third day in September detailed existing and proposed models for sustained citizen action, how to finance them, and new proposals to facilitate people banding together. In the afternoon, we applied these models by holding a rally for DC statehood, with former DC mayors, the chair of the DC City Council, and the nonvoting DC representative to Congress, along with leading grassroots advocates and legal experts.

The final day of Breaking Through Power was a first-ever national civic event recognizing the law of torts and the civil justice system. The law of wrongful injury and trial by jury in open courts of law was one of the great liberation movements coming out of medieval England and was refined in our country for over 250 years to keep up with changing values and technologies. Historian Eric Foner has rightly called tort law the "weapon of the weak." We hoped that a program dedicated to the many dimensions of tort law, including the relentless attack to weaken its remedies by the insurance and tortfeasors' lobby, would be worthy of attention from the media and the legal community.

The program featured national experts on many aspects of this important pillar of civil law—invoked by wrongfully injured plaintiffs without having to ask permission from any authority—which is a form of initiatory democracy. The agenda featured numerous stories for the press—especially on the declining state of the civil jury, the use of tort law to break through the Catholic Church's cover-up of sexual abuse, the importance of class actions as a tool for consumer protection, the relevance of contemporary issues such as climate change and cybertorts, the increasing use of fine-print contracts to take away people's day in court, human interest stories by successful plaintiffs, and proposals for advancing this form of justice.

Neither the general media nor the specialized legal media bothered to show up. As with the other days, the fact that the proceedings were livestreamed and could be viewed by those reporters who could not attend in person made absolutely no difference.

What of C-SPAN? It came for one day in May and one day in September. As the only unedited, national media outlet for serious events, C-SPAN was heavily committed to covering and replaying, over and over, the often redundant speeches and utterances of candidates running in the presidential primaries. Since the Republican primary had far more candidates, they received far more C-SPAN time than the Democratic presidential candidates, whose field was quickly reduced to Hillary Clinton and Bernie Sanders. It would seem that C-SPAN, for balance, would cover progressive gatherings with many proposals and redirections pertinent to any electoral campaign. If anything, C-SPAN, a creation of the cable industry responding to Brian Lamb's bold public service idea, offers right-wing events the type of extensive coverage that most progressive groups can only envy.

The afternoon devoted to DC statehood was most revealing of the local DC media. Supported by 71 percent of DC residents in a recent poll, "New Columbia" becoming our fifty-first state should have been a natural for coverage by local public radio stations, the *Washington Post*, the *Washington Times*, and other media in the Maryland and Virginia suburbs. Hitherto there had been no comparable convocation with so many notable advocates and officials present. Nonetheless, the event received no coverage, not even from the popular *Kojo Nnamdi Show* on WAMU public radio. For a cause so important to the residents of the District of Columbia, the local media did a gross disservice to their audience by ignoring it.

The same disinterest came from the business media—print and electronic—regarding movements and unique proposals to have the people, who own the commons, and shareholders and pensioners, who own the greatest accumulation of wealth in the US, acquire more control from the iron grip of corporations and their managers. Eminent presenters included the legendary mutual fund innovator, John Bogle, as well as victorious lawyers, corporate campaigners, and strategists, such as Ray Rogers, Jeffrey Clements, Dennis Kelleher, James Henry, and David Bollier. The leading advocate of state public banking, Ellen Brown, surveyed rising activities in several states, including California. The business press, with their expansive cable time, was not there. Neither was anyone from Bloomberg News—TV or radio—there to cover any one of the newsworthy presenters.

ORGANIZING FULL–TIME CIVIC GROUPS

Throughout the eight days of the conference there were proposals to organize full-time civic groups. On the media day, an authors' organization was proposed to monitor systemic lack of coverage across all media of books challenging power, alerting society to what's going on beyond entertainment and advertising. Similarly, Lloyd Constantine outlined a proposal to form a "Penny Brigade," whereby a tiny number of shareholders—individual and institutional—could contribute one cent per share owned each year to fund five hundred full-time watchdogs of five hundred leading corporations. The mere publicizing by me a few years ago of this mechanism of accountability on cable TV prompted cash-rich Cisco Systems to announce for the first time a solid annual dividend (nearly 3 percent) to its investors.

The most consequential proposal, made on May 25, 2016, was our plan to establish a nonprofit anti-war, pro-peace Secretariat staffed mostly by high ranking veterans to enable fast responses and actions whenever the warfare state and its warmongering ideologues drive the country toward wars of aggression. The fabricated drumbeat toward the criminal war of aggression against Iraq in 2003 and beyond by George W. Bush and Dick Cheney served as our Exhibit A.

The staff of the Secretariat would enable retired officials from the military, national security, and diplomatic services, backed by a mass media campaign, to meet with and testify before members of Congress, organize around the country, hold news conferences, and publish op-eds in the press. They would constitute an aggregating formidable public opposition to unconstitutional, illegal, unwise wars and military adventures that are boomeranging against the security, economic well-being, and liberties of the American people, along with the millions of civilian victims abroad.

In the months before the March 2003 invasion of Iraq, at least three hundred retired, high-level establishment, military, national security, and diplomatic officials spoke out against the looming invasion. Among the most outspoken was retired General Anthony Zinni, as well as retired General William Odom, who also was head of the NSA, and Brent Scowcroft and James Baker, two of former President George H.W. Bush's closest military security advisors.

They and others expressed their opinions publicly, but no one was aggregating, coordinating, and facilitating such retirees to constitute a daily broad-based momentum against the lies, deceptions, and cover-ups of the Bush/Cheney regime and their intimidation, post-

9/11, of both the mass media and the opposition party day after day. The results and spread of the war on Iraq have been catastrophic for the region, for our soldiers, and for the next generation of Americans, all of whom will continue to pay the terrible price for this immense war crime.

I was not the only one who believed that such a Secretariat, with a hundred-million-dollar annual budget—which could have easily been provided by an equally outspoken anti–Iraq War megabillionaire, George Soros—could have stopped the deadly rush to Iraq. Later the Secretariat could have more easily turned the tide against the reckless 2011 undeclared war on Libya, opposed by Secretary of Defense Robert Gates. Spearheaded by the hawkish secretary of state, Hillary Clinton, the chaotic, violent attacks in Libya have destabilized other countries in Africa ever since.

It is not surprising that, without previews or coverage by the mass media, getting those ideas to the vast audience beyond the podium has been difficult indeed. For those modernists who think that email lists, Facebook, and Twitter accounts are a substitute, think again. Serious engagement requires serious media well beyond the frenzied, cluttered overload of hyper-micro messaging. While social media platforms can play an important role in generating attention and turnout for serious causes, coverage by the mass media and established institutions is essential for taking these efforts to the next level.

Despite the media blackout, all sixty-four hours of the Breaking Through Power gatherings are available to citizens, scholars, and students at www.breakingthroughpower.org. It is my hope that the recorded presentations will come to serve as a valuable brain trust for future advocates and students of policy and action.

However, in light of our experiences in the Breaking Through Power conference, it's important to note that even reaching reporters and editors to give them timely notices of events, scoops, leads, and alerts is much harder than in the pre-Internet era. Contemporary newsrooms, once noisy with human interchanges, have grown eerily quiet. The telephone is rarely answered for the kind of two-way personal exchanges that were so crucial to citizen groups in past decades. Reporters now look at their screens, post newsy bits online, and check their smartphones for emails and text messages. While the sheer variety and scope of the Breaking Through Power mobilizations illuminated just how completely in absentia the mass media can be, progressive citizen groups in Washington, speaking truth and facts to power and myths, have mostly resigned themselves to appearing rarely in the national print media, apart from a quote now and then, and almost never on the national television news or weekday afternoon TV shows. The latter have become little more than caricatures, with confessions, comedic exhibitions, personal masochisms, and self-indulgences introverting a mass audience largely made up of the unemployed and millions of other marginalized people seeking a little excitement in their lives.

Their predecessor shows were mildly mindful of the 1934 Communications Act, which allowed broadcasters free use of our public airwaves only if they performed in the "public interest, convenience and necessity." That background awareness allowed occasional invitations for the major justice movements in America—civil rights, women's rights, environment, civil liberties, consumer and labor rights, along with more local oppressed groups that were given a voice. I can look back and call Phil Donahue the greatest practitioner and enabler of the First Amendment in the twentieth century, and I'd challenge anyone to provide a rebuttal. He so believed in the First Amendment that he had Rev. Jerry Falwell, as well as others with whom he disagreed, on his show numerous times.

Apart from independent media, which offer few opportunities to reach mass audiences, there are hardly any venues today that highlight honest representation of national civic action. Public radio and public TV, while better in most cases than their pathetic commercial counterparts on the public's right to know, are also heavily reliant on business advertisements and their own fear of right-wingers in Congress and elsewhere. Consequently, they don't come close to providing programming that helps a democracy to function, deepen, and renew itself.

CONCLUSION: RECLAIMING THE PUBLIC AIRWAVES

In 1979, we proposed an audience network using regular prime-time hours daily, by returning time to the radio and television audience from the free 24/7 license of the broadcast industry. We later proposed that cable time should be given to channels for workers, students, patients, consumers, civil servants, and other groups deprived of coverage, to facilitate organizing, publicizing, and collaborating with one another. There are over six hundred cable channels devoted to infomercials and frivolity, including low-grade, canned entertainment. Since *we the people* provide both network and cable businesses their licenses and franchises (that keep we the people off their stations), we can, through legislation and ordinances, change the terms of this surrender into partial acquisitions of our public airwaves—locally, regionally, and nationally. Funding for studios, reporters, editors, producers, and equipment would come from starting to charge these media companies rent for the lucrative use of our public property that they have been getting free since their origins.

Otherwise, the "vast [media] wasteland," to recall Federal Communications Commission (FCC) Commissioner Newton Minow's famous address in 1961 to the National Association of Broadcasters, will continue to distance itself from the urgent civic needs of the citizenry. In the process, they will cover elections as very profitable entertainment, closing out the civic arenas that have been the wellsprings and reservoirs of our justice and freedoms. Meanwhile, reporters, editors, and television and radio producers can be forced to produce at least a modest expansion in coverage. Complaining formally to the FCC, especially around station license renewal time, gets the attention of the broadcasters, even if the FCC does little or nothing.

Always remember the public airwaves and cable licenses are our property. In the early deliberations over licensing the public airwaves during the 1920s, conservatives like Herbert Hoover thought radio should be a public trust without any advertisements. Today, over 90 percent of the time on radio and TV is devoted to entertainment, music, and advertisements. We need to raise our expectations, at least to the level of the 1934 Communications Act, and exercise our First Amendment rights to demand serious attention for grassroots civic action.

NOTE: For a complete list of noted civic leaders brought together for the May and September 2016 Breaking Through Power sessions, see https://www.breakingthroughpower.org/speakers/.

RALPH NADER has spent his lifetime challenging corporations and government agencies to be more accountable to the public. His 1965 book *Unsafe at Any Speed* permanently altered the safety standards of the US automobile industry. He successfully lobbied in 1974 for amendments to the Freedom of Information Act, which gave increased public access to government documents. Over the years he has founded many public interest groups, including Public Citizen, Critical Mass Energy Project, Public Interest Research Groups, and the Center for Study of Responsive Law. He continues to be a relentless advocate for grassroots activism and democratic change.

ACKNOWLEDGMENTS

Mickey Huff and Andy Lee Roth

We continue to be humbled by the many wonderful teachers, students, and committed activists who make the work of Project Censored possible. And we are extremely grateful for the vibrant energy, creativity, persistence, and dedication of all of those who helped make *Censored 2018*—our twenty-fifth annual book in our forty-two-year history.

In an era when the president of the United States refers to the free press as "enemies of the American people," we salute the courageous journalists and independent publications that continue to dig deep below the surface to report on the most important issues of our time. Project Censored exists to honor, highlight, and support your work, while helping educate the next generation of intrepid reporters. Faculty evaluators and student researchers at the Project's college and university affiliate campuses make it possible for us to cover the increasingly extensive, dynamic networked fourth estate as well as to diversify our reach and coverage. The authors who contributed to chapters and sections of *Censored 2018* inspire us with challenging questions and new perspectives. We are proud that this year's volume also represents the work of contributors ranging in age from those in their teens and twenties to an octogenarian *and* a nonagenarian. The members of our international panel of judges once again assured that our Top 25 list includes only the best, most significant validated independent news stories.

At Seven Stories Press, our extraordinary publishers in New York, Dan Simon, Jon Gilbert, Stewart Cauley, Ruth Weiner, Lauren Hooker, Allison Paller, Noah Kumin, Silvia Stramenga, Sanina Clark, and Yves Gaston have our great respect and gratitude for their steadfast commitment to publishing the Project's research. Michael Tencer and Veronica Liu are agile, trustworthy editors whose resolute efforts on behalf of *Censored 2018* go above and beyond.

Hilary Allison created the original artwork for the cover of *Censored 2018*. We are delighted to work with her again and appreciate her clear vision.

We thank our friend and ally, Khalil Bendib, whose cartoons have long accentuated our annual book, and continue to do so with unrivaled wit and wisdom.

We are hugely grateful to Peter Phillips, outgoing president of the Media Freedom Foundation, whose twenty-year support of the Project and ongoing teaching and research contributions make him a major force for social justice and equality in the world. Peter continues to be an inspiration to all of us.

We recognize the vision of our late founder, Carl Jensen (1929–2015). We acknowledge his tireless optimism, unwavering support for a free press, and commitment to critical media literacy education. We are honored to carry on the legacy he started in 1976.

The members of the Media Freedom Foundation's board of directors, listed below, continue to provide organizational structure and invaluable counsel, and help sustain us and keep us on course in pursuing Project Censored's mission.

Adam Armstrong is the long-time maestro of our Internet presence. As webmaster, he works tirelessly to maintain and expand our work at projectcensored.org, as well as our sister sites, including the Global Critical Media Literacy Project, at gcml.org. We could not reach our increasingly global audience without his great skills and dedication to our shared cause. He is also the force behind our new online video series as well as our podcast, *The Project Censored Show*, and our new Patreon page. Please visit and consider supporting our video and podcast work at patreon.com/projectcensored.

We thank Christopher Oscar and Doug Hecker of Hole in the Media Productions for their vision and support as filmmakers and allies. Their award-winning documentary, *Project Censored The Movie: Ending the Reign of Junk Food News*, brought Project Censored's message to new audiences and is now easier than ever to view online in many popular platforms. (See projectcensoredthemovie.com for viewing details.) We continue working with them, encouraging student and classroom production of video shorts on Project Censored news stories and analysis.

We are grateful to the friends and supporters of *The Project Censored Show*, now also a podcast, coming up on its seventh year. We thank our amazing producer at KPFA Pacifica Radio, Anthony Fest, and our live broadcast engineer, Erica Bridgeman. We also wish to thank all the volunteers there who support the overlapping missions of Project Censored and Pacifica; Bob Baldock for his work on public events; and all of the nearly forty stations from Maui to New York that carry our weekly public affairs program across the US. We thank cofounder and cohost of the program Peter Phillips, who continues to do monthly shows, as we also thank those who stepped up to be part of our expanding on-air team, including Nolan Higdon, Nicholas Baham III, Desiree McSwain, Michael Levitin, interns Aimee Casey and Alisha Huajardo, as well as Mitch Scorza at California State University, East Bay, for technical support.

We are grateful to the people who have hosted Project Censored events or helped to spread the word about the Project's mission over the past year, including John Bertucci of Petaluma Community Access Television, along with videographers Mark Jaramillo and Michael Martin; John Crowley, Diane Gentile, Paul Coffman, and everyone at Aqus Café; Larry Figueroa, Jennifer Jensen, and the crew at Lagunitas Brewing Company; Chase Palmieri and family at Risibisi; Raymond Lawrason, Grace Bogart, and all at Copperfield's Books; James Preston Allen and the team at *Random Lengths News*; Michael Nagler, Stephanie Van Hook, and the Metta Center for Nonviolence; Margli and Phil Auclair and everyone at the Mount Diablo Peace and Justice Center in Walnut Creek; Attila Nagy, the Petaluma Progressives, and all those at the Peace and Justice Center of Sonoma County; the Sociology Social Justice and Activism Club at Sonoma State University; Steven Jay at The World's Stage and Media Democracy in Action; Matthew Witt at the University of La Verne; Elizabeth Blakey at California State University, Northridge; Jason Houk, Kathleen Gamer, and all at Independent Media Week in Ashland, OR; the California Conference of the American Association of University Professors (CA-AAUP); Kenn Burrows; Susan Rahman; Kevin Pina; Chris McManus; David Talbot; Mark Crispin Miller; Marc Pilisuk; Peter Dale Scott; Davey D; Sharyl Attkisson; Abby Martin of *The Empire Files* and Media Roots; Mnar Muhawesh and the team at MintPress News; Free Speech TV; Arlene Engelhardt and Mary Glenney, hosts of *From a Woman's Point of View*; Lee Camp; Elaine Holtz; Linda Sartor; Jason Bud; Eric Draitser; John Barbour; Jon Gold; Ken Walden; John Collins and the team at Weave News; Chase Palmieri, Jared Fesler, and the Tribe at Tribeworthy.com; Maggie Jacoby and everyone involved in the Banned Books Week Coalition, including those at the National Coalition Against Censorship and James LaRue at the American Library Association's Office for Intellectual Freedom; Ralph Nader, the Center for Study of Responsive Law, and the organizers of "Breaking Through Power" in Washington, DC; and Peter Ludes and Hektor Haarkötter at the German Initiative on News Enlightenment—each of whom helps the Project to reach a broader audience.

We are grateful for our relationships with the Action Coalition for Media Education (ACME) and the graduate program in Media Literacy and Digital Culture at Sacred Heart University (SHU), as well as our collaborative effort, the Global Critical Media Literacy Project (gcml.org), which officially launched at the Media Freedom Summit for Project Censored's fortieth anniversary in October 2016. Special thanks to Rob Williams, Julie Frechette, Bill Yousman, and Lori Bindig Yousman. We will continue to promote critical media literacy education with our partners through the GCMLP.

Also, we give special thanks to everyone who helped organize and celebrate the Project's fortieth anniversary Media Freedom Summit, held at Sonoma State University (SSU), October 21–22, 2016. We are grateful to SSU president Judy K. Sakaki and the dean of the School of Social Sciences, John Wingard, for their support.

Colleagues and staff at Diablo Valley College provide Mickey with tremendous support and informed dialogue. Thanks to Lisa Martin and History Department cochairs Matthew Powell and Melissa Jacobson, as well as John Corbally, Bridgitte Schaffer, Lyn Krause, the late "Buzz" Holt, Greg Tilles, Manuel Gonzales, Katie Graham, Marcelle Levine, Adam Bessie, David Vela, Jacob Van Vleet, Steve Johnson, Jeremy Cloward, Amer Araim, Mark Akiyama, Bruce Lerro, Toni Fannin, Laury Fischer, Albert Ponce, Adam Perry, Frank Ortega, Mary Mazzocco, Richard Robinson, Todd Farr, English and Social Sciences dean Obed Vazquez, vice president of Student Services Newin Orante, interim president Ted Wieden, and outgoing chancellor Helen Benjamin, along with current and former teaching and research assistants and Project interns Thomas Field, Elsa Denis, Brittany Ayala, Ama Cortes, Jess Parry, Sierra Shidner, Kelly Van Boekhout, Brandy Miceli, Kamila Janik, Miya McHugh, and Aimee Casey. We also thank Mary Fitzpatrick, adjunct college skills instructor at the College of Marin, and Brian Covert, lecturer at Doshisha University in Kyoto, for their incredible editorial assistance.

Mickey would also like to thank all of his students for the inspiration they provide, as they are a constant reminder of the possibilities of the future and how privileged we are as educators to have such an amazing role in contributing to the public sphere.

Andy thanks the students in his Summer 2016 and Spring 2017 Introduction to Sociology courses at Citrus College. At Citrus College, Dana Hester, Brian Waddington, Gayle Allen, and Olivia Canales provide support and encouragement. Sarah Bosler, Vivian Linderman, and Sandy Krause from the College's Hayden Memorial Library are experts when it comes to helping students hone their research and critical thinking skills.

The generous financial support of donors and subscribers, too numerous to mention here, sustains the Project. This year, we are especially thankful to Marcia Annenberg, George Appell, Sharyl Attkisson, John Boyer, Sandra Cioppa, Dwain A. Deets, Jan De Deka, Margaret Guyder, Michael Hansen, Gillian G. Hearst, Neil Joseph, Sergio and Gaye Lub, Robert Manning, Sandra Maurer, David Nelson, Christopher Oscar, Melissa Pitts, Donald Plummer, Patrick Reilly, Lynn and Leonard Riepenhoff, John and Lyn Roth, Basja Samuelson, Marc Sapir, T.M. Scruggs, Bill Simon, Jan and Tom Vargo, Derrick West and Laurie Dawson, and Elaine Wellin.

On a personal note, we are indebted to and thankful for the love and support of our families and close friends, as they oft make sacrifices behind the scenes so we can continue to do the work we do. Mickey especially thanks his wife, Meg, as he could not do all that he does without her amazing work, counsel, and patience. Andy would like to thank Larry Gassan, Nick Wolfinger, and Liz Boyd for encouragement, inspiration, and loyalty.

Finally, we are grateful to you, our readers, who cherish and demand a truly free press. Together, we make a difference.

PROJECT CENSORED 2016–17 JUDGES

ROBIN ANDERSEN. Professor of Communication and Media Studies, Fordham University. She has written dozens of scholarly articles and is author or coauthor of four books, including *A Century of Media, A Century of War* (2006), winner of the Alpha Sigma Nu Book Award. Writes media criticism and commentary for the media watch group Fairness and Accuracy In Reporting (FAIR), The Vision Machine, and the *Antenna* blog.

JULIE ANDRZEJEWSKI. Professor Emeritus of Human Relations and cofounder of the Social Responsibility program, St. Cloud State University. Publications include *Social Justice, Peace, and Environmental Education* (2009).

OLIVER BOYD-BARRETT. Professor Emeritus of Media and Communications, Bowling Green State University and California State Polytechnic University, Pomona. Publications include *The International News Agencies* (1980), *Contra-flow in Global News: International and Regional News Exchange Mechanisms* (1992), *The Globalization of News* (1998), *Media in Global Context* (2009), *News Agencies in the Turbulent Era of the Internet* (2010), *Hollywood and the CIA: Cinema, Defense, and Subversion* (2011), *Media Imperialism* (2015), and *Western Mainstream Media and the Ukraine Crisis* (2017).

KENN BURROWS. Faculty member at the Institute for Holistic Health Studies, Department of Health Education, San Francisco State University. Founder and director of the Holistic Health Learning Center and producer of the biennial conference, Future of Health Care.

ERNESTO CARMONA. Journalist and writer. Chief correspondent, teleSUR Chile. Director, Santiago Circle of Journalists. President of the Investigation Commission on Attacks Against Journalists, Latin American Federation of Journalists (CIAP-FELAP).

ELLIOT D. COHEN. Professor of Philosophy and chair of the Humanities Department, Indian River State College. Editor and founder of the *International Journal of Applied Philosophy*. Recent books include *Technology of Oppression: Preserving Freedom and Dignity in an Age of Mass, Warrantless Surveillance* (2014), *Theory and Practice of Logic-Based Therapy: Integrating Critical Thinking and Philosophy into Psychotherapy* (2013), and *Philosophy, Counseling, and Psychotherapy* (2013).

GEOFF DAVIDIAN. Investigative reporter, war correspondent, legal affairs analyst, editor, photojournalist, and educator. Founding publisher and editor of the *Putnam Pit* and *Milwaukee Press*. Contributor to Reuters, UPI, magazines, newspapers, and online publications.

JOSÉ MANUEL DE PABLOS COELLO. Professor of Journalism, Universidad de La Laguna (Tenerife, Canary Islands, Spain). Founder of *Revista Latina de Comunicación Social* (RLCS), a scientific journal based out of the Laboratory of Information Technologies and New Analysis of Communication at Universidad de La Laguna.

LENORE FOERSTEL. Women for Mutual Security, facilitator of the Progressive International Media Exchange (PRIME).

ROBERT HACKETT. Professor of Communication, Simon Fraser University, Vancouver. Codirector of NewsWatch Canada since 1993. Cofounder of Media Democracy Days (2001) and OpenMedia.ca (2007). Publications include *Remaking Media: The Struggle to Democratize Public Communication* (with W.K. Carroll, 2006) and *Journalism and Climate Crisis: Public Engagement, Media Alternatives* (with S. Forde, S. Gunster, and K. Foxwell-Norton, 2017).

KEVIN HOWLEY. Professor of Media Studies, DePauw University. He is author of *Community Media: People, Places, and Communication Technologies* (2005) and editor of *Understanding Community Media* (2010) and *Media Interventions* (2013). Dr. Howley is currently working on a new monograph, *Drones: Media Discourse and the Public Imagination*.

NICHOLAS JOHNSON.* Author, *How to Talk Back to Your Television Set* (1970). Commissioner, Federal Communications Commission (1966–1973). Former media and cyber law professor, University of Iowa College of Law. More online at www.nicholasjohnson.org.

CHARLES L. KLOTZER. Founder, editor, and publisher emeritus of *St. Louis Journalism Review* and *FOCUS/Midwest*. The *St. Louis Journalism Review* has been transferred to Southern Illinois University, Carbondale, and is now the *Gateway Journalism Review*. Klotzer remains active at the *Review*.

NANCY KRANICH. Lecturer, School of Communication and Information, and special projects librarian, Rutgers University. Past president of the American Library Association (ALA), and convener of the ALA Center for Civic Life. Author of *Libraries and Democracy: The Cornerstones of Liberty* (2001) and "Libraries and Civic Engagement" (2012).

DEEPA KUMAR. Associate Professor of Journalism and Media Studies, Rutgers University. Author of *Outside the Box: Corporate Media, Globalization, and the UPS Strike* (2007) and *Islamophobia and the Politics of Empire* (2012). Currently working on a book on the cultural politics of the war on terror.

MARTIN LEE. Investigative journalist and author. Cofounder of Fairness and Accuracy In Reporting, and former editor of FAIR's magazine, *Extra!*. Director of Project CBD, a medical science information nonprofit. Author of *Smoke Signals: A Social History of Marijuana—Medical, Recreational, and Scientific* (2012), *The Beast Reawakens: Fascism's Resurgence from Hitler's Spymasters to Today's Neo-Nazi Groups and Right-Wing Extremists* (2000), and *Acid Dreams: The Complete Social History of LSD: The CIA, the Sixties, and Beyond* (with B. Shlain, 1985).

DENNIS LOO. Professor of Sociology, California State Polytechnic University, Pomona. Coeditor (with Peter Phillips) of *Impeach the President: The Case Against Bush and Cheney* (2006).

PETER LUDES. Professor of Mass Communication, Jacobs University, Bremen, 2002–2017. Founder of the German Initiative on News Enlightenment (1997) at the University of Siegen, publishing the most neglected German news (Project Censored, Germany). Recent publications include "Updating Marx's Concept of Alternatives," in *Marx and the Political Economy of the Media* (2016), "Long-Term Power Presentation Shifts: From Key Audio-Visual Narratives to an Update of Elias's Theory on the Process of Civilization," in *The Humanities between Global Integration and Cultural Diversity* (2016), and "Das Internet der verzerrten Wahrnehmungen und abgeklärte Aufklärung" (The Internet of Distorted Perceptions and Detached Enlightenment), in *Nachrichten und Aufklärung: Medien- und Journalismuskritik heute* (*News and Education: Media and Journalism Criticism Today*, forthcoming).

WILLIAM LUTZ. Professor Emeritus of English, Rutgers University. Former editor of the *Quarterly Review of Doublespeak*. Author of *Doublespeak: From Revenue Enhancement to Terminal Living: How Government, Business, Advertisers, and Others Use Language to Deceive You* (1989), *The Cambridge Thesaurus of American English* (1994), *The New Doublespeak: Why No One Knows What Anyone's Saying Anymore* (1996), and *Doublespeak Defined* (1999).

SILVIA LAGO MARTÍNEZ. Professor of Social Research Methodology and codirector, Research Program on Information Society at the Gino Germani Research Institute, Faculty of Social Sciences, Universidad de Buenos Aires.

CONCHA MATEOS. Professor of Journalism, Department of Communication Sciences, Universidad Rey Juan Carlos, Spain. Journalist for radio, television, and political organizations in Spain and Latin America. Coordinator for Project Censored research in Europe and Latin America.

MARK CRISPIN MILLER. Professor of Media, Culture, and Communication, Steinhardt School of Culture, Education, and Human Development, New York University. Author, editor, and activist.

JACK L. NELSON.* Distinguished Professor Emeritus, Graduate School of Education, Rutgers University. Former member, Committee on Academic Freedom and Tenure, American Association of University Professors. Author of seventeen books, including *Critical Issues in Education: Dialogues and Dialectics*, 8th ed. (with S. Palonsky and M.R. McCarthy, 2013), and about two hundred articles.

PETER PHILLIPS. Professor of Sociology, Sonoma State University, since 1994. Director, Project Censored, 1996–2010. President, Media Freedom Foundation, 2010–2016. Editor or coeditor of fourteen editions of *Censored*. Coeditor (with Dennis Loo) of *Impeach the President: The Case Against Bush and Cheney* (2006). Author of four chapters in recent *Censored* yearbooks on the Transnational Capitalist Class.

T.M. SCRUGGS. Professor Emeritus (and token ethnomusicologist), University of Iowa. Executive producer, the Real News Network.

NANCY SNOW. Pax Mundi Professor of Public Diplomacy, Kyoto University of Foreign Studies, Japan. Professor Emeritus of Communications, California State University, Fullerton. Public affairs and media relations advisor to Langley Esquire, a leading Tokyo public affairs firm. Author or editor of eleven books, including *Japan's Information War* (2016) and *The Routledge Handbook of Critical Public Relations* (with J. L'Etang, D. McKie, and J. Xifra, 2015).

SHEILA RABB WEIDENFELD.* President of DC Productions Ltd. Emmy Award–winning television producer. Former press secretary to Betty Ford.

ROB WILLIAMS. Founding president of the Action Coalition for Media Education (ACME). Teaches media, communications, global studies, and journalism at the University of Vermont and Champlain College. Author of numerous articles on critical media literacy education. Publisher of the *Vermont Independent* online news journal. Coeditor of *Media Education for a Digital Generation* (with J. Frechette, 2016) and *Most Likely to Secede* (with R. Miller, 2013), about the Vermont independence movement.

*Indicates having been a Project Censored judge since our founding in 1976.

ANNUAL REPORT FROM THE MEDIA FREEDOM FOUNDATION PRESIDENT

Project Censored was founded in 1976 by Carl Jensen at Sonoma State University (SSU). He developed the Project for twenty years, releasing an annual report of the top censored stories, which he called "Censored: The News that Didn't Make the News and Why." In 1993, Jensen published the list along with accompanying analysis in the form of a book, and in 1996 began what is now a twenty-one-year relationship with Seven Stories Press in New York. Jensen served as the Project's director for twenty years, then appointed as his successor sociologist Peter Phillips, who expanded the breadth and scope of the Project's research. In 2000, Phillips created the Media Freedom Foundation (MFF), a 501(c)(3) nonprofit organization, to oversee and promote the mission of Project Censored and to ensure its independence. As early as 2003, the Project began to grow beyond SSU, in what would later become a more robust extension of the Project's critical media literacy curriculum. Phillips served as president of the board until late 2016. In 2010, I (Mickey Huff) became director of the Project, and since 2012 I've worked with associate director Andy Lee Roth on producing the annual *Censored* volumes. In 2016, the MFF board elected me as its second president.

With the launch of Project Censored's Campus Affiliates Program in 2010, the Project officially expanded from its original base at SSU. Since then, Project Censored has developed to include approximately two dozen colleges and universities across the US and around the world, involving scores of faculty and hundreds of students each year. Also in 2010, Phillips and I started *The Project Censored Show* on Pacifica Radio, which airs on some forty stations across the US, streams online around the world, and is now available as a podcast. Additionally, Christopher Oscar and Doug Hecker's *Project Censored The Movie: Ending the Reign of Junk Food News*, the second feature film about the Project, debuted at film festivals in 2013, winning numerous awards, and serving as the genesis for our video series, which continues to grow. Both *Project Censored The Movie* and its predecessor, Steven

Keller's *Is the Press Really Free?* (1998), are excellent for community and classroom use and are available online.

Over the years, MFF has supported media literacy education in many ways. In 2015, MFF members oversaw and assisted in the creation of a joint educational effort, the Global Critical Media Literacy Project (GCMLP), with the Action Coalition for Media Education (ACME) and the graduate program in Media Literacy and Digital Culture at Sacred Heart University. The GCMLP website is an online source for faculty and students to bring their research, essays, and video content to a wider public. Through the website, we also make available the GCMLP's *Educators' Resource Guide*, which members of the aforementioned parties, including Project Censored, coedited and coauthored.

In the past year, as public interest in so-called "fake news" spiked, the Project received invitations to speak about our work fighting censorship and raising awareness around critical media literacy education as an antidote to propaganda. The number one question we are still asked when we speak around the country is "Who do you trust in the news media?" Although there is no single, simple *answer* to this question, there is a *process*—one we have taught for over forty years now—centered around critical media literacy and involving fact-checking, source transparency and veracity, and basic critical thinking skills. It is not up to anyone to tell the public *what* to think or whom to trust. It is, however, our job as educators to help people understand *how* to think about the news, including how to form critical questions about news content and how to establish whether news outlets and specific news stories are trustworthy or not.

The Project continues to do this, promoting media democracy in action, through our annual book, weekly radio/podcast program, public speaking series and events, short film projects, campus and classroom visits, interviews with media outlets, and various forms of education and consultation. As an example of the latter, in 2016 I began consulting with the online startup Tribeworthy.com, which does something they call Crowd Contested Media. As described in Chapter 3 of this volume, Tribeworthy's goal is to build trust in news sites based on principles of critical media literacy. MFF also helps spread the work of numerous scholars, including, for example, Susan

Maret's information integrity checklist; resources produced by MFF's newest board members, including Allison Butler's work on changing definitions of "fake news" after the 2016 election; Ben Boyington's efforts to introduce the Project to a K–12 audience; and Nicholas Baham III and Mary Cardaras's help with podcast production and publications at California State University, East Bay. Cardaras and Baham are making that campus a new stalwart Project Censored affiliate.

In addition, MFF continues to partner with numerous community organizations, cosponsoring many public events, in efforts to raise awareness of the importance of a truly free press, one that rejects censorship in its many increasingly insidious guises and promotes social justice for all. The Project continues to support other anti-censorship efforts, including Banned Books Week, the National Coalition Against Censorship, and the national Whistleblower Summit for Civil and Human Rights.

Project Censored persists in these many endeavors through MFF, but we cannot do so without the dedication of a small but committed core group, including one part-time staff member, bookkeeper, and webmaster. Most of the people who work with us do so as a labor of love, with little to no financial compensation, but that is simply not enough to sustain the Project.

Over the past few years, we have gathered a modest number of dedicated monthly supporters (most of whom pledge five to ten dollars per month) and a smaller pool of generous donors. MFF does not receive or accept corporate funding or advertising money—not only to avoid conflicts of interest, but also to remain truly independent. As a result, over the years, luminaries including I.F. Stone, Walter Cronkite, Ralph Nader, Diane Ravitch, Noam Chomsky, Howard Zinn, Medea Benjamin, Daniel Ellsberg, and Naomi Wolf, to name a few, have heralded Project Censored's work and significance.

Nevertheless, remaining truly independent comes with financial consequences that increasingly challenge the Project's sustainability. Despite the Project's long and vaunted history, not to mention the diversity of new programs in development, financial pressures increasingly push us to focus on fundraising efforts in order to continue and expand the Project's vital work. We do all that we do on a five-figure budget, but in order to sustain all that we do, we must double our current support levels.

It is my assumption that you, dear reader, holding this book in your hands, appreciate the craft of research and writing, as well as the importance of critical thinking and higher education. It is my hope that you will consider supporting Project Censored's work in whatever way(s) that you can. Whether that means purchasing a book for yourself, a family member, or friend, or donating a copy to your library or school; becoming a monthly supporter; or, for those who are more financially well-endowed, making a tax-deductible donation— your financial support ensures that Project Censored will be able to continue to fight censorship and advocate for the maintenance of a free press, while helping to educate the next generation of intrepid muckraking journalists. Together, we can create a more informed and inspired society, one not fooled by fake news or alternative facts, but rather empowered to restore integrity to our "post-truth" world.

Sincerely,

Mickey Huff
President, Media Freedom Foundation
Director, Project Censored

HOW TO SUPPORT PROJECT CENSORED

NOMINATE A STORY

To nominate a *Censored* story, send us a copy of the article and include the name of the source publication, the date that the article appeared, and the page number. For news stories published on the Internet, forward the URL to mickey@projectcensored.org or andy@projectcensored.org. The deadline for nominating *Censored* stories is March 15 of each year.

Criteria for Project Censored news story nominations:

A censored news story reports information that the public has a right and a need to know, but to which the public has had limited access.

The news story is recent, having been first reported no earlier than one year ago. For *Censored 2018* the Top 25 list includes stories reported between April 2016 and March 2017. Thus, stories submitted for *Censored 2019* should be no older than April 2017.

The story has clearly defined concepts and solid, verifiable documentation. The story's claims should be supported by evidence—the more controversial the claims, the stronger the evidence necessary.

The news story has been published, either electronically or in print, in a publicly circulated newspaper, journal, magazine, newsletter, or similar publication from either a domestic or foreign source.

MAKE A TAX–DEDUCTABLE DONATION

Project Censored is supported by the Media Freedom Foundation, a 501(c)(3) nonprofit organization. We depend on tax-deductible donations to continue our work. To support our efforts on behalf of independent journalism and freedom of information, send checks to the address below or donate online at projectcensored.org. Your generous donations help us to oppose news censorship and promote media literacy.

Media Freedom Foundation
PO Box 750940
Petaluma, CA 94975
mickey@projectcensored.org
andy@projectcensored.org
Phone: (707) 241-4596

ABOUT THE EDITORS

ANDY LEE ROTH is the associate director of Project Censored and coeditor of seven previous editions of the *Censored* yearbook. He coordinates the Project's Validated Independent News program. His research, on topics ranging from ritual to broadcast news interviews to communities organizing for parklands, has been published in such journals as the *International Journal of Press/Politics; Social Studies of Science; Media, Culture & Society; City & Community;* and *Sociological Theory.* He reviews books and films for *YES! Magazine.* He earned a PhD in sociology at the University of California, Los Angeles, and a BA in sociology and anthropology at Haverford College. He teaches sociology at Citrus College, and serves on the boards of the Claremont Wildlands Conservancy and the Media Freedom Foundation.

MICKEY HUFF is director of Project Censored and the new president of the Media Freedom Foundation. To date, he has edited or coedited nine volumes of *Censored* and contributed numerous chapters to these annuals since 2008. Additionally, he has coauthored several essays on media and propaganda for other scholarly publications. He is currently professor of social science and history at Diablo Valley College in the San Francisco Bay Area, where he is cochair of the History Department; he is also a lecturer in the Communications Department at California State University, East Bay. Huff is executive producer and cohost with former Project Censored director Peter Phillips of *The Project Censored Show,* the weekly syndicated public affairs program that originates from KPFA Pacifica Radio in Berkeley, CA. He is a cofounding member of the Global Critical Media Literacy Project (gcml.org), sits on the advisory board for the Media Literacy and Digital Culture graduate program at Sacred Heart University, and serves on the editorial board for the journal *Secrecy and Society.* For the past several years, Huff has worked with the national outreach committee of Banned Books Week alongside the American Library Association and the National Coalition Against Censorship, of which Project Censored is a member. Most recently, he became the critical media literacy consultant for a new educational Internet startup, Tribeworthy.com, which is a Crowd Contested Media interactive online platform that allows users to rate news articles and sources for trustworthiness using critical media literacy skills. He has been interviewed by numerous media outlets around the world regarding critical media literacy, propaganda, and censorship issues as well as contemporary historiography in the US. He is a longtime musician and composer and lives with his family in Northern California.

For more information about the editors, to invite them to speak at your school or in your community, or to conduct interviews, please visit projectcensored.org.

INDEX

174

Chester, Jeffrey, 94, 230
Chevron, 90, 91
Chicago, IL, 93, 163
Chicago Defender, 93
Chicago Tribune, 149, 152, 167
Children's Hospital at Montefiore, 43
Chile, 168
China, 55, 56, 164
Chomsky, Noam, 26, 100n7, 139, 209
Christianity, 74, 118
Chrome (Internet browser), 157
CIA (Central Intelligence Agency), 21, 47, 217, 219, 220
Cisco Systems, 235
citizen action, *see* activism
Citizens for Tax Justice, 227
Citizens United v. Federal Election Commission (2010), 52, 208n17
Citron, Danielle, 130
Citrus College, 59, 64, 71, 75, 82, 86, 92, 94, 139, 141, 149, 152
CityLab, 69, 70
civic mobilization, *see* activism
civil liberties, 23, 81–84, 98–100, 235, *see also* Constitution (US), *see also* surveillance
Civil Rights Act (1964), 52, 165, 169
Civil War (US), 22, 123
Clean Power Plan, 78
Clements, Jeffrey, 234
Cleveland, OH, 42, 43, 167
climate change, 35, 77–84, 104n64, 110, 111, 114–16
    denial, 11, 12, 52, 74, 78, 79, 111
    displacement, 77, 80, 81
    environmental impacts, 79, 80, 82–84, 90
    policy, 80, 82, 89, 92
Climate of Concern, 77, 78
Clinton, Bill, 12, 52
    crime bill (1994), 12
Clinton, Hillary,
    and the Democratic National Committee, 62, 63, 234
    and the media, 124, 125, 170
    as secretary of state, 220, 236
    emails, 63, 125
    fake news, 52, 121, 124, 128
    presidential campaign (2016), 12, 53, 54, 63, 103n47, 121, 124–26
CNBC (television network), 112
CNN (television network), 19, 21, 67, 112, 115, 121, 123, 125, 140, 163, 169, 170, 173
Coffin, Thomas, 82, 83
Cohen, Elliot D., 47, 48
Cohen, Roger, 221
Cohn, Roy, 174
Colbert, Stephen, 17, 175, 177
Cold War, 126
Cole, Teju, 165
College of Marin, 73, 80, 89
colleges, *see* education system
Collier, Kevin, 65

Colorado, 74, 75, 122
Combined Tactical Systems (CTS), 87
Comedy Central (television network), 174
Committee to Protect Journalists (CPJ), 22
Common Dreams, 98, 115
Communications Act (1934), 237, 238
communism, 20, 126, 128, 209, 210
COMPAS (Correctional Offender Management Profiling for Alternative Sanctions), 76, 77
Conca, James, 82, 83
Concordia Summit, 53
Conger, Jack, 113
Congress (US), 22, 45, 46, 230, 231, 233, 235, 237
Connecticut, 72
Conservative Political Action Conference (CPAC), 228
conservatives, 11, 12, 23, 74, 75, 118, 119, 123, 171, 228
Consortium News, 72
Constantine, Lloyd, 235
Constitution (US), 23, 35, 81, 82, 130
    First Amendment, 26, 68, 70, 71, 74, 130, 132, 197–03, 208n17
    Fourth Amendment, 68, 70, 71
    Fifth Amendment, 83
    Ninth Amendment, 83
Constitution Hall, 225, 227, 229
Conway, Kellyanne, 19, 29n12, 32, 33, 122, 123
Cooper, Matthew, 168
Cordova, AK, 58
Cornell University, 23
corporate greed, 55–57, 77–79, 82, 83, 87–92, 119, 120, 129, 151, 152, 170, 226
Coulter, Ann, 163, 174
CounterPunch, 47, 126
Cousins, Farron, 43, 44
Cramer, Ruby, 63
crime rate, 12, 75–77, 84–86, 88, 89, 163, 164
Crimea, 210, 221
critical thinking, 23–28, 31, 32, 36, 108, 109, 118–20, 122, 131
"Crowd Contested Media," 25, 141, 146–48
Cruz, Ted, 53, 173
CS, *see* weapons, chemical
Current, 228
Custodio, Gabriella, 107–38
Daily Show, 174
Damascus, 154
Danner, Mark, 28, 29
Dark Ages America, 108
data collection, *see* big data
Davies, Madlen, 55, 56
Davies, Sally, 55
Dawes Gay, Elizabeth, 59
De Correspondent, 78
Dean, John, 165
debtors' prisons, 98–100
defamation, *see* libel law
Defense Finance and Accounting Service, 45
DeGennaro, Rafael, 46
Delaware, 75, 198

Heartland Institute, 52, 102n33
Hedges, Thomas, 45
Hellmann, Melissa, 89
Hemisphere (surveillance program), 68, 69
Henry, James, 234
Heritage Foundation, 75, 171
Herman, Edward S., 26, 100n7, 209–23
Hernandez, Hector, 75–77
Hersh, Seymour M., 117
Higdon, Nolan, 25, 107–38, 163–83
Hightower, Jim, 230
Hitler, Adolf, 122, 164, 168
Holder, Eric, 75, 76
Holland, Joshua, 63
Hollywood, CA, 112
Honduras, 26, 220, 221
Hoover, Herbert, 238
Hotchkiss, Ralf, 228, 229
House of Representatives, 22, 73, 163
housing, 44, 45, 80, 81, 88, 89
HSBC (Hongkong and Shanghai Banking Corporation Limited), 78
HTTPS Everywhere, 25, 142, 158, 159
Huajardo, Alisha, 107–38
Huff, Mickey, 17–30, 44–47, 61–64, 67–73, 107–38, 230
Huffington Post, 47, 52, 121, 125, 129, 216
Human Rights Council, 66
Hungary, 145
hunger, 58, 113, 133n18
Hurricane Katrina, 115
Hussein, Saddam, 217–19
iCloud, 70
Idaho, 198
Idiocracy, 108, 110, 133n5
ignorance, 23, 108, 120, 122, 169, 174, 211, 214, *see also* agnotology
Illinois, 74, 92, 93
Illinois Department of Corrections, 35, 92, 93
Illinois River Correctional Center, 92
immigrants, 109, 122, 163, 164
incarceration, *see* prisons
"inconvenient facts," 31–36, 121
Index on Censorship, 25, 139, 140, 142–45
India, 17, 35, 55, 65, 80, 145
Indian River State College, 47
inequality,
  economic, 44, 59, 86, 98–100, 129, 130, 232
  gender, 84–86
  health, 41–44, 59–61
  racial, 20, 42, 50, 59, 75–77, 84–86, 114, 129, 130, 164, 165, 170, 172
Influence Map, 79
Infowars, 123, 173
infrastructure (US), 41–44
Instagram, 18, 207n10
Intelligence Authorization Act (2015), 73
Inter Press Service (IPS), 64, 65
Intercept, 97, 98
Intergovernmental Panel on Climate Change (IPCC), 80

International Atomic Energy Agency (IAEA), 218
International Fact-Checking Network, 129
International Telecommunications Union, 66
Internet, 103n51, 114, 221, 236, *see also* social media
  and law, 197–208
  privacy, 48, 94, 95, 142, 156–59, 216
  propaganda, 18, 23, 122, 124, 127, 146–48, 166, 173, 175, 177, 215, 216
  shutdowns, 64–67, 160n8
Iowa, 198
Iran, 26, 220, 221
Iraq,
  and US propaganda, 20, 47, 48, 53, 116–18, 168, 210, 217–21
  invasion of, 26, 210, 219, 235, 236
  sanctions against, 12, 210
Iraqi National Congress, 219
ISIS (Islamic State of Iraq and the Levant), 110, 111
Islam, 30n27
Italy, 28, 164
Iyer, Pico, 30n30
Jackson, Andrew, 123
Jacobin, 174
Jacobs, Ben, 22
Jaffe, Amy Myers, 90
Jamail, Dahr, 57, 58, 109
Japanese Americans, 30n27
Jarecki, Eugene, 230
Jensen, Carl, 24, 33, 39, 109
Jolley, Rachael, 139, 140, 142–45
Jones, Alex, 123, 173, 174
Jones, Olivia, 51–54
Jordan-Aparo, Randall, 88
Joseph, George, 69, 70
Jost, Jonathan, 165
journalists, 13, 14, 24, 69, 112, 126, 128, 214, 236, *see also* media
  as watchdogs, 32, 34, 36, 117, 121, 165, 209
  fear of appearing too liberal, 171, 172, 237
  hostility toward, 19–23, 143, 144, 154, 171, 212
  sources, 118, 119, 141, 146, 150, 152, 219, 231, 232
Judaism, 74, 164
Judge, Mike, 108, 133n5
judicial system, 35, 52, 58, 61, 62, 69, 70, 81–84, 130, 197–203, 233
  inequality, 49–51, 75–77, 85, 86, 98–100
  prisoner treatment, 86–88, 92, 93
Juliana v. United States, 82–84
Junk Food News, 24, 25, 107–16, 130–32
jurisprudence, 200–02, 207n13
JURIST, 83
Juvenile Law Center, 98–100
Kaiser Permanente, 60
Kamel, Hussein, 217, 218
Kansas, 198
Kardashian family, 229
Kasapligil, Nora, 57, 58
Kaye, David, 66, 67, 71
Kelleher, Dennis, 234

White House Correspondents' Association, 24, 109, 110, 112, 113

white privilege, 59, 76, 96, 114, 118, 163, 170, 174

white supremacy, 74, 164, 165, 169, 173, 176, 177

Wiebe, Kirk, 230

WikiLeaks, 63, 125

Wilkinson, Francis, 165

Williams, Brian, 117

Williams, Rob, 49–57, 61–64, 73–75, 77–79

Wilson, Ralph, 74

Wilson, Scott, 229

Wintrich, Lucian, 123

Wisconsin, 50, 54, 75, 198

Witness Against Torture, 87

women, 12, 80, 81, 87, 117, 229, *see also* feminism, *see also* health, of women, *see also* inequality, gender, *see also* transgender people

Women's Policy Inc., 59

Woodruff, Judy, 227

World Health Organization (WHO), 43, 55, 59

World War II, 30n27, 210

Wrase, Sarah, 44

Writers and Scholars International, 142

Wuerker, Matt, 230

Yacka, Sue, 85

Yahoo, 215

Yandle, Staci, 93

Yates, Sally Q., 87

Yelp, 147

Yeltsin, Boris, 214, 222n11

Yemen, 113, 133n18, 154

YES! Magazine, 80, 81, 89, 98

Yiannopoulos, Milo, 168

Yolangco, Mark, 107–38

Yoss, Caroline, 80, 81

YouGov, 121

Yousman, Bill, 30n36

YouTube, 197, 200

Zaitchik, Alexander, 165

Zambrano, Jonnie, 94, 95

Zika virus, 42

Zimbabwe, 145

Zinn, Howard, 13, 139, 140

Zinni, Anthony, 235

Zuckerberg, Mark, 129

PROJECT CENSORED THE MOVIE
ENDING THE REIGN OF JUNK FOOD NEWS

AVAILABLE AT VIMEO, ITUNES, GOOGLE PLAY, AND
AMAZON PRIME VIDEO, STREAMING OR DOWNLOAD.
ALSO AVAILABLE FOR PURCHASE IN DVD FORMAT!
SEE PROJECTCENSOREDTHEMOVIE.COM FOR DETAILS.

Determined to break the grip of Junk Food News on the American public, two California fathers uncover the true agenda of the corporate media while they investigate the importance of a free and independent press.

This award-winning documentary, six years in the making, takes an in-depth look at what is wrong with the news media in the US and what we can do about it. The film highlights the work of forty-year veteran media democracy organization Project Censored and their commitment to providing solutions through media literacy and critical thinking education while celebrating the best in underreported, independent journalism.

Project Censored: The Movie, made by former PC Sonoma State University student Doug Hecker and longtime Project supporter Christopher Oscar, features original interviews and montages (edited by Mike Fischer) about the Project and media censorship with Noam Chomsky, Howard Zinn, Daniel Ellsberg, Michael Parenti, Oliver Stone, Cynthia McKinney, Nora Barrows-Friedman, Peter Kuznick, Khalil Bendib, Abby Martin, Project-affiliated faculty and students, as well as Project founder Carl Jensen, former director and president of the Media Freedom Foundation Peter Phillips, current director Mickey Huff, and associate director Andy Lee Roth. Plus much, much more!